YOUNG GENERATION AWAKENING

Young Generation Awakening

ECONOMICS, SOCIETY, AND POLICY ON
THE EVE OF THE ARAB SPRING

Edited by Edward A. Sayre and Tarik M. Yousef

OXFORD
UNIVERSITY PRESS

OXFORD
UNIVERSITY PRESS

Oxford University Press is a department of the University of Oxford.
It furthers the University's objective of excellence in research, scholarship,
and education by publishing worldwide. Oxford is a registered trade mark of
Oxford University Press in the UK and certain other countries.

Published in the United States of America by Oxford University Press
198 Madison Avenue, New York, NY 10016, United States of America.

Library of Congress Cataloging-in-Publication Data
Names: Sayre, Edward, editor, author. | Yousef, Tarik, editor, author.
Title: Young generation awakening : economics, society, and policy on the eve
    of the Arab Spring / edited by Edward A. Sayre and Tarik M. Yousef.
Description: New York : Oxford University Press, 2016. | Includes
    bibliographical references and index.
Identifiers: LCCN 2016008352 | ISBN 9780190224615 (alk. paper)
Subjects: LCSH: Youth—Arab countries—Economic conditions—21st century. |
    Youth—Arab countries—Social conditions—21st century. | Arab Spring,
    2010—Economic aspects. | Arab countries—Economic conditions—21st
    century. | Arab countries—Social conditions—21st century. | Arab
    countries—Politics and government—21st century.
Classification: LCC JQ1850.A91 .Y675 2016 | DDC 909.097492708342—dc23
    LC record available at http://lccn.loc.gov/2016008352

9 8 7 6 5 4 3 2 1
Printed by Sheridan Books, Inc., United States of America

To Wendy, Gillian, Owen, Hend, Aya, and Layla for all of your patience and support.

Contents

Acknowledgments

DRAFT PAPERS THAT became the chapters of this book were first presented and discussed in a workshop titled "The Social-Economic Situation of Middle East Youth on the Eve of the Arab Spring," hosted by the Issam Fares Institute of Public Policy and International Affairs at the American University of Beirut, December 8–9, 2012. The papers presented included a range of disciplinary perspectives and empirical techniques, and one of the goals of this book has been to bring together these varied approaches into a coherent narrative. Some of the papers originally presented did not get included in the book; other chapters arose out of combining two papers. The original workshop depended heavily on the administrative and financial support of Silatech, without which this book would not have been possible. The participants in the workshop who do not have chapters in this book nonetheless contributed significantly to the ideas contained herein. These participants include Ragui Assaad, University of Minnesota; Jad Chaban, American University of Beirut; Magda Kandil, International Monetary Fund; Cengiz Erisen, TOBB University of Economics and Technology; Noura Kamel, Silatech; Qazi Rashid, Silatech; Nadia Zrelli Ben Hamida, Higher School of Economic and Commercial Sciences, Tunis; Chaimaa Yassine, University of Paris 1 Pantheon Sorbonne; and Sara Bitter, Issam Fares Institute. The workshop was graciously hosted by Rami Khouri of the Issam Fares Institute, who also participated in the workshop and contributed significantly to our thinking about the issues surrounding the role of youth in the Arab Spring.

This book also received significant support from the University of Southern Mississippi, where Edward Sayre is an associate professor of economics. Critical stages of the preparation of the manuscript were completed during a sabbatical, for which the support of the Department of Political Science, International Development, and International Affairs and the College of Arts and Letters is greatly appreciated. The financial support of the Qatar National Research Foundation, the Dr. Ronald and Mrs. Charlie Graham Economics Support Endowment at the University of Southern Mississippi, and the College of Arts and Letters at the University of Southern Mississippi helped sustain this project at various times. Elizabeth Hughes Cranford provided meticulous and thorough editorial and administrative assistance throughout the early stages of this project.

During most of the time this book was being written, Tarik Yousef was CEO of Silatech, and the team at Silatech helped in innumerable ways throughout this time. Nader Kabbani, director of research and policy at Silatech, helped refine and strengthen many of the ideas in this book with his sage commentary and guidance. Thomas Chidiac provided excellent research assistance for several of the chapters. David Beck helped to significantly restructure chapters in ways that strengthened the authors' arguments. And Paul Dyer, while he coauthored two of the chapters, was also instrumental in coordinating the resources from Silatech for those who were working on this project from the United States.

Contributors

GHADA BARSOUM is Assistant Professor in the Department of Public Policy and Administration of the School of Global Affairs and Public Policy at the American University in Cairo. Her research focuses on issues of youth, gender, employment, and higher education policy. She was recently principal investigator of a study on the informal economy in Egypt in collaboration with the UNDP regional office. Prior to joining the American University in Cairo she was a research associate at the Population Council, West Asia and North Africa Office. She is the author of a book on the employment crisis of female graduates in Egypt and a number of articles in peer-reviewed journals. Her teaching and research interests include youth and gender policies, research methods, and social service reform. She also consulted for the International Labor Organization, UNICEF, and UNFPA. She obtained her Ph.D. in Sociology from the University of Toronto in 2005 and her master's degree from the American University in Cairo in 1999.

DAVID BECK, prior to his current work as a project manager at Madeo Digital Studio, was a research analyst at Silatech, where his work focused on demographic and labor force dynamics related to youth in the Middle East and North Africa. Beck has worked in the United States, India, and the UAE and has experience related to global education, conflict resolution, public policy, and social entrepreneurship. He received a bachelor's degree in politics from Bates College and is currently based in New York.

BRAHIM BOUDARBAT is Professor of Labor Economics at the School of Industrial Relations, University of Montreal. He holds a Ph.D. in economics from the University of Montreal. Prior to his current position, he was a postdoctoral and teaching fellow in the Department of Economics at the University of British Columbia. His main fields of interest are economics of immigration, economics of education, labor economics, and applied econometrics. His publications include *Why are the Relative Wages of Immigrants Declining? A Distributional Approach* (2014); *Education–job Match among Recent Canadian University Graduates* (2012); *The Evolution of the Returns to Human Capital in Canada, 1980–2005* (2010); *Vocational Training in Morocco: Social and Economic Issues for the Labour Market* (2009); and *Moroccan Youth in an Era of Volatile Growth, Urbanization, and Poverty* (2009). He is affiliated with several centers and research groups, including the Institute for the Study of Labor, the Center for Interuniversity Research and Analysis on Organizations, and the Canadian Labor Market and Skills Researcher Network.

ANITA BREUER is a senior researcher at the German Development Institute/Deutsches Institut für Entwicklungspolitik, Bonn, Germany, where her research focuses on the role of the Internet and social media in democracy promotion and international development cooperation. She holds a master's degree in Latin America area studies and received her doctoral degree in political science from the University of Cologne in 2008. Her primary research interests revolve around the role of information communication technologies in processes of democratic transition and the impact of social media on patterns of individual political behavior. She has published on these issues in journals such as *Democratization, Journal of Information Technologies and Politics, Representation,* and *Latin American Politics and Society.* She is coeditor (with Yanina Welp) of *Digital Technologies for Democratic Governance in Latin America* (2014). She acts as reviewer for numerous peer-reviewed journals, including *American Political Science Review, Comparative Political Studies, British Journal of Political Studies,* and *Democratization.*

RAJ M. DESAI is Associate Professor of International Development at the Edmund A. Walsh School of Foreign Service and in the Department of Government at Georgetown University and is a nonresident senior fellow at the Brookings Institution. He is a specialist on problems of economic reform, foreign aid, and international development. In addition to coauthoring *A Better Investment Climate for Everyone* (2005), he coedited *Can Russia Compete?* (2008) and *Between State and Market: Mass Privatization in Transition Economies* (1997). He has also authored articles on economic reform, entrepreneurship, and poverty alleviation in the *American Political Science Review, Economics and Politics,* the *Journal of Comparative Economics, IMF Staff Papers, Economics of Transition,* the *World Bank Research Observer,* the *International Studies Review,* the *European Journal of Political Economy,* the *Journal of International Law and Politics,* the *National Interest,* and *Survival.* He has received fellowships from the Qatar Foundation, the Social Sciences Research Council, the Andrew Mellon Foundation, and the National Science Foundation. He has served as occasional consultant to the World Bank Group, the Asian Development Bank, the UNDP, and other international organizations. He was previously a private sector development specialist at the World Bank, where he worked on the privatization and restructuring of public enterprises in eastern Europe and the former Soviet Union and on the recovery of financial systems following economic crises in East Asia and Latin America. He received his Ph.D. and M.A. degrees from Harvard University, where he was a National Science Foundation fellow, and his B.A. from the University of California, Irvine.

ISHAC DIWAN is currently affiliated with Dauphine University and the Paris School of Economics in France. His current research interests focus on political economy issues in the Middle East and include a focus on the study of crony capitalism and of opinion surveys. He is directing the Economic and Political Transformation program of the Economic Research Forum, and he is a fellow at the Harvard University Middle East Initiative. He earned his Ph.D. in economics from the University of California, Berkeley, in 1984. He taught international finance at the New York University Business School between 1984 and 1987, before joining the World Bank in 1987, where he worked in the Research Complex (1987–1992), the Middle East Department (1992–1996), and the World Bank Institute (1996–2002). He lived in Addis Ababa (2002–2007) and Accra (2007–2011) while serving as the World Bank's country director for Ethiopia and Sudan and then for Ghana, Liberia, Sierra Leone, Burkina Faso, and Guinea. During 2011–2014, he taught at Harvard Kennedy School.

PAUL DYER is knowledge program manager at Silatech, supporting external research projects aimed at enhancing general knowledge about youth in the Arab world, the economic challenges facing them, and how best to provide them with increased economic opportunities. He also serves on the Taqeem Evaluation Council and is participating in two ongoing impact evaluation studies in Morocco and Yemen. Prior to joining Silatech, Paul was a fellow at the Dubai School of Government in the UAE, where he codirected the Middle East Youth Initiative, a program jointly developed with the Wolfensohn Center for Development at the Brookings Institution. He has also served as a consultant to the Office of the Chief Economist, Middle East and North Africa Region, at the World Bank. He holds a master's degree in Arab Studies from Georgetown University. In addition to evaluating the impact of youth programs, his research interests include demography, labor market reforms, and the impact of regulations on job creation.

DANIEL EGEL is an Economist at the RAND Corporation and Professor at the Pardee RAND Graduate School. His research uses qualitative and quantitative methods to study policymaking in fragile and instability-prone countries, with a focus on development- and stability-focused programming. His work at RAND focuses on policymaking at the nexus of development and stability and includes a calculation of the economic costs of the Israeli-Palestinian conflict, analyses of US counterinsurgency and counterterrorism efforts, and an assessment of the economic value of US international security commitments. His development-focused research includes randomized control trials of development programming in Yemen, an exploration of the role of Yemen's tribes in economic development, and assessments of the school-to-work transition in Iran and Morocco; his stability-focused research has included an analysis of the drivers of Tunisia's revolution and a history of US efforts to develop Afghan security forces. He served as an embedded analyst with the NATO Special Operations Component Command-Afghanistan, a postdoctoral scholar at the University of California Institute for Global Conflict and Cooperation, a consultant for the Middle East Youth Initiative at the Brookings Institution, and a consultant with the Yemeni Social Fund for Development since 2009. He earned his Ph.D. in economics from the University of California, Berkeley.

RANA HENDY has a Ph.D. from the University of Paris, Pantheon-Sorbonne, in the fields of labor and gender economics. During her doctoral program she benefited from a full fellowship from the Centre de Recherche en Economie et Statistiques, based in Paris. Currently, she is Assistant Professor in the College of Business and Economics at Qatar University. On a commuting basis, she works closely with the Economic Research Forum (Cairo), where she is managing two major projects on inequality and gender issues in Middle Eastern and North African countries. Her academic articles cover various research areas such as women's empowerment, time and resource allocation in the household, inequality of opportunity, and firm dynamics, as well as issues related to trade policies. Her latest publications appeared in *Applied Economics,* the *International Trade Journal,* and the *International Journal of Entrepreneurship and Small Business.* She has also contributed to three volumes on the Jordanian and Egyptian labor markets. On a consultancy basis, she works closely with international organizations such as the World Bank, the Organisation for Economic Co-operation and Development, and the United Nations.

SAMER KHERFI is an Assistant Professor of Economics at the American University of Sharjah, UAE, where his teaching includes courses on Middle East economics, international economics, labor economics, and econometrics. His current research interest focuses on education and labor market outcomes in the Middle East. He has served as an economic and statistical consultant in the UAE. He holds a Ph.D. in economics from Simon Fraser University.

JEFFREY B. NUGENT is a development economist who has worked on a wide variety of issues, problems, and analytical techniques and in and on a variety of countries in Latin America, Africa, South and East Asia, and especially the Middle East and North Africa. In recent years, much of his work has made use of new institutional economics and political economy perspectives. His most important books are *Economic Integration in Central America: Empirical Investigations* (1974), *Economics of Development: Empirical Investigations* (with Pan Yotopoulos, 1976), *New Institutional Economics and Development: Theory and Applications to Tunisia* (with Mustapha Nabli and others, 1989), *Fulfilling the Export Potential of Small and Medium Firms* (with Albert Berry and Brian Levy, 1999);

his recent coedited books are *Trade Policy and Economic Integration in the Middle East and North Africa* (with Hassan Hakimian, 2003) and *Explaining Growth in the Middle East* (with Hashem Pesaran, 2006). Among his most recent research interests are the measurement, determinants, and effects of rigidity in labor regulations, trade and economic integration, and the effects of natural resources on institutions, volatility, and growth.

ANDERS OLOFSGÅRD is currently deputy director at the Stockholm Institute of Transition Economics and Associate Professor at the Stockholm School of Economics. Before that he was Associate Professor at the Edmund A. Walsh School of Foreign Service, Georgetown University. He earned his Ph.D. in economics from the Institute for International Economic Studies, Stockholm University, in 2001. His primary research areas are political economy, development, and applied microeconomics, and he has published widely in both economics and political science journals. He has also been a visiting scholar at the research department of the International Monetary Fund and has served as a senior consultant for the World Bank, USAID, and the Swedish Parliament, among others.

MONA SAID is Associate Professor of Economics at the American University in Cairo and Faculty Affiliate and visiting fellow at the London Middle East Institute, School of Oriental and African Studies, University of London. Prior to joining the American University in Cairo, she was a Lecturer (Assistant Professor) in Economics, with reference to the Middle East, at the University of London and an economist at the International Monetary Fund. Her research interests include labor and human resource economics, gender-based inequality in earnings, equity implications of trade policy, youth employment, and migration, with a regional focus on the Middle East and North Africa and the Euro-Mediterranean. Some of her most recent publications have appeared in refereed outlets that have included the *Journal of Developing Areas*, *Comparative Economic Studies*, and *Economic Development and Cultural Change* and in books: *Europe and the Mediterranean Economy* (2011); *Monetary Poverty and Social Exclusion around the Mediterranean Sea* (2012); *The Jordanian Labor Market in the New Millennium* (2013); and *The Egyptian Labor Market in the Era of Revolution* (2015). She obtained her M.Phil. and Ph.D. degrees in economics from the University of Cambridge.

DJAVAD SALEHI-ISFAHANI is currently Professor of Economics at Virginia Tech, nonresident senior fellow at the Brookings Institution, and research fellow at the Economic Research Forum in Cairo. He has taught at the University of Pennsylvania (1977–1984) and has served as visiting faculty at the University of Oxford (1991–1992), the Brookings Institution (2007–2008), and Harvard Kennedy School (2009–2010). He has served on the Board of Trustees of the Economic Research Forum, on the Board of the Middle East Economic Association, and as Associate Editor of the *Middle East Development Journal*. His research has been in energy economics, demographic economics, and the economics of the Middle East. He has coauthored two books, *Models of the Oil Market* and *After the Spring: Economic Transitions in the Arab* World, and edited two books, *Labor and Human Capital in the Middle East* and *The Production and Diffusion of Public Choice*. His articles have appeared in the *Economic Journal,* the *Journal of Development Economics, Health Economics, Economic Development and Cultural Change*, the *Journal of Economic Inequality*, the *International Journal of Middle East Studies,* the *Middle East Development Journal,* and *Iranian Studies*, among others. He received his Ph.D. in economics from Harvard University.

EDWARD A. SAYRE is Associate Professor of Economics and Chair of the Department of Political Science, International Development and International Affairs, at the University of Southern Mississippi. He received his Ph.D. in economics from the University of Texas, Austin, in 1999. In recent years, he has served as the director of research and visiting fellow at the Brooking Institution's Middle East Youth Initiative at the Wolfensohn Center for Development (2010–2011) and as senior research fellow at Fikra Policy and Research in Doha (2011–2015). His research focuses on the economics of the Palestinian-Israeli conflict, labor issues in the Gulf Cooperation Council countries, and the economic concerns of young people in the Middle East. Before starting his current position at the University of Southern Mississippi, he was a Visiting Research Associate at the Palestine Economic Policy Research Institute in Jerusalem (1996–1997) and taught at Kenyon College (1999–2001) and Agnes Scott College (2001–2007). He has also served as treasurer of the Middle East Economic Association, and he was on the Board of Directors from 1999 to 2015.

TARIK M. YOUSEF served as the CEO of Silatech between 2011 and 2015, a regional initiative that promotes the economic empowerment of Arab youth through employment and entrepreneurship. Prior to that, he was the founding dean of the Dubai School of Government between 2007 and 2011, after serving on the faculty of Georgetown University, Washington DC, as Associate Professor of Economics and as the Sheikh Al Sabah Professor of Arab Studies in the School of Foreign Service between 1998 and 2007. He cofounded the Middle East Youth Initiative at the Brookings Institution in 2007, where he has since served as nonresident senior fellow. He received his Ph.D. in economics from Harvard University. An expert on youth inclusion and policy reform in the Arab world, he has contributed over 50 articles and book chapters and coedited several books and reports, including *Generation in Waiting: The Unfulfilled Promise of Young People in the Middle East* (Brookings, 2009) and *After the Spring: Economic Transitions in the Arab World* (Oxford University Press, 2012). His policy experience includes working at the African and Middle East Departments of the International Monetary Fund, the Middle East and North Africa Region of the World Bank, and the UN's Millennium Project. He has served on numerous boards of national and regional organizations in the Arab world.

Introduction

Edward A. Sayre and Tarik M. Yousef

THE MIDDLE EAST and North Africa (MENA) region is at a critical juncture. Starting with the self-immolation of street vendor Mohammed Bouazizi in the provincial town of Sidi Bouzid in the Tunisian interior, the MENA region has witnessed street protests, revolutions, limited democratic progress, political collapse into civil war, and local conflicts that threaten to engulf the entire region. Before the protests, however, young people in the region had been enduring years of economic and social exclusion. The region has had the highest youth unemployment rates in the world for decades as a result of institutional rigidities, education systems that fail to provide appropriate skills, and a demographic "youth bulge" that has increased supply pressures on the education systems and labor markets. Once these young people eventually found jobs, institutional rigidities prevented them from making the full transition to adulthood due to obstacles arising from the region's marriage and housing markets. In fact, in the context of the region's growing youth bulge, such negative outcomes have persisted for decades, with youth facing social, economic, and political exclusion. Beginning in December 2010, this frustration arising from this exclusion has seemed to be erupting, and young people across the region have been at the forefront of the social unrest that was quickly dubbed the Arab Spring.

This book will examine the conditions of youth in the MENA region on the eve of the Arab Spring, in an effort to document the causes of continued youth exclusion and the factors that enabled the uprisings that swept the region during 2011. Recently, several microdata sets have become available that better allow researchers to understand the socioeconomic situation of Arab youth in 2009, 2010, and early 2011 as the Arab Spring began unfolding. The chapters included in this book make use of youth surveys from Morocco and Tunisia and of labor force surveys from several countries (including Egypt, Jordan, and Tunisia) to explore the lives of young people in countries across the Middle East. Although several of the countries examined in this book have not experienced full revolution, their experience during the Arab Spring was marked by protests and demands for economic redistribution and more accountable government. To give broader context to these demands, the book also includes analyses of available data on public opinion about social and political factors, cross-country data on entrepreneurship, cross-country data on educational outcomes, and cross-country data on economic and social conditions.

Background

From 2005 to 2010, many of the contributors to this book (including the editors) collaborated to produce research on Middle East youth through the Middle East Youth Initiative at the Wolfensohn Center for Development at the Brookings Institution. The research agenda coalesced in the 2009 book *Generation in Waiting: The Unfulfilled Promise of Young People in the Middle East*. The book's main argument was that unprecedented social, demographic, and economic pressures on young people in the Middle East existed during this first decade of the twenty-first century. High and then falling birthrates in nearly all Middle Eastern countries, combined with economic and political institutions that could not adapt to the "youth bulge," confronted Middle Eastern governments with unique challenges in dealing with so many potentially unemployed youth. These youth were not able to make the successful transition to adulthood that their parents and grandparents had been able to make and instead found themselves excluded from transitions from school to work and to marriage and family formation.

In 2013 the Middle East Youth Initiative was re-launched under the auspices of Silatech, a government-supported NGO based in Doha, Qatar. One of the agenda items of this project, known as MEYI 2.0, has been to develop a follow-up to *Generation in Waiting*. The need for such a book is threefold. First, new data from 2009 and 2010 has now been collected, released, and analyzed by researchers. The time period for *Generation in Waiting* was before the global financial crisis occurred. As such, it was silent on what the ramifications of the crisis might be for Middle East youth. Toward this effort, the editors of this book held a conference in Beirut on December 6 and 7, 2012. The papers presented at that conference have become the basis for the chapters of this book. Not all of the presented papers made it into the book, and in a few cases two or more papers have been synthesized into a single chapter.

Second, it was clear that while the recommendations and insights of *Generation in Waiting* had been prescient, it had missed many aspects related to the foundations of the

Arab Spring. Specifically, the role of technology and social media in the lives of young people had not been examined. Yet anecdotal evidence from the early days of the Arab Spring suggested the importance of social media in the political lives of youth. Data sets were beginning to be developed that allowed micro-level analysis of the role of social media, allowing us to analyze this phenomenon.

Third, at the time, data were simply not available from some Arab Spring states, most important Tunisia. Because *Generation in Waiting* focused on country studies, little was said in it about the countries not examined in a case study. Thus, there was a need to expand coverage in North Africa to include Tunisia and, to the degree that we could, the Gulf states, where youth—despite these states' relative wealth—have experienced similar outcomes in regard to education, employment, and delays in marriage and family formation.

Because of the variety of data sources and topics covered in this book, our purpose is not to claim what definitively caused the Arab Spring but to focus on the most important aspects of the economic and political environment of the Middle East prior to the Arab Spring. For this reason, we see three distinct threads inherent in the arguments the various authors make. Some of the arguments are made explicitly; others are part of the background to the story. These threads are (1) the use of microeconomic analyses, (2) the importance of relative outcomes, and (3) the primacy of institutions.

This book advances the development literature by using the microeconomic approach to development that includes using randomized experiments, official local labor force data, and newly available microeconomic data. This trend in the development field has allowed researchers to examine the factors that are seen to cause differences in growth rates between countries at the microeconomic level, not just the macroeconomic level. Thus, the emphasis is not just on what causes growth rates to differ but also on why those factors are important.

The analyses found in this book focus on microeconomic approaches rather than cross-country methods. We argue that to fully understand the conditions that created the environment in which the Arab Spring erupted, one must examine the microeconomic conditions and the policy environment of individual states. Some similarities will be worth mentioning, and many countries face similar economic issues, but the similarities and differences are best understood by using microdata. This microeconomic comparative approach will be conducted both explicitly in specific chapters of the book and indirectly by comparing results between chapters.

Without claiming to have the only explanation of the genesis of the Arab Spring, this book offers a deeper analysis of the origins of the Arab Spring than any book that is currently available. The focus is on relative differences in economic conditions between groups and the socioeconomic factors that lead to revolution. This relationship is spelled out more clearly in specific chapters, and while the authors of individual chapters may differ in their particular approach, certain elements are consistent.

Two works in particular are important in framing our analysis about relative outcomes and how the demographic challenge has manifested itself into a state of revolution.

Richard Easterlin in *Birth and Fortune* (1980) made the argument that relatively large birth cohorts were faced with a set of economic and social disadvantages when compared to relatively small birth cohorts. Beginning with the overcrowding of schools and the lack of sufficient resources in the education system in the United States, Easterlin argued, the relatively bad economic outcomes for young people in the baby boom were likely to stick with them for the rest of their lives.

In *Why Men Rebel,* Ted Gurr (1970) developed what he called the relative deprivation hypothesis. According to Gurr, to understand why revolution occurs, one must consider psychological factors and not merely, political, economic, and social factors. This is similar to the arguments made by Hamermesh and Soss (1974) in their economic theory of suicide, which drew on Henry and Short (1954). All of these researchers focus on the importance of relative rather than absolute conditions when determining when economic conditions push individuals into action. For Henry and Short and Hamermesh and Soss, they were considering individual actions directed against other individuals and groups. However, Gurr focuses on the importance of the psychological features of groups of people who may have similar complaints against the established economic and political order. This *relative deprivation* is defined as the perceived discrepancy between value expectations and value capabilities. The perceived discrepancy is between the group undergoing the deprivation and a reference group. In the case of Middle East youth, the parents' generation serves as the reference group.

In this book, we focus not on absolute conditions of youth as being deterministic or even salient to the story of revolt but on the relative conditions of young people and their perception of future well-being. While we will acknowledge that it was not only the youth that participated in the revolts, without the preconditions of the relative deprivation of the educated, young generation, the critical elements for revolt would not have coalesced the way they did.

The institutional approach to economic development has been emphasized since North and Thomas (1973), though evidence for the importance of institutions goes back to Adam Smith. Institutions are seen as one of the primary causes of economic growth and simultaneously as being a consequence of economic conditions. More broadly, institutions matter because they determine the incentives for agents in an economy. They set the rules of the game and determine the constraints by which households, businesses, and organizations are bound. As Acemoglu and Robinson (2013) show, there is increasing evidence that cross-country economic analysis needs to take institutions into account in a way that fully incorporates the effects of institutions on constraining behavior and the incentives they produce.

In our institutional approach, it will also be important to highlight the roles played by specific economic, political, and social actors, which are generally going to be defined as *organizations* in the economy. These organizations interact in the institutional framework to help manifest the specific incentives that individual actors respond to. One such organization is the education system. While education systems vary from state to state,

Middle East education systems often have certain characteristics that allow us to speak of their role very broadly in the story of the lives of young people there. In the transition from youth to adulthood, the education system helps connect young people to good jobs. Part of the specific characteristics of Middle East education systems were that in order to fit into the broader institutional framework seen in the authoritarian bargain, jobs were guaranteed to all those who possessed at least a secondary education, and even better government jobs were guaranteed to those who received a university education. As a result of this institutional framework, through the specific organization known as the education system, a perverse incentive structure was created. It created an incentive to only acquire the credential of a particular degree, not the skills that the possession of that degree usually implied. As such, the Middle East education system became part of the problem, as it would only produce credentials that were of no use to private employers who wanted to hire workers on the basis of their marginal productivity.

The institutional approach found in this book includes evidence to explain the current social and economic conditions of the Middle East and to highlight possible areas of progress or stagnation in the future. First, this book clearly shows the primacy of institutions in determining the tensions in generations that will not end simply due to the deposing of particular dictators. Institutional failure was the source of the crisis, and this book highlights those institutions that have failed. They include the structure of the educational system; the system of strict labor market regulations; and a social welfare system that discourages formal employment. Second, these analyses highlight likely areas of institutional reform with the establishment of new regimes. Finally, this book highlights areas of persistence of the institutional structures of Middle Eastern societies that will continue to slow development in the future.

Outline

Demography, Education, and Employment

In chapter 1 David Beck and Paul Dyer review the evidence on demographic change and delayed transitions in the Middle East. Due to declining state budgets, Arab states have failed to deliver on promised education and employment benefits to the burgeoning population of Arab youth. This failure by states has led to poor quality of education, high youth unemployment rates, and resultant delays in marriage. The private sector is largely not an option for these young people, as the education that they received from the state focused on rote skills with little applicability to the demands of a modern dynamic workplace.

Beck and Dyer trace the source of the youth bulge in the Middle East and report on its current status. Specifically, they show how birthrates and death rates diverged after World War II to lead to sharply rising population growth. The traditional pattern of the demographic transition from less developed to more developed societies is that soon after mortality rates decline, birthrates also begin to fall. In the Middle East this process was delayed. By the early 1980s, however, fertility also began to fall and fell at a very rapid rate, exceeding the rate of change experienced by most regions in the world. This persistent high level and then rapid decline in the birthrate led to the dramatic relative size of the youth bulge. Beck and Dyer conclude by discussing the impact that this youth bulge (or youth wave) has had on labor markets that are trying to absorb so many new entrants.

In chapter 2, Djavad Salehi-Isfahani reviews the growth and equity in accumulation of human capital in the MENA region, dividing human capital in terms of its quantity and quality and examining the roles of the state and family in determining educational gains. In doing so, he highlights the efforts and (quantitative) success of the state in promoting proeducation policies, improving educational attainment through compulsory education, and improving equity in terms of access to school. He highlights public expenditure on education as being relatively high in states across the region, also noting the impact—albeit indirect—the state has had in improving attainment through public sector hiring and policies aimed at helping families reduce fertility.

Despite these efforts, outcomes in terms of quality of education remain poor. The poor quality of education and learning across the region is demonstrated in results from the Trends in Mathematics and Sciences Study (TIMSS) examination. Notably, no countries in the MENA region produce scores on this examination that reach the world average, and between 1999 and 2011 no significant gains were made in scores. Moreover, there is a striking lack of correlation between public spending on education and test results.

In addition, a striking inequality in learning remains. In decomposing results from the 2007 TIMSS study, Salehi-Isfahani finds that students from more privileged backgrounds have a much better chance of securing higher education than those from more disadvantaged backgrounds. In turn, there is limited intergenerational mobility in terms of attainment across the region. Here family plays a decided role: more advantaged families are able to invest more, both in financial terms and in terms of parental time, in the education of their children. Moreover, the role of the state in production of human capital has diminished over time relative to that of families, as the role of the public sector as employer for new graduates has declined.

The greater role of family resources means that the inequality of outcomes translates into inequality of opportunity. The same state policies that have led to success in attainment (meritocratic education with state hiring of graduates) are to some extent responsible for the high degree of inequality of opportunity. In the future, to combat rising inequality, state policies must focus on leveling the playing field for education, moving beyond efforts to provide educational opportunities to efforts to favor the disadvantaged. This includes efforts to improving public schools, investing in preschool programs, providing free tutoring to disadvantaged children, and reforming selection methods for university in ways that improve the chances of high-ability poor youth to remain in school.

In chapter 3 Mona Said examines the labor market conditions on the eve of the Arab Spring by studying the effects of the global financial crisis on the Middle East. This chapter summarizes the changes in employment and unemployment for Middle East youth in a broad set of countries from Morocco to Syria. The author uses various data sets to analyze how changes in the global economy have affected local labor market conditions. While the Middle East was not as directly affected by the 2008 downturn as Europe or the United States, the financial crisis did negatively impact several Arab countries because of their dependence on the financial sector, tourism, remittances, and foreign direct investment. Moreover, since youth are the most vulnerable members of the labor force in these countries, they were the most negatively impacted by the downturn.

The primary factors that caused the downturn in the Middle East were the negative impacts of the financial crisis on the price of oil and on remittances from Europe. Looking at figures from the entire region, Said shows that the youth unemployment rate increased by an entire percentage point from 2008 to 2010, doubtless as a result of the financial crisis. However, the years leading up to the crisis were also particularly good ones: when examining the longer term prospects for the Middle East, such indicators actually pointed toward improvements in conditions.

By examining a set of individual case studies, Said is able to give a detailed picture of the various impacts of the financial crisis throughout the region. For example, while unemployment rates increased for all young men in Jordan between 2006 and 2009, unemployment rates for young men in Egypt declined. Likewise, Syria appears to have been harder hit than most other countries, as it saw its GDP growth rate reduced significantly, largely due to the decline in remittances. Tunisia saw an overall decrease in its unemployment rate but an increase in the unemployment rate for young people.

Said concludes by discussing various policy interventions that impacted the global downturn on the region. Labor migration policies are critically important in understanding the transmission of shocks from one part of the region or from Europe to the MENA region more broadly. While some Gulf countries are looking at reducing their dependence on expatriate labor, the demand for workers from the Middle East appears to have remained high. In addition, specific labor market interventions, especially in the area of closing the skills and expectations mismatch, do not seem to have had much of an impact thus far, although new regional initiatives may have more of an impact in the future.

The topic of chapter 4, by Edward Sayre and Rana Hendy, is female labor supply in the MENA region, with a special focus on the labor market decisions of young women. Many researchers make the connection between women's opportunities in the workforce and economic development. If women are unable to work outside the home because of cultural, legal, or other institutional barriers, then the country is not able to use all of its resources effectively. This issue is particularly relevant in the Middle East, where female labor force participation rates are some of the lowest throughout the world. Female participation rates range from a high of 52 percent in Qatar to a low of 13 percent in Syria.

This chapter begins by examining the different experiences with female labor supply in countries in the Middle East. Several countries have particularly low female participation, including Algeria, Syria, the West Bank and Gaza, and Jordan, all of which have participation rates lower than 20 percent. These countries are followed by North African countries like Egypt, Morocco, and Tunisia, which along with Yemen and Lebanon have female participation rates of around 24–26 percent. The highest participation rates are seen in the Gulf states, with participation rates in the 30, 40, and 50 percent range, but these are biased upward by the presence of expatriate workers.

The determinants of participation by country include age, marital status, and education level. The most educated women are also the most likely to seek work. This is also part of the reason why they also suffer from the highest unemployment rates, especially for women in their twenties looking for their first jobs. A critical issue becomes what happens when women get married. This chapter explores the case studies of Jordan and Egypt; using labor market panel surveys from each country, the authors are able to estimate the likelihood of women to stay in the labor market after marriage.

The authors find that the experience in Jordan is very different from that in Egypt, in terms of the probability of dropping out of the labor force after marriage. In both countries, women who work for the public sector generally do not drop out of the labor force when they get married. However, in Jordan, women in the private sector prior to marriage become inactive at marriage. On the other hand in Egypt, women do not have many opportunities in the private sector for wage work, but when they get married they often go from inactivity to private sector nonwage work, which implies that they are moving into the informal sector.

A critical question the authors also attempt to answer is whether it is the husbands or social norms that keep married women out of the workforce. Using the case of Tunisia, the authors examine the difference in labor force participation for women by both husband's and wife's education level and find that female labor force participation of married women depends heavily on the education level of the husband.

Paul Dyer and Samer Kherfi examine labor market issues of Arab youth in the Gulf states in chapter 5. The countries of the Arab Gulf have particular labor force issues that are either not as severe or are completely absent in other countries in the region. Specifically, high per capita income derived from hydrocarbon earnings leads to a set of issues concerning the redistributionist social contract, the incentives of workers to attain human capital, and the presence of a large expatriate population. With these issues in mind, the authors examine several case studies in the Gulf, paying particular attention to the UAE, Qatar, and Bahrain.

For the UAE, the authors have access to the only microdata set available to labor economists working in the Gulf, and thus the authors use results from the case study to draw wider conclusions about the region. Qatar is an important case: the pace of economic development in the country is causing particular strains that are worth exploring. From 2000 to 2010, Qatar increased its population from 600,000 to 1.6 million; most of the new residents were expatriate workers. In contrast, Bahrain is worthy of special attention due to declining oil resources and the political conflict that continues there as of this writing.

Using microdata from the UAE and aggregate data from other countries, Dyer and Kherfi explore the transition from education to employment for Arab youth in the Gulf. In nearly all the Gulf states, unemployment rates of young people are three times higher than unemployment rates for adults (aged 30–64). The relatively higher levels of education for youth, especially women, have contributed to higher levels of labor force participation, but also greater relative unemployment for Gulf female youth more than for other young women. Women aged 15–29 have unemployment rates of over 40 percent in the UAE, much higher than in several other countries in the Gulf.

The authors find that the generous provisions found in public sector employment in the Gulf imply that few Gulf citizens work in the private sector. The public sector offers such better pay and benefits that there are limited incentives to find a private sector job, which will have longer hours, a more competitive work environment, and fewer benefits. The authors indicate that due to saturation of the public sector, however, the main policy challenge of the Gulf states will be to make private sector jobs more attractive while at the same time not burdening the private sector with regulations that halt job creation.

Social Media, Youth, and Protest

In chapter 6 Anita Breuer explores the effect of social media use by protesters during the Tunisian revolution. Breuer begins her study with an examination of the general role digital media plays in the political process. She emphasizes that while there is a widespread popular belief that the Internet will undermine authoritarian rule, the political implications of the Internet in the context of authoritarian or democratizing political systems are still largely unknown. In the context of Tunisia, it is a widely shared assumption that the revolution's joining of disparate forces would not have been possible without modern communication technology and social media. Breuer conducts both a quantitative and a qualitative study to fully understand the role of social media in the revolution.

Breuer traces both the development of and subsequent access to the Internet in Tunisia and the attempts to censor the Internet there. President Zine el-Abidine Ben Ali, in order to promote his image as a modernizer, widely expanded communication technology infrastructure and allowed for access to the Internet through state-run Internet cafés. Despite the international community's encouragement of the expansion of Internet access, Ben Ali kept close control of everything that happened on the web in Tunisia. In August 2008, he responded to protest movements centered on a strike concerning working conditions by blocking Facebook. In 2009, censorship expanded extensively, leading many of the web-based activists in Tunisia to increase their activities and to find ingenious new ways around the censors. Breuer notes that Tunisia's cyber avant-garde, with some exceptions, was initially dominated by affluent, well-educated, polyglot individuals with high amounts of cultural capital.

Breuer draws on evidence from the popular protests in Tunisia between December 2010 and January 2011, using expert interviews with Tunisian bloggers and a web survey conducted among Tunisian Facebook users. Breuer argues that the social media allowed a "digital elite" to form personal networks and circumvent the national media blackout by brokering information outside the mainstream media. Furthermore, social media helped to overcome the "free rider" problem of collective action by reporting the magnitude of protest events. Finally, Breuer shows how social media facilitated the formation of a national collective identity that was supportive of protest action and transcended geographical and socioeconomic disparities by providing a shared, mobilizing element of emotional grievance.

In chapter 7 Ishac Diwan uses World Values Survey data on Egypt from 2000 and 2008 to explore the underlying factors that drove the Egyptian revolution of 2011, testing competing theories that have been put forward as bases for understanding the revolution. These include theories that Egypt's uprising was a middle-class-led effort to modernize; that it was a poor- and middle-class-led effort at redistributing wealth; that it was, in essence, an Islamic revolution; and finally that it was a youth-driven uprising influenced by demographics. Diwan identifies changes in public opinion related to preferences for democracy, income equality, and political Islam among individuals of differing age groups, social classes, and educational backgrounds. These changes help to explain the uprising and the path forward as Egypt struggles with implementing a democratic system.

In his analysis, Diwan finds little support for the theory that the Egyptian revolution and preferences for democracy were driven by the country's youth population. While acknowledging the key role played by youth in the uprising's initial mobilization, Diwan observes little difference between the views of youth and older individuals regarding preferences for democracy and income equality. Moreover, youth opinions in the lead-up to the revolution reflect a decrease in interpersonal trust, suggesting a declining belief that governance along democratic lines would be more feasible or credible.

Along similar lines, despite the relative success of Islamist parties in the elections following the revolution, Diwan finds little evidence to suggest that the revolution's success was driven by mobilization along religious lines. In comparing differences in support for democracy and support for autocracy along the religious/secular divide, Diwan notes few differences in the aggregate. Instead, support for political Islam operates as a veil for class differences, with middle-class supporters of political Islam favoring democracy in roughly equal measure with middle-class secularists. In fact, support for political Islam in the population as a whole declines slightly over time.

Diwan does find evidence of deep societal frustration with growing inequality and of preferences for equality increasing over time. Not only does he describe an increase in the number of respondents identifying themselves as poor rather than middle class, he finds preferences for income equality increasing greatly among the poor and the middle class over time. Similarly, there is growing support for democracy among both the poor and the middle class. In both aspects, the increase in support among youth is weaker than support among older groups. And while the rich favor more equality over time, their support for democracy erodes.

Such findings suggest that modernization theory and redistribution theory are both at work in setting the foundations for the Egyptian revolution. The World Values Survey results demonstrate a rise in popular grievances and in aspirations of a more educated population simultaneously. This concurrence explains why the middle class, at the intersection of these forces, has served as the principal champion of democratization. While this phenomenon may include, inherently, a restless middle-class youth frustrated with poor labor market outcomes, their growing frustration with such outcomes is matched by that of their parents. At the same time, the divide in this seemingly united middle class suggests that Egypt's revolution risks devolving in the absence of natural coalitions among the new ruling elite.

In chapter 8 Raj Desai, Anders Olofsgård, and Tarik Yousef seek to explain the roots of the Arab Spring and the youth-led unrest that occurred across the Arab region. The authors apply simple game theory to Gallup World Poll data from low and middle-income countries, including behavioral data related to socioeconomic status, nonviolent political engagement, and support for violent rebellion, as well as demographic characteristics such as age, education, gender, employment status, and income. In applying their model, the authors find that while marginalized groups are known to participate in acts of violent rebellion, they tend to remain bystanders in other aspects of civic and political life, including participation in political parties, signing petitions, and demonstrations.

The key theoretical argument is that political actions signal preferences for political change and that the credibility of those signals depends on the opportunity cost of political action. This opportunity cost varies depending on the socioeconomic situation: if you are unemployed or have low labor productivity (correlated to income and education), the opportunity cost of partaking in nonviolent street protests and strikes is low. This would suggest that one would be more likely to participate, but since the signaling value of such activities is low, the regime pays little attention to them, and political change is unlikely to follow. Thus, marginalized groups may refrain from peaceful political action in the (correct) belief that the political elite pay little attention to their protests anyway. What follows is a potential vicious cycle of withdrawal from peaceful political engagement, leading to further socioeconomic marginalization, leading to further withdrawal, and so on.

On the other hand citizens who are more politically connected and better off—the more educated, the employed, and the middle class—face a higher opportunity cost of political action. This is partly due to their higher labor productivity but also because their relative position in society may be more dependent on the tacit acceptance of their status by the regime. This group thus faces a higher initial cost of taking to the streets in peaceful demonstrations. However, if they do, they send a much stronger signal of discontent to the regime. Given their role, they are therefore more likely to be able to instigate policy change through peaceful means and are therefore more likely to choose this option despite the higher costs. The model thus suggests that while the relatively better off are more likely to engage in peaceful political action, the worse off are more likely to turn to violent political action to instigate change.

When one applies this perspective to attempts to understand the Arab Spring, it is notable that the initial spark of what was later labeled the Arab Spring came from the self-immolation of a marginalized vendor in Tunisia. This spark generated protests from other marginalized groups, often turning violent, but the big push came when members of the middle class and even the relatively affluent in Tunisia started protesting the regime, typically in less violent forms. Spreading to Egypt, the uprising was initially led by educated, urban youth of the middle and upper classes engaging in peaceful demonstrations and protests. While positioning themselves as being for the resolution of poverty and inequality, they had the means by which to organize and mobilize against the state, and the state paid attention. Mass support for the uprisings came as the more marginalized joined in with an assessment that the signaling value of mostly peaceful protests was higher when they joined forces with the middle class.

Economic and Social Policy in the Wake of the Arab Spring

In chapter 9, Ghada Barsoum explores the issue of young people working in the informal economy in Egypt. The issue of informal work and limited access to social protection among working youth is a critical issue, yet these issues have not been sufficiently addressed by Egyptian policy. Barsoum claims that policymakers have instead focused on the more immediate issue of youth unemployment. The concern about the unemployed arises from the political volatility of this group, and the demonstrations of January 25, 2011, showed that government officials' fear that employment issues could lead to political action against the regime was rightly placed. Barsoum emphasizes that it is important to remember that the Arab Spring was sparked by a frustrated street vendor, someone working informally. By focusing on broader issues of unemployment rather than informal work and job quality, Egyptian policymakers may have failed to address the most prescient concerns in this area.

Barsoum examines this issue by using qualitative long-form interviews with young people in Cairo who are working in the informal economy. Building on these interviews, the chapter describes the lived experience of informal work and lack of social protection among youth. Young people who work informally are not governed by work contracts in the same way formal sector workers are. This chapter seeks to provide an understanding of the process of informal work as experienced and described by working youth themselves. How do they perceive their lack of social protection and social security? If the needs of the present are barely covered by the income that comes from their work, how do they foresee their future? What policies need to be put in place to address this situation of vulnerability? In addition to the qualitative data, Barsoum uses quantitative data from the 2009 Survey of Young People in Egypt to contextualize interview results.

Barsoum finds that young people in Egypt still want the benefits of government jobs. When working in the informal sector, they are not receiving the social insurance and protection the Arab social contract has promised. Instead they find that they are kept off of the social insurance rolls because otherwise they would be too expensive as workers. In looking at potential policy solutions, Barsoum examines several examples, including recent reforms in postrevolutionary Indonesia, that could offer ways forward in postrevolutionary Egypt. However, Barsoum notes that it is not clear that the political will exists to implement such reforms and that the continued valorization of the government job by Egyptian youth may continue to be a policy hurdle. Without some degree of understanding of the unsustainable nature of the previous work-life course, young people may resist any policy that falls short of what previous generations received.

In chapter 10 Jeffrey Nugent examines the role that labor market regulations play in decreasing demand for young workers. Many researchers claim that labor market deregulation can help increase demand for young workers, as the costs of employment and the even higher costs of dismissing workers make employers reluctant to hire new workers. Nugent highlights that it is also possible that because of the tendency of these labor market regulations to discourage firing, at least in the short run, deregulation of the labor market could increase unemployment by giving firms a free hand in dismissing employees.

Nugent reviews the literature that demonstrates the relative rigidities of labor markets in many of the countries in the Middle East, most notably Morocco, Egypt, Syria, and Tunisia. These rigidities take the form of ambiguous government reviews of intended dismissals, the outlawing of dismissals for pecuniary reasons, high mandatory severance and retirement benefits, and generous workplace benefits concerning hours, working conditions, and mandatory leaves. What is unknown, however, is the actual effectiveness of these labor laws, since there is a large degree of noncompliance and there are large informal sectors that do not adhere to any of these labor laws.

Nugent then uses the World Bank's Enterprise Surveys (WBES) in two separate analyses. The first uses the WBES from Morocco and Egypt to assess what the effect of liberalizing labor markets in these regimes would be. Due to the slow pace of reform and the large degree of noncompliance by firms, the hypothetical questions found in the WBES allow for a better understanding of this issue. In his empirical analysis, Nugent finds that companies that claim that labor law rigidity is more of an obstacle are more likely to respond to an elimination of all labor laws. In addition, they are relatively more likely to increase dismissals rather than hiring as a response to reforms. This lends credibility to some observers' worries that short-term costs of labor market reform may manifest in higher unemployment.

In his second stage of analysis, comparing WBES results in a large cross-section of countries, Nugent finds that deregulation could lead to substantially higher employment of young people, particularly at certain types of firms. Firms with a greater degree of export orientation and those that are more labor intensive, such as those in the garment and textile industry, are likely to increase employment the most.

In chapter 11, Brahim Boudarbat and Daniel Egel look at the impact of vocational training reforms in Morocco. Morocco has implemented policies to close the skills mismatch that is at the root of youth unemployment, including creating programs for vocational education and training that are widely supported by the public. The goal of these programs is to improve the attractiveness of recent graduates to private sector employers and decrease these graduates' dependence on the public sector work.

This chapter analyzes three types of program that were implemented as part of these reforms. These programs include co-operative training, apprenticeship programs, and a skills-based approach. The data used is in this chapter is from two longitudinal surveys conducted by the Moroccan Department of Vocational Training to explore the apparent failure of these programs. By using data on graduates from urban vocational training facilities who completed their studies in 2000, the authors are able to present the longer term impact of reforms rather than simply focusing on the short-term job market effects.

While Boudarbat and Egel find that both the privatization of vocational training and policies designed to encourage small business formation were largely ineffective, they also show that participation in a traineeship program after graduation has a lasting and strongly positive impact on subsequent labor market outcomes. The authors also provide evidence suggesting that the failure of the program that was designed to provide incentives to small business formation in the formal sector can be largely attributed to two factors. The first is that the program seems to have been poorly publicized, as nearly 80 percent of the eligible individuals were simply unaware that it existed. Second, this program was unable to adjust for the increased costs associated with joining the formal sector. The lesson from the Moroccan experience is that there is still a role for vocational training, but the outcomes are far from certain, and the institutional arrangements are critical for the potential success of any training program.

In the final chapter, we explore the possibilities of economic reforms in light of the Arab Spring and put forward challenges to policy makers and researchers. The first challenge is to not squander the unique opportunity that has presented itself with the Arab Spring. The initial feelings of support for change could allow policy innovations by new democratically elected governments. Unfortunately, this honeymoon period will not last long, and some may claim that it is already over. The second challenge is to researchers of microeconomic development in the Middle East. The impact of the first few years of the post–Arab Spring Middle East will likely determine the long-run development conditions throughout the region. For that reason, it is imperative that researchers develop new tools and research questions to fully understand the challenges of the new realities in the Middle East.

After presenting these challenges, we focus on the areas where policy reform is needed most dramatically. The need arises from increasing youth inclusion and fully taking advantage of the youth bulge to turn the demographic challenge into a true demographic gift. The main areas of policy reform are educational equality, job creation and job quality, and access to credit markets.

The key policy impediment is a continued focus on rote learning and centrally controlled education systems that reward students on the basis of their performance on standardized tests. It is imperative that the education system move from credential development to skill development to make workers more attractive to private sector employers. Moreover, policymakers must take steps to level the playing field for youth from poorer families, enabling them to secure the educational quality gains that are open now only to those with access to tutoring and other aids in promoting better educational gains.

In an environment with a young, dynamic, and creative workforce, employers still must be compelled with the correct incentives to be willing to hire these young people. As Nugent outlines in chapter 10, a major area of employers' concern is that of labor market regulations. Labor market reforms will need to balance providing basic social protections with allowing firms the ability to respond to market signals to determine whom to hire.

Finally, access to credit is extremely limited in the region, so freeing up credit markets will allow the young person with a bright future but without a high-paying first job to start taking the steps toward family formation and true adulthood. Financial reform is just a small part of general freeing up of markets (along with the removal of tariffs and housing market reforms) that can open up the potential of the Arab private sector.

REFERENCES

Acemoglu, D., and J. A. Robinson. 2013. Economics versus politics: The pitfalls of policy advice. http://economics.mit.edu/files/8741.

Easterlin, R. A. 1987. *Birth and fortune: The impact of numbers on personal welfare.* Chicago: University of Chicago Press.

Gurr, T. R. 1970. *Why men rebel.* Princeton, NJ: Princeton University Press.

Hamermesh, D. S., and Soss, N. M. 1974. An economic theory of suicide. *Journal of Political Economy* 82(1): 83–98.

Henry, A. F., and J. F. Short. 1954. *Suicide and homicide: Some economic, sociological and psychological aspects of aggression.* New York: Free Press.

North, D. C., and R. P. Thomas. 1973. *The rise of the western world: A new economic history.* Cambridge: Cambridge University Press.

1 Demographic Transitions across the Middle East and North Africa

David Beck and Paul Dyer

OVER THE PAST three decades, a youth wave has washed over the Middle East and North Africa (MENA) region, with those aged 15–29 making up an increasing share of the region's total population. In 1990, youth formed 26.9 percent of the MENA region's total population. By 2010, on the eve of the Arab Spring, they formed 30.4 percent. With so many young people concurrently making the transition to adulthood, this youth wave has put significant pressures on the region's education systems and labor markets. As such, the region's youth are weighing their options about investments in school and career in a constrained economic environment. The inability of the MENA region's economies to fully incorporate this emerging generation has fueled a growing frustration among the region's young people and an increasing sense of urgency among its policymakers.

To best address the needs of the region's youth, it is important to understand that they are the contemporary manifestation of a historic demographic transition that has been unfolding for decades. Further, throughout this transition, the youth cohort has remained important, both underscoring the pressures that accompany a growing population and personifying the potential economic boons that can follow. With these pressures and potentials in focus, this chapter provides an overview of the changing demographic dynamics of the MENA region since the end of World War II, the resultant rise of a regional youth wave, and the effects these developments have had on the economic inclusion of the region's youth.

The Demographic Transition in the Middle East and North Africa Region and Other Developing Regions

The youth wave—or "youth bulge" as it is more commonly termed—in the MENA region has formed in the context of gradual demographic changes experienced throughout the developing world since the end of World War II. Over the last half century, this demographic transition, fueled by sharp declines in mortality and comparatively delayed declines in fertility, has led to incremental but impactful shifts, both in the growth of particular populations and the structure of their respective age structures. Further, it has triggered significant socioeconomic changes, which, while a shared and general feature of the demographic transition, have differed greatly across the world.

Across the developing world, rapid declines in the rate of mortality, particularly among infants and young children, triggered the beginning of the demographic transition. In the early 1950s, the mortality rate in less developed regions was over twice that of more developed regions, with 23 deaths per 1,000 people in the former compared with 11 per 1,000 in the latter.[1] At the same time, for every 1,000 infants born in a developing country, 153 died within their first year, compared to 60 out of 1,000 in more developed countries. In the postwar period, governments, as well as international agencies such as the World Health Organization, moved to improve food security and reduce the impact of disease by improving sanitation, expanding preventative health care, and utilizing newly available antibiotics and vaccinations (World Bank 2004).[2] In part as a result of these efforts, mortality rates among less developed countries decreased to 10 per 1,000 people, and infant mortality declined to 79 per 1,000 births by 1980.

The MENA region's experience with declining mortality is striking. At 25.3 deaths per 1,000 in the early 1950s, the region's mortality rate was notably higher than the average among less developed regions, at 23.1. At that time, rates in East Asia, Latin America, and Sub-Saharan Africa were 20.3, 15.5, and 27.7, respectively. Since then, the aggregate mortality rate in the MENA region has steadily declined, falling firmly below the average among less developed regions in the 1980s. By the early 1990s, the MENA region's mortality rate had decreased to 6.5, equaling the rate of Latin America and falling below that of East Asia.[3] In contrast, mortality in Sub-Saharan Africa has remained high, falling only to 16.2 deaths in the early 1990s and to 13 by the early 2000s.

In terms of changes in infant mortality, the experience of the MENA region is perhaps more significant. In the early 1950s, the region's infant mortality rate was much higher than the average among developing regions, with 214 deaths per 1,000 births in the former compared to 153 per 1,000 in the latter. At that time, the rates of East Asia, Latin America, and Sub-Saharan Africa were 116, 126, and 183, respectively. Over the next 30 years, the MENA region's infant mortality rate fell dramatically, and in the 1980s it went below the average among less developed regions. By the late 2000s, the MENA region's infant mortality rate, at 25 per 1,000 births, was nearly half that of the developing regions as a whole, at 46.

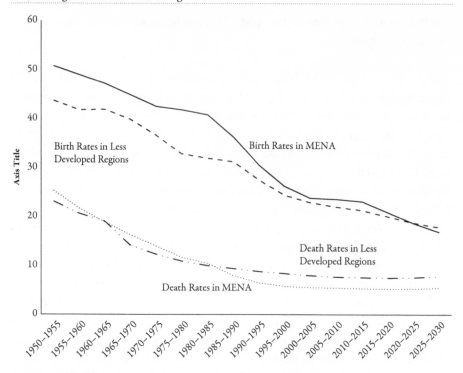

FIGURE 1.1 The demographic transition in MENA and developing regions, 1950–2030.
Source: United Nations (2013).

As shown in figure 1.1, mortality in the MENA region started at a fairly high point compared with that of other middle-income regions, and the region's gradual mortality decline generally followed global patterns. In contrast, its experience with declining fertility has been unique, with a pattern characterized by a prolonged delay in the decline of its already comparatively high fertility rates and a rapid acceleration of that decline beginning in the mid- to late 1980s.

In the early 1950s, the average fertility rate in less developed regions, at 6.1 children per woman, was more than double that of the more developed regions, at 2.8. At that time, the MENA region maintained an even higher fertility rate of 6.9 children per woman, compared to rates of 5.6 in East Asia, 5.9 in Latin America, and 6.5 in Sub-Saharan Africa. The MENA region's high fertility supported a birthrate of nearly 51 births per 1,000, notably higher than the average among the developing countries, at less than 44 births per 1,000.[4]

By the early 1980s, the overall fertility rate of less developed regions had fallen to 4.2 children per woman. During the 1970s the fertility rates of East Asia and Latin America, middle-income regions like MENA, began to fall dramatically, such that by the early 1980s these rates had decreased to 2.6 and 3.9, respectively. It was not until the late 1980s, however, that fertility began to fall significantly in the MENA region. In the early 1980s, the region's average fertility rate was 6.1 children per woman, and the region's birthrate

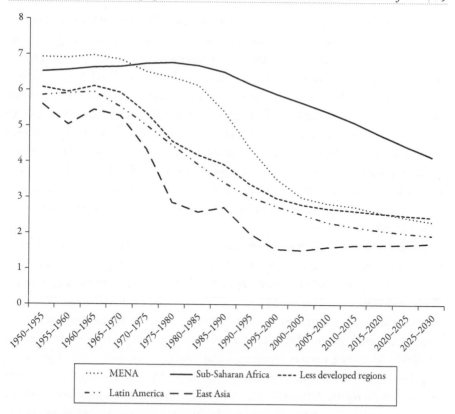

FIGURE 1.2 Total fertility rate in MENA and developing regions, 1950–2030.
Source: United Nations (2013).

was 41 births per 1,000. By the early 1990s, however, average fertility in the MENA region had fallen to 4.4 children per woman, and within the next 15 years, it reached 3.0 children per woman, nearly matching the average among less developed regions, at 2.8.[5] Similarly, the region's birthrate declined below 24 births per 1,000 population by the early 2000s. Since then, the MENA region's fertility rate has decreased further, albeit at a more gradual rate. The 2013 estimate for the fertility rate is 2.8 children per woman, while the region's birthrate is estimated at 23.1 births per 1,000.

When compared with that of other regions, the MENA region's fertility decline is remarkable (see fig. 1.2). The region's fertility rate remained among the highest in the world through the early 1980s, while those of other middle-income regions, such as East Asia and Latin America, were experiencing significant declines. After declining only slightly for decades (or even increasing in some countries during the 1960s and 1970s), the MENA region's fertility rate has dropped rapidly since the late 1980s.

There is a wide body of literature on the determinants of fertility, with explanations for its change focusing on proximate determinants related to individual behavior and biological factors, such as sterility, contraceptive use, and postpartum abstinence, which affect fertility directly, or to institutional, economic, or cultural factors, which may affect fertility decisions more indirectly.[6] Within the latter factors, attention has been given to the roles that income variation, urbanization, and differing access to education and health services have played in decreasing fertility (Behrman, Duryea, and Székely 1999; Kremer and Chen 2000; Schultz 1997). Toward explaining the MENA region's unique fertility experience, scholars have additionally suggested that the patriarchal nature of traditional Arab culture has had an influence on the region's fertility (Hoodfar 1997; Papps 1993) or that Islam itself may have a distinctly pronatal bias when compared with other religions (Jones and Karim 2005; Lucas and Meyer 1994; Omran and Roudi 1993). Explanations that build on unique cultural or religious drivers are largely discounted, however, when controlled for other determining factors, such as income and education (Dyer and Yousef 2008).

It is more likely that the region's relationship with oil, and the means by which states have redistributed the wealth it supported, has played a disproportionately important role in shaping the region's unique fertility experience (Dyer and Yousef 2008; Fargues 2003). With funds flooding the region during the oil boom of the 1960s and 1970s, the region's oil-producing states redistributed wealth to their populations in the form of public sector employment and high subsidies, while non-oil-producing states were able to offer similar benefits by leveraging workers' remittances and strategic rents from their oil-producing neighbors, as well as from the United States and the Soviet Union, both of which sought influence in the region. Across the MENA region, governments subsidized food and fuel and guaranteed free access to education and health care.[7] In many MENA states, policies ensured that the wages for public sector employees increased with the number of their child dependents (Bulmer 2000). Further, even in the absence of such guarantees, high public sector wages for men incentivized many women to stay home instead of joining the labor market. This development, like the wide availability of subsidies, likely decreased perceptions of the opportunity costs associated with having additional children.

The collapse of oil prices in the mid-1980s and the slowdown of economic growth in the early 1990s spurred budget reforms across the region. As such, many MENA countries significantly reduced public sector investment, reforming many subsidy programs and slowing public sector employment (World Bank 2004). In addition, many governments instituted family planning programs in an effort to counter mounting population pressures, while at the same time strengthening and formalizing social safety nets (Roudi 2001). These changes likely impacted many of the aforementioned perceptions regarding the relative costs and benefits of having additional children playing a considerable role in accelerating the MENA region's fertility decline after the mid-1980s.

Importantly, the region's individual country experiences reflect a lot of variety within the region's overall demographic narrative. Generally, while most of the region's countries saw mortality transitions much like that experienced by the region as a whole, there have been notable variations. Yemen, for example, a largely rural country that has long suffered from high rates of poverty and a lack of health services, as well as periodic conflict both at the local and national level, had the region's highest mortality rate in the early 1950s, at over 41 deaths per 1,000. In stark contrast, Lebanon, a largely urban country that long benefited from a historically robust economy, had a mortality rate that, at roughly 13 deaths per 1,000, was less than half that of the region's average; in fact, its mortality rate was more in line with those found in more developed countries at the time. Despite lowering its mortality rates considerably since the 1950s, Yemen still has the region's highest mortality rate, currently over 7 deaths per 1,000. Even though its mortality rate has declined significantly in this time, the fact that it remains at the bottom of the region underscores the effects that slow economic development and conflict can have on mortality rates.[8] Importantly, despite having comparatively low mortality rates in the 1950s, Lebanon saw its fertility rate, while still decreasing, eventually intersect with the region's average, as its civil war and subsequent instability impacted its mortality transition.[9]

Perhaps nowhere has conflict been more influential on mortality transitions than in Iran and Iraq, where the nearly decade-long Iran-Iraq War in the 1980s led to hundreds of thousands of deaths on both sides, reversing the mortality declines of both countries. Prior to the war, Iran's mortality decline had generally followed the region's pattern, while Iraq's, after an initial delay, had accelerated through the 1960s and 1970s. Conflict, in fueling poverty and family income security and limiting the development of health infrastructure, has also affected mortality indirectly. This has been evidenced among Palestinian children, especially those in Gaza, who suffer among the region's highest infant mortality rates.[10] The ongoing civil war in Syria will likely significantly influence Syria's mortality transition, as violence continues to devastate the country's people and infrastructure.

A fairly significant mortality trend can be identified in some of the region's major oil producers, particularly Libya, Oman, and Saudi Arabia, underscoring the influence of more direct economic factors on changing mortality. In the early 1950s, largely before the development of productive oil fields, each of these countries maintained relatively high rates of mortality, particularly infant mortality. Libya, for example, had the second highest mortality rate in the region in the early 1950s, at 30 deaths per 1,000; further, the country's infant mortality was estimated at 254 deaths per 1,000 births, much higher than the region's average of 214. By the late 1960s, however, mortality in each of these countries had fallen well below the region's average, driven largely by their governments' ability to direct increasing oil revenues toward improved health infrastructures and increased economic opportunities for their citizens.

Fertility transitions across the region have perhaps shown greater diversity than those of mortality, in regard to both the levels of variance in the region's fertility rates before their declines and the rates at which they have changed since the 1950s. Further, it has been these differing trends, more than those evidenced in the region's mortality experience, that have more directly influenced population growth, age structure changes, and the emergence of youth waves across the region.

Lebanon's fertility rate has remained one of the region's lowest since the 1950s. In the early 1960s the country's fertility averaged 5.7 children per woman, and by the early 1990s it had declined considerably to 2.8. Distinguishing this country from much of the region, Lebanon's fertility rate fell below the population replacement rate of 2.1 before 2000.[11] By 2010, the country maintained the region's lowest fertility rate, at 1.5 children per woman.

Like Lebanon, Egypt experienced fairly early declines in fertility. Egypt's fertility rate in the early 1950s, however, was higher than that of Lebanon, at 6.6 children per woman, and the pace of its decline has been slower. By the early 1980s, for example, Egypt's fertility rate had declined only slightly, to 5.2. By the early 2000s, it had fallen to 3.2. While Egypt's fertility rate is still declining, the country is not expected to reach population replacement rates until after 2040.

The fertility rates of Morocco and Tunisia, at 6.6 and 6.7 in the early 1950s, respectively, actually increased into the 1960s. After their fertility rates both surpassed 7.0 children per woman in the early 1960s, differentiating them from much of the region, both countries experienced consistent and accelerated declines in fertility, a process that slowed in the 2000s. Like Lebanon, Tunisia's current rate of 2.0 children per woman is below the population replacement rate. Morocco maintains a current fertility rate of 2.8, and that rate is expected to fall below the replacement level around 2035.

The high-population, oil-producing countries of Algeria, Iran, and Syria stand out for their delayed, but eventually accelerated, fertility declines. Algeria and Syria, to start, maintained fertility rates above 7.0 children per woman well into the 1970s. During the 1980s and 1990s, however, those rates declined rapidly. In Algeria, for example, the fertility rate fell from 7.2 children in the late 1970s to 2.9 in the late 1990s. Syria's decline was less rapid than Algeria's but followed a similar pattern, falling from 7.3 in the late 1970s to 4.3 in the late 1990s. Algeria and Syria have current rates of 2.8 and 3.0 children per woman, respectively, and are expected to reach replacement rates by 2035.

While Iran followed a fertility trend similar to those of other high-population, oil-producing countries, the peculiarities of Iran's experience merit particular attention.[12] Prior to the country's 1979 revolution, Iran's fertility had declined gradually. Throughout the 1950s and 1960s, the total fertility rate in Iran remained at about 6.9 children per woman, and by the late 1970s it had declined only slightly to just below 6.3. After the revolution, the state introduced policies aimed at bolstering its population in the context of its war with Iraq. In turn, Iran's fertility rate edged upward to above 6.5 children per woman over the early 1980s. Following the end of the war and the government's recognition of the growing costs of its rapidly expanding population, the government reversed course on pronatal policies put in place following the revolution.[13] In turn, Iran's fertility rate fell rapidly to just under 4.0 children per woman by the early 1990s, and below 2.0 by the early 2000s. Iran maintains one of the region's lowest fertility rates, at a current 1.9 children per woman.

The low-population, oil-producing countries of Libya and the Gulf Cooperation Council (GCC) generally maintained relatively high fertility rates of roughly 7.0 children per woman through the late 1960s. During the early 1980s, the fertility rate of Saudi Arabia remained relatively high, while those of Libya and Oman actually increased to nearly 8.0

children per woman. Around the 1970s, smaller GCC states (Bahrain, Kuwait, Qatar, and the UAE) began to show fertility declines closer to those of the rest of the region. It is important to note, however, that fertility declines in these countries have been timed with the oil boom and the related influx of foreign workers: while these expatriate populations are largely male, the fertility norms of foreign women have influenced these countries' fertility declines. In the UAE, for example, total fertility in 2008 was estimated at 1.9 children per woman, while for local Emirati women, it was estimated at 3.5 (UAE NBS 2008). Similarly, in Qatar in 2011, total fertility was estimated at 2.0 children per woman, while fertility among Qatari women was estimated at 3.4 children (QMPS 2014).

When compared with other MENA countries, Iraq, Jordan, and Palestine all have seen limited fertility declines. Iraq and Jordan maintained fertility rates above 6.0 children per woman into the late 1980s, while Palestine held a similar rate into the early 1990s. While their fertility rates have declined since that time, they are still among the region's highest. Current fertility rates in Iraq and Palestine are both at 4.1 children per woman, and neither country is expected to reach replacement rates of fertility until after 2050. Jordan, which saw a fertility decline generally steeper than those of Iraq and Palestine through the 1980s and early 1990s, has a current fertility rate of 3.3. Still, Jordan is not expected to reach replacement fertility rates until after 2040.

Yemen's fertility transition has differed greatly from those of other MENA countries. In the early 1960s, the country had a fertility rate of 7.3 children per woman, similar to those of other countries in the region. However, as the rates of many of those countries subsequently declined, Yemen's rate notably increased, reaching 9.2 in the early 1980s. Since that time, it has declined considerably, but at a current 4.2 it remains the region's highest. Further, according to current projections, Yemen, like Egypt and Jordan, is not expected to reach replacement rates of fertility until after 2040, implying the existence of a large youth cohort for years to come.

Population Growth and the Formation of a Regional Youth Wave

Through the 1970s and 1980s, with mortality rates continuing to fall as fertility remained high, the MENA region's population growth accelerated, with average annual population growth rates of 2.8 percent and 3.1 percent in the 1970s and 1980s, respectively (see fig. 1.3).[14] To put this in a comparative context, the population in less developed regions as a whole grew by an average 2.3 percent a year during the 1970s and an average 2.1 percent a year over the 1980s. In the late 1980s and 1990s, as the region's fertility decline gained momentum, population growth slowed dramatically. From 1990 to 2010, the region's population growth averaged roughly 2 percent a year. From 2010 to 2020, average population growth is projected to be 1.7 percent a year. While this rate is somewhat higher than that seen among less developed regions overall, which averages 1.3 percent a year, it is notably lower than it was at its peak.

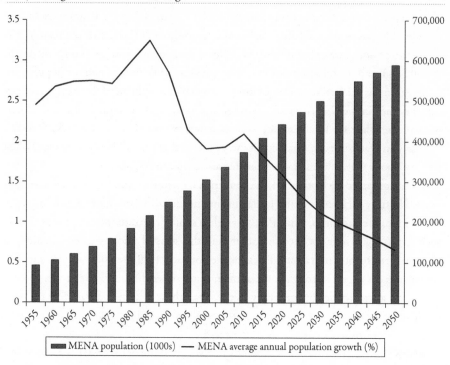

FIGURE 1.3 Population growth, MENA countries, 1950–2050.
Source: United Nations (2013).

During the region's high-population-growth years, its population's age structure typi-
fied that of high-fertility populations in general, with children forming the bulk of the
region's demographic structure. In 1980, 44 percent of the population was under the age
of 15, and 71 percent was under the age of 30 (see fig. 1.4). At that time, the working-age
population (those aged 15–64) made up less than 52 percent of the total. This age distribution ensured that the population carried a heavy dependency burden (the ratio of
working-age adults to children and elderly), made all the more burdensome by the
region's low rates of female labor force participation at the time.[15] As the region's fertility
rates declined through the late 1980s and early 1990s, the generation born during the
high-fertility years of the 1970s and 1980s, the future Arab Spring generation, matured.
In 1990, youth aged 15–29 formed 26.9 percent of the total MENA region population. By
2005, around the time the youth wave reached its peak, that share had increased to
31 percent.

By and large, the formation of youth waves in individual MENA countries has tracked
their experiences with declining fertility: the differing intensity, longevity, and timing of the
region's fertility declines have affected similarly varied characteristics in the region's youth
waves. Lebanon, for example, an early leader in the region's fertility decline, saw its youth
wave initially rise in the 1970s. After reaching roughly 29 percent in 1980, however, the
country's youth share largely declined.[16] Notably, since the mid-2000s, Lebanon's youth

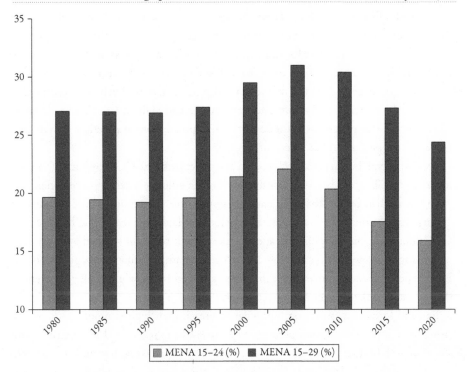

FIGURE 1.4 Youth as a share of total population, MENA countries, 1980–2020.
Source: United Nations (2013).

share has once again increased, forming a secondary wave (or echo) made up of the children of the now older initial wave. The echo cohort is expected to surpass 29 percent of the country's total population in 2015 before falling steeply in population share shortly thereafter.

Egypt, which initially experienced a gradual decline in fertility, saw its youth population increase at a similarly gradual initial rate. In fact, the youth population even decreased as a share of population from 1985 to 1995, a decrease driven by the continued and substantial birth of new children and, to some degree, labor migration out of Egypt.[17] In the late 1990s and early 2000s, however, the country's youth share expanded rapidly, increasing from roughly 26 percent in 1995 to 29 percent in 2005. Egypt's current youth population is estimated at around 27 percent of the country's total population.[18]

As in the case of their experiences with changing fertility, Morocco and Tunisia have had notably similar experiences with the youth wave. With their fertility rates increasing into the 1960s, the youth population shares of Morocco and Tunisia rose from 23.4 and 24.7 percent, respectively, in the early 1970s, to over 29 percent in both a decade later. Between 1980 and 2010 those rates fluctuated only slightly. Since 2010, both Morocco and Tunisia have seen their youth cohorts decline steeply as a share of total population. Morocco's 2015 youth population is estimated at 26.3 percent and Tunisia's at 24.8 percent.

In Algeria, Iran, and Syria, where fertility declines were initially delayed but eventually accelerated, there are pronounced, if somewhat delayed, youth waves. This pattern is most clearly illustrated in Iran, which stands as an example of how dramatically the dynamics of a youth population can change. After seeing some fluctuation in the population share of its youth cohort for some time, the youth share spiked in the 2000s, rising from roughly 26 percent in 1990 to 36 percent in 2005. That same year, the youth population shares of Algeria and Syria reached 33 and 31 percent, respectively. The youth shares in each of these countries have since declined but remain high: in Iran those aged 15–29 currently make up 27 percent of the country's total population; in Algeria and Syria they make up 26.4 percent and 28.2 percent, respectively.

As with overall fertility rate declines, the age structure of the GCC countries (and to a lesser extent Libya) has been more influenced by the influx of foreign workers, generally young men, than by the changing national population. Determining specific patterns among Gulf nationals is complicated by a lack of available data over time; however, the GCC countries' youth populations aged 15–29 continue to be outweighed by larger populations aged below 15. Statistics from the UAE, for example, show that 35 percent of the Emirati population, not including expatriates, are aged 15–29, while a full 73 percent of the Emirati population is under 30 (see chapter 5 here).

Iraq and Jordan saw their youth populations reach their highest points in the 1990s, rising to 29.4 percent and 31.3 percent, respectively, in 1995. Since that time the youth shares of both have declined, albeit slowly, reaching 27.8 percent in Iraq and 29.4 percent in Jordan in 2010. In Iraq, more than in Jordan, the relatively slow rate with which fertility declined has ensured that the youth cohort will maintain a considerable population share into the foreseeable future. The current youth populations of Iraq and Jordan form 28.2 percent and 27.5 percent of each country's total population, respectively.

The youth populations of Palestine and Yemen are still increasing in share. Palestine's youth wave is only now reaching its crest, with over 30 percent of its current population aged 15–29. Further, it is estimated that in 2020 youth will make up more than 30 percent of Palestine's total population. Importantly, while the youth shares of Gaza and West Bank are similar, the notably high population share of those below the age of 15 within Gaza, at 43.4 percent, in 2013—that year, they made up 38 percent of the population of West Bank—ensures that Gaza's youth share will remain particularly high for the foreseeable future.[19] Given its historically high fertility rates, Yemen has seen a pronounced and prolonged youth wave. From 1970 through the 1990s, Yemen's youth share fluctuated at around a quarter of the country's total population. Starting in the late 1990s, however, that share expanded dramatically, reaching 31.7 percent in 2010. By 2020 it will have decreased only slightly to an estimated 31.1 percent, a prescient factor in the country's ongoing political and economic instability.

Challenge, Opportunity, and the Arab Spring

While large youth populations are often seen through the lens of the socioeconomic challenges they present, the rise of the region's youth wave has offered the countries of the

MENA region a historic opportunity to capitalize on the potential economic boons of an expanding working-age population and declining dependency ratios, an opportunity similar to that seized by East Asian economies during the 1980s.[20] The potential gains of such an opportunity, however, are far from guaranteed. To best leverage this opportunity, an economy must first weather the pressures that accompany an expanding dependent population as it enters school and then must incorporate it into the labor market as it ages. For the MENA region's governments, the tasks of expanding national infrastructures and economic opportunities to incorporate their countries' growing populations has been daunting, and perhaps nowhere has this been more important and more difficult than in the region's schools and labor markets.

Shifting dynamics in these sectors have had an important influence on the shaping of the Arab Spring generation. From 1960 to 1990, the region's primary-school-aged population (age 5–14) increased from 26.3 million to 67.6 million, growing at an average annual rate of 3.1 percent. In contrast, during that time, the region's total population grew at an average annual rate of 2.9 percent. Despite the challenges that came with incorporating this expanding youth cohort into classrooms, progress in this regard was significant. Supported by increasing oil revenues, strategic rents, and remittance income throughout the 1970s and 1980s, governments across the region invested heavily in their countries' education systems.[21] In 1960, roughly 84 percent of the MENA region's population had received no schooling, with the regional average for total years of schooling at 1.07, well below the world average of 3.65.[22] Further, the region's 1960 female-to-male educational attainment ratio, at 41.5 girls for every 100 boys, was far below the world average of 74.2. By 1990, however, educational attainment had notably increased, with the regional average for total years of schooling reaching 4.58 and the share of the region's population with no schooling falling to 45.2 percent. Further, the female-to-male educational attainment ratio had increased to 63.1.

In many ways, when considering the demographic pressures that have resulted from the region's rapid population growth in the postwar era, the expansion of educational opportunities across the region has been remarkable. Educational quality, however, remains a pressing issue throughout the region, a fact that has had important implications for each country's ability to prepare its youth for employment in a changing and increasingly globalized economy. (See chapter 2 here.) Further, as educational attainment continued to increase through the 1990s, the crest of the region's demographic wave continued to move into older cohorts, compounding pressures already building with the region's labor markets.

The region's highly oil-dependent economy has consequentially affected the dynamics of its labor markets. To start, oil revenues and related rents allowed governments across the region to greatly expand their public sectors through the 1960s and 1970s, a process that supported considerable public sector employment. In addition, the rapidly growing oil economies of the GCC, countries with relatively small national populations, absorbed some of the initial labor force pressures that had been building across the region. It is estimated, for example, that just under 10 percent and 15 percent of the labor forces of Egypt and Yemen, respectively, migrated for work in the 1980s (World Bank 2004). Similarly, migration to Europe provided a vent for labor pressures building throughout North Africa.

While natural resource rents in the region's economies have supported many positive developments, such as infrastructure investment and expansive welfare services, these developments have come with costs. The resultant and pervasive presence of the state in the region's economies undermined the emergence of diversified and dynamic private sectors. The region's citizenry became accustomed to and dependent on public sector employment and the primary role of government in service delivery, both of which would impose increasing challenges on government budgets as populations grew (World Bank 2004). Further, the historically expansive availability of public sector work with significant nonwage benefits, as well as families' ability to depend on worker remittances from migrating family members, reduced potential incentives for women to join the workforce: by 1990, only 18.6 percent of working-age women in the region were economically active.[23]

Importantly, in the mid-1980s a prolonged collapse in international oil prices undermined the ability of states across the region to maintain their traditional roles as employers and economic providers. As a result, the region's oil-producing countries were forced to cut large government budgets or accumulate large deficits, and the region's non–oil producers began enacting large-scale reforms of their expansive public sectors (World Bank 2004). Within this context, as the region's traditionally state-dominated labor markets slowed and shifted, the youth wave matured into working age and started looking for work.

Through the 1990s, as labor force growth increased progressively with the growing number of young new entrants (fig. 1.5), many of the primary employment avenues that had been available for decades closed. In addition, conflict and its resultant migration affected labor force pressures; for example, labor force growth soared in Jordan, Palestine, and Yemen during the 1990s in part because of the influx of refugees and returning workers from Iraq and the Gulf states during the first Gulf War (World Bank 2004). Employment opportunities for Arab youth in the Gulf never returned to their pre-1990 levels, as Gulf employers increasingly turned to the Indian subcontinent and other regions for their labor force needs (Kapiszewski 2006).

Joining a changing and challenging labor market, the MENA region's youth wave faced poor labor market outcomes, including high rates of unemployment and underemployment, as they tried to build the foundations of their careers, even in the context of a return to high international oil prices in the mid-2000s. In 2005, when the region's youth formed 31 percent of the region's total population and 44 percent of its labor force, the unemployment rate among those aged 15–24 was estimated at roughly 27 percent. In 2010, on the eve of the Arab Spring, the unemployment rate

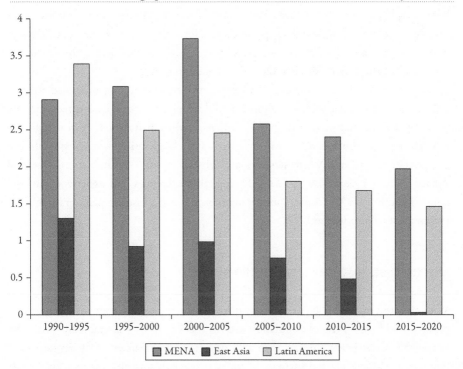

FIGURE 1.5 Labor force growth in MENA and comparison regions, 1990–2020.
Source: International Labour Organization (2011).

for youth remained over 25 percent, with roughly 6.2 million youth actively looking for work and failing to find it (see chapter 3 here).[24] Further, for those able to find work, an increasing number were able to do so only in the region's growing informal sectors (see chapter 9 here).

While a large share of the MENA region's youth wave has struggled with economic exclusion, young women have perhaps borne the highest burden. In terms of unemployment, female youth have maintained unemployment rates roughly double those of their male counterparts. In 2010, the unemployment rate among women ages 15–24 was estimated at 42 percent, compared with a rate of 21 percent among young men. Moreover, labor force participation rates among young women remain exceptionally low, despite increasing educational attainment among them and apparent generational shifts in attitude toward the appropriateness of women's participation in the labor force. In 2010, the region's overall female labor force participation rate was estimated at 21.3 percent, compared with an international average of nearly 50 percent. Further, labor activity was highest among women aged 25–29, a group that includes many women who had completed their educations, at a mere 28.5 percent. This limited economic participation among women has kept the region's labor supply pressures below their potentials.[25] But the inability of economies across the region to create employment opportunities for more young women continues to undermine the ability of these countries' governments to fully grasp the economic potentials of their increasingly educated female populations.

As evidenced, the experiences of many of the region's young men and women during the past few decades of economic and demographic change have been marked by social and economic exclusion and underscored by frustration. Accordingly, by 2010 the region's youth had become, in many ways, a "generation in waiting" (Dhillon and Yousef 2009), and while scholars and observers will continue to analyze and debate the exact causes of the Arab Spring, the influences and experiences of the region's youth wave, the contemporary manifestation of a historic demographic transition, must be considered.

After the Crest: The Future of the Youth Wave

With the crest of the MENA region's youth wave having passed, some of the pressures that resulted from the rapid population growth that created it will gradually recede. By 2020, while those below the age of 30 will form roughly 53 percent of the region's total population, those aged 15–29 will make up 24.4 percent, a notable contrast to their 31 percent share in 2005. Policymakers faced with concerns both for the material welfare of youth and the potential political instability suggested by their disproportionate unemployment and underemployed may greet the declining youth wave with a sigh of relief. It should be noted, however, that the region's demographic wave is not going away—it is only aging. As such, addressing the challenges facing the region's youth should remain a priority. If not, the economic exclusion they face today may become cemented for the region's adults tomorrow.

Further, in some MENA countries, youth shares are still increasing. In the near future, Oman, Yemen, and Palestine (especially in the Gaza Strip) are expected to see their youth populations reach their highest points in decades, with youth at roughly 40 percent in Oman, and over 30 percent in both Yemen and Palestine, in 2015. In addition, many MENA countries are expected to see secondary youth waves forming and reaching crests in the 2030s, as the children of the boom generation become youth themselves.

Finally, it is important to note that with youth expected to form a substantial share of the region's total population for years to come, the potentials of the demographic gift are not yet lost. Moreover, it may be the young who are best placed to shepherd those potentials to fruition. Accordingly, and as this book underscores, while the youth wave of the MENA region may be receding, policies for the young will remain an imperative across the region as it adjusts in the wave's wake.

REFERENCES

Barro, R. J., and J. W. Lee. 2013. A new data set of educational attainment in the world, 1950–2010. *Journal of Development Economics* 104 (September): 184–198.

Becker, G. S., and R. J. Barro. 1988. A reformation of the economic theory of fertility. *Quarterly Journal of Economics* 103: 1–25.

Becker, G. S., and N. Tomes. 1976. On the interaction between the quality and quantity of children. *Journal of Political Economy* 84: S143–S162.

Behrman, J. R., S. Duryea, and M. Székely. 1999. Decomposing fertility differences across world regions and over time: Is improved health more important than women's schooling? Working paper 406. Washington, DC: Inter-American Development Bank.

Bloom, D. E., and J. G. Williamson. 1998. Demographic transitions and economic miracles in emerging Asia. *World Bank Economic Review* 12(3): 419–455.

Bongaarts, J. 1978. A framework for analyzing the proximate determinants of fertility. *Population and Development Review* 4(1): 105–132.

Bongaarts, J. 1987. The proximate determinants of exceptionally high fertility. *Population and Development Review* 13(1): 133–139.

Bulmer, E. R. 2000. Rationalizing public sector employment in the MENA region. Middle East and North Africa region working paper series 19. Washington, DC: World Bank.

Chaaban, J. 2009. The impact of instability and migration on Lebanon's human capital. In *Generation in waiting: The unfulfilled promise of young people in the Middle East*, ed. N. Dhillon and T. Yousef, 120–141. Washington, DC: Brookings Institution.

Dhillon, N., and T. Yousef, eds. 2009. *Generation in waiting: The unfulfilled promise of young people in the Middle East*. Washington, DC: Brookings Institution.

Dyer, P., and T. Yousef. 2008. The tyranny of demography: Exploring the fertility transition in the Middle East and North Africa. Working paper 08-11. Dubai: Dubai School of Government.

Easterlin, R. A. 1975. An economic framework for fertility analysis. *Studies in Family Planning* 20: 254–263.

Fargues, P. 2003. Women in the Arab countries: Challenging the patriarchal system? Population and societies working paper no. 387. Paris: Institut National d'Études Démographiques.

Hoodfar, H. 1997. *Between marriage and the market: Intimate politics and survival in Cairo*. Berkeley: University of California Press.

International Labour Organization (ILO). 2011. Economically active population, estimates and projections. 6th ed. Geneva: International Labour Organization.

International Labour Organization (ILO). 2014. Key indicators of the labor market (KILM). 7th ed. http://ilo.org/empelm/pubs/WCMS_114060/lang--en/index.htm.

Jones, G. W., and M. S. Karim, eds. 2005. *Islam, the state and population*. London: Hurst.

Kapiszewski, A. 2006. Arab versus Asian migrant workers in the GCC countries. United Nations expert group meeting on international migration and development in the Arab region. http://www.un.org/en/development/desa/population/migration/events/expertgroup/2006/index.shtml.

Kremer, M., and D. L. Chen. 2002. Income distribution dynamics with endogenous fertility. *Journal of Economic Growth* 7(3): 227–258.

Lucas, D., and P. Meyer. 1994. *Beginning population studies*. Canberra: National Centre for Development Studies, Research School of Pacific Studies, Australian National University.

Omran, A. R., and F. Roudi. 1993. The Middle East population puzzle. *Population Bulletin* 48(1): 1–40.

Papps, I. 1993. Attitudes towards female employment in four Middle Eastern countries. In *Women in the Middle East: Perceptions, realities and struggles for liberation*, ed. H. Afshar and M. Maynard, 96–116. London: Macmillan.

Palestinian Central Bureau of Statistics. 2014. Population statistics. http://www.pcbs.gov.ps/site/881/default.aspx#Population.

Palestinian Central Bureau of Statistics, 2012. *Annual report. Palestine children: Issues and statistics*. Child statistics series no. 15. Ramallah-Palestine: Palestinian Central Bureau of Statistics.

Qatar Ministry of Planning and Statistics (QMPS). 2014. *Social statistics: 2003–2012*. Doha: Ministry of Planning and Statistics. https://www.qsa.gov.qa/eng/publication/Social_publications/QatarSocialStatistics/QatarSocialStatistics-2003-2012-Pub-May-2014-Eng.pdf.

Roudi, F. 2001. *Population trends and challenges in the Middle East and North Africa*. Washington, DC: Population Reference Bureau.

Roudi-Fahimi, F. 2002. *Iran's family planning program: Responding to a nation's needs*. Washington, DC: Population Reference Bureau.

Schultz, T. P. 1997. The demand for children in low income countries. In *Handbook of population and family economics*, ed. M. Rosenzweig and O. Stark, 350–430. Amsterdam: North Holland.

United Arab Emirates National Bureau of Statistics (UAE NBS). 2008. Population Statistics: 2008. Abu Dhabi: UAE National Bureau of Statistics. http://www.uaestatistics.gov.ae/EnglishHome/tabid/96/default.aspx.

United Nations. 2013. World Population Prospects: The 2012 revision. Department of Economic and Social Affairs, Population Division. http://esa.un.org/unpd/wpp/unpp/panel_population.htm.

World Bank. 2004. *MENA Development Report. Unlocking the Employment Potential in the Middle East and North Africa: Toward a New Social Contract*. Washington, DC: World Bank.

World Bank. 2008. *The road not traveled: Education reform in the Middle East and Africa*. Washington, DC: World Bank.

Williamson, J., and T. Yousef. 2002. Demographics transitions and economic performance in the Middle East and North Africa. In *Human capital: Population economics in the Middle East*, ed. I. Sirageldin, 16–36. London: I. B. Tauris.

Williamson, J. 2013, March. Demographic dividends revisited. CEPR discussion paper no. DP9390. London: CEPR.

NOTES

1. Demographic data for this chapter are drawn from United Nations (2013), unless otherwise noted. Accordingly, the UN's semantic characterization of region types has been adopted. In addition, "Latin America and the Caribbean" and "Eastern Asia" have been shortened to "Latin America" and "East Asia," respectively.

2. Penicillin was discovered in 1928, but its availability for public health use expanded after World War II (Dyer and Yousef 2008).

3. Mortality in East Asia has risen slightly since the 1990s, due to the aging of its population.

4. Fertility rates measure the number of children that women aged 15–49 within a given population are predicted to have over their lifetimes. Birthrates measure the number of actual births in a given year in a given population.

5. From the 1950s to the early 2000s, the fertility rate of Latin America closely paralleled the declining average among developing regions. The aggregate fertility rate of East Asia, while remaining below the average during that time, fluctuated greatly during this period due to differing country experiences. In particular, the rapid decline evident in East Asia between 1975 and 1985 is aligned with the implementation of China's one child policy in 1979.

6. For frameworks of proximate determinants of fertility, see Bongaarts (1978, 1987). Theoretical models for such determinants of fertility are provided by Easterlin (1975) and Becker and Tomes (1976); both of these articles focus on the economic utility of children as well as the trade-offs between quantity and quality of children in the context of economic development. See also Becker and Barro (1988).

7. See World Bank (2004) for a more expansive review of the effects of oil revenues on state spending and policy across the MENA region.

8. "Current," as used in this sentence and henceforth with regard to both mortality and fertility rates, refers to UN estimates for 2010–2015.

9. During the 1990s, Lebanon's mortality rates rose just slightly above the MENA average.

10. Overall infant mortality in Palestine was reported as 27.6 deaths per 1,000 live births during the 2002–2006 period: 30.7 in Gaza and 25.5 in West Bank (Palestinian Central Bureau of Statistics 2012).

11. The population replacement rate refers to the fertility rate needed to maintain natural population size (not accounting for migration). Generally, a country's replacement rate is assumed to be 2.1 children per woman, but its actual replacement rate might vary, reflecting its experience with changing mortality.

12. For a more detailed assessment of the fertility decline in Iran and the role of population policy therein, see Roudi-Fahimi (2002).

13. Population growth rates in Iran averaged 3.2 percent a year in the late 1980s.

14. Average annual population growth is calculated using data drawn from United Nations (2013). Growth rates in figure 1.3 represent average annual population growth over five-year periods.

15. Regional estimates for female labor force participation in 1980 are not available. World Bank (2004), using ILO estimates from 1996, puts regional female labor force participation at 25 percent. However, these figures have since been revisited, and the ILO's most recent estimates and projections are only available from 1990, at which point, the ILO (2011) estimates, the MENA region's female labor force participation (aged 15–64) was 19.1 percent.

16. Further, conflict and war, as well as economic opportunities abroad, have incentivized many of Lebanon's youth to leave the country for long periods of time, if not permanently (Chaaban, 2009).

17. In the mid-1980s, nearly 10 percent of Egyptians, mostly young male workers, emigrated to other countries, predominantly the Gulf states, for employment opportunities (World Bank, 2004).

18. "Current," as used in this sentence and henceforth with regard to youth population shares, refers to UN estimates for 2015.

19. While the overall youth share for Palestine is drawn from ILO (2011), demographic data regarding West Bank and Gaza, specifically, are drawn from the Palestinian Central Bureau of Statistics (2014).

20. According to Bloom and Williamson (1998), changes in the population age structure of East Asia between 1965 and 1990 are responsible for as much as a third of per capita GDP growth seen during that period. See also Williamson (2013) and Williamson and Yousef (2002).

21. On average, the MENA governments spent nearly 5 percent of their GDP on education during the period 1965–2003 (World Bank 2008).

22. All data regarding educational attainment are drawn from Barro and Lee (2010).

23. Unless otherwise noted, labor force statistics are drawn from ILO (2011).

24. Unemployment rates are drawn from ILO (2014).

25. If participation rates among women in the MENA region had grown by 15 percentage points between 1990 and 2010, as they did in Latin America (from 41.8 percent in 1990 to 56.8 percent in 2010), the region's labor force would have grown by nearly 16 million additional workers.

2   Schooling and Learning in the Middle East and North Africa

THE ROLES OF THE FAMILY AND THE STATE

Djavad Salehi-Isfahani

THE TWO WELL-KNOWN, stylized facts about education in the Middle East and North Africa (MENA) region are that schooling has been increasing rapidly and that the productivity of this schooling is low (Salehi-Isfahani 2013; United Nations 2003; World Bank 2008). Two other features of MENA education, for which evidence is still accumulating, are that access to both quantity and quality of education is unequal and that intergenerational mobility in education is quite low (Salehi-Isfahani et al. 2013). These features of MENA education are important not only for economic growth but also for social and political stability. The widening gap between the expectations of youth regarding the rewards to education and the reality of high unemployment of educated youth, coupled with the feeling that these outcomes are unfair, adversely influences the politics of the region in the post-uprising years (Salehi-Isfahani 2012).

In this chapter I review the evidence on the increase in schooling and equitable access to it in the MENA countries. I frame the discussion in terms of a key distinction between the roles of the two "principals" in the education of youth: the family and the state. It is common to think of MENA educational outcomes in terms of successes or failures of government policy, underplaying the fact that families not only are important producers of human capital but also make important decisions about the investment in education for the next generation (Becker 1992; Carneiro and Heckman 2005; Heckman 2011). Governments influence those decisions by enforcing compulsory education laws, by investing in public infrastructure, especially in building schools, and by adopting rules and labor market policies that affect the returns to education. In the MENA region, the rule-setting role of the state has been as important as its school-building function in promoting schooling. In most countries, implicit or explicit guarantees of public sector jobs to graduates have been instrumental in encouraging families to send their children to school. Education was closely identified with government employment, tilting the balance of investments by families in favor of the quantity of education—that is, diplomas and credentials—rather than its quality, that is, productive skills (Salehi-Isfahani 2013).

The distinction between the roles of families and states helps us better understand the evolution of quantity and quality of education in the MENA countries. Governments are better suited for the production of quantity rather than quality of education. The quantity of education is easily monitored by tests, grade promotion, and education certificates. Education quality is less easily observed, so it is subject to severe agency problems that put the government, as the principal, in a disadvantaged position. In contrast, families are better suited to investing in quality because they either do not have the agency problem, as when they do the teaching, or they can monitor the quality of the teaching—by schools or private tutors—more closely. Governments depend on a long chain of command that links teachers and school administrators to ministries of education, so their ability to observe and influence learning is limited. This is particularly relevant for skills that do not lend themselves to testing. It is very costly to motivate teachers to instill, say, self-confidence in children and to be able to determine that the teachers' investment has actually been made. Parents on the other hand can more easily monitor learning and are able to make the needed investments in less observable skills directly themselves.

Another important distinction between what parents and governments do is related to equity. Governments are in principle acting in the interest of the public and have equity as one of their objectives, whereas parents act selfishly in their education investments. Parental investments therefore often reproduce existing inequality across generations, whereas governments can promote equality of opportunity by leveling the playing field (Pop-Eleches and Urquiola 2013). Although the provision of school resources is often inequitable to begin with, governments can be more equitable than families in investing educational resources; thus, the transmission of inequality of education is often greater where education is more privately funded. More educated parents are naturally able to invest more in their children and, when school resources are inadequate, use their own resources. Because of this built-in source of inequality, as Roemer (1998) has argued, equality of opportunity requires governments not just to provide equal access to schooling for all children but to actually favor those from disadvantaged backgrounds. Such compensating behavior by governments is the foundation of education policies in many Western countries but it has been rarely discussed in regard to the MENA region.

The Increase in Schooling

The large role of the state in the MENA countries is often seen as an impediment to the accumulation of productive human capital (World Bank 2008). But education policies of postindependence Arab governments aimed at modernizing their bureaucracies were mainly responsible for the rapid growth of schooling in the last two decades (Assaad 2014; Salehi-Isfahani 2012). Traditional theories of economic development attribute greater investment in education to rising returns on human capital (Becker 1975). These returns in turn depend on the cost of schooling and the wage premium for educated workers, both of which the MENA governments have contributed to by building schools and offering graduate jobs in the public sector.

Schooling has increased faster in the Arab region than in other developing regions, increasing from fewer than two years in 1970 to more than seven years in 2010.[1] But most Arab countries, in relation to their GDP per capita, have a less impressive record of educational attainment. If we draw a straight line representing the predicted average years of schooling from a regression of schooling on GDP per capita, only three MENA countries (Algeria, Jordan, and Iran) would place above it; all others would be below it, indicating too little educational attainment for their income level.

The rise of schooling is a consequence of decisions by the state and families to invest in education. Economic theory suggests that education decisions for the family are closely associated with their decisions on the number of children (Becker 1992). As parents increase their demand for child education, they have less time and other resources to devote to having a larger family. Recent theories of economic growth (Becker, Murphy, and Tamura 1990; Lucas 2002) place the trade-off between quantity and quality of children at the center of their models of economic and demographic transition. According to these theories, the transition of European countries to sustained economic growth during the Industrial Revolution required a change in the behavior of the average family from high fertility and low investment in children to low fertility and high investment in children. In these models an exogenous increase in the returns to human capital, spurred by technological change, changes the incentives of families and is the impetus for the demographic transition. Lucas (2002) argues that without the fertility decline, technological shifts that raise incomes without increasing the returns to human capital, such as those occurring before the Industrial Revolution, dissipate into larger populations rather than raising per capita incomes because they fail to change the incentives for high fertility.

This view of economic development can be described with the help of a simple graph that combines three data characteristics of each country: fertility, education, and income (fig. 2.1). The first two quantify the choices made by the average family in the MENA countries over the period 1980–2010. The y-axis in each of the four graphs measures the average number of births per woman, or the total fertility rate (TFR), and the x-axis

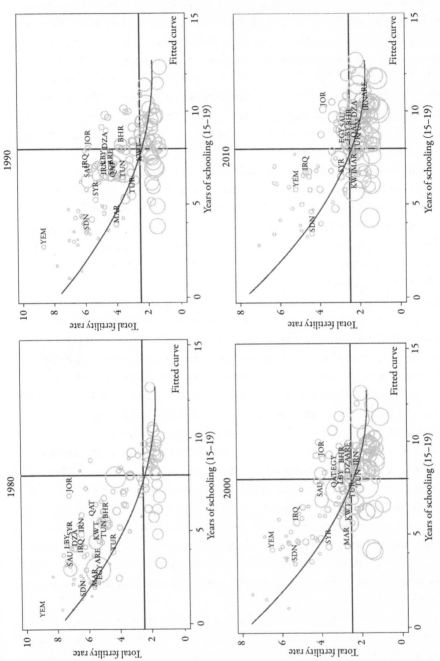

FIGURE 2.1 Years of schooling and total fertility rates, the MENA countries, 1980–2010. The size of the circles reflects the size of per capita GDP. Total fertility rates (TFR) are the average number of births per woman. The thresholds of 2.5 for TFR and 8 for average years of schooling indicate low fertility and education.

Source: Barro and Lee (2012); World Bank (2014).

measures the average years of schooling of the population aged 15–19. The level of economic development is approximated by per capita GDP and is reflected in the size of the marker circle. For the purpose of comparison, figure 2.1 shows the fitted regression line of TFR on years of schooling, using the data on all the countries for all years, a sort of global average family behavior representing the "normal" growth path. The charts also mark two thresholds that delineate what one might call modern family behavior, a TFR of 2.5 (for low fertility) and 8 for the average years of schooling representing basic education, which is also the minimum level of compulsory education for many countries. These thresholds define four quadrants, each representing a phase of development. The upper left quadrant is the "underdeveloped phase," characterized by large families and low investment in education. The bottom right quadrant represents the "developed phase," in which families are small and investment in children is high. The other two quadrants contain countries with average fertility and education that is different from the "normal path" where most countries are situated. These two quadrants do not have many observations, which reinforces the idea that the fitted regression line represents long-run equilibrium. There is also a close correlation between family behavior and economic development—the circles that mark per capita income get larger as we move down the line. The notable exceptions to this pattern are the oil-rich countries, notably Oman and Saudi Arabia, that have experienced rising incomes but lag in terms of demographic transition.

The most interesting observation to be made with the help of this graph is that that the traditional family behavior in the MENA region of high fertility and low education persisted for a fairly long time. Until 2000 the MENA countries were primarily in the underdeveloped quadrant, much later than were the countries of East Asia and Latin America (not marked on these charts). Since 2000, most have moved into the "developed" lower right quadrant, where countries with low fertility and high education are located.

What is governments' contribution to these long-term changes in family behavior? Clearly, progress along the "normal path," which is at the heart of the process of economic development and modernization of the family, is not possible without public investment in school-building that enables families to do their part with more investment in education. Female education has been instrumental in reducing fertility, which has in turn contributed to greater investment in child education. State interventions to reduce fertility with investments in health and family planning have also been critical. Lower infant mortality has been decisive in reducing childbearing (Preston 1978). In addition, there is evidence of direct influence on fertility through family planning in Iran's rapid fertility decline (Salehi-Isfahani et al. 2010). Finally, governments have provided the most effective incentives for formal schooling by hiring the graduates of the educational system, even promising them guarantees of employment after graduation (Assaad 2014; Salehi-Isfahani 2012).

Public Resources in Education

The level of public support for education can be measured by the share of expenditures that governments devote to education. As a group, the MENA countries spend amounts roughly similar to what other countries spend, though within the region public expenditures on education vary widely, in terms of both total resources allocated and how they are allocated to various levels of schooling. Per pupil expenditures for selected MENA countries range from $785 (USD purchasing power parity) in Egypt to $10,114 in Qatar. On average the region spends about $1,583, which is higher than the average for Latin America, but this favorable comparison is mostly due to the oil-rich countries of the Gulf.

Public expenditures on education in the MENA region appear higher than the global average when considered in relation to the years of schooling they generate. Figure 2.2 shows that, conditional on per pupil expenditures, the MENA countries achieve fewer years of schooling than the international average represented by the fitted regression line. All the MENA countries in the sample lie below the line of predicted years of schooling, indicating that their expenditures are less efficient than the world average in generating years of schooling.

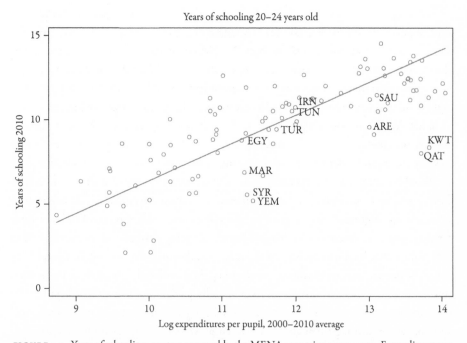

FIGURE 2.2 Years of schooling, 20- to 24-year-olds, the MENA countries, 2000–2010. Expenditures per capita are population-weighted averages for 2000–2010. Sources: Author's calculations using World Bank (2014) and TIMSS data files available at http://timssandpirls.bc.edu/timss2011/international-database.html.

Spending on early childhood education is more efficient than spending on education later in life. Most education experts believe that the most important use of public resources is early in a child's life: preschool and primary education. Thus, in measuring efficiency of educational expenditures, one should focus on the relative spending at the primary, secondary, and tertiary levels. During the period 2005–2010, the non–Gulf Cooperation Council (GCC) countries of the MENA region on average spent 2.5 times at the tertiary level what they spent at the primary level. In contrast, during the same period the Korean government spent twice as much per primary-level student and *less* per tertiary student, $2,474 (USD Purchasing Power Parity) compared to $2,940. Similarly, compared to Latin America, non-GCC MENA countries spend more per tertiary student than primary.

From Quantity to Quality of Education

The MENA countries have done well in terms of attainment or quantity of education but not in terms of quality. The most often cited evidence in support of the latter claim is the high unemployment of educated youth. The Arab Human Development Report (United Nations 2003) criticizes education quality in the Arab world, describing it as focused on rote learning. The World Bank flagship report on education (World Bank 2008) also laments the low quality of education in the MENA countries and blames it on the importance of the public sector in the provision of education. Others have linked rote memorization and diploma-seeking behavior of the MENA region's students to the incentives implicit in public sector hiring (Assaad 2014; Salehi-Isfahani 2012). The MENA countries' public spending on education is about the world average, and in terms of inputs, such as class size and teacher quality, it is not easy to blame low quality on low public support for education. In fact, expenditures are very imperfectly correlated with education quality if one measures quality by student learning.

Evidence from international tests in which the MENA countries participate, conducted by the international consortium Trends in Mathematics and Science Studies (TIMSS) shows that eighth grade students in the MENA countries lag behind their counterparts globally in learning, and the countries performing worst are not the poorest.

The TIMSS tests are given to random groups of eighth graders in mathematics and science and are standardized so that the global average in 1995 is 500, with a standard deviation of 100. According to these standardized scores, MENA students have consistently performed below the international average, and in several MENA countries even below the intermediate benchmark of 475. Table 2.1 presents the averages for the MENA countries since 1999 for math and science for boys and girls, showing that only a few of the MENA countries came close to the international average of 500 (science scores for girls in Bahrain and Jordan). Even more disappointing, there is no obvious trend of improvement. Several countries actually did worse in later years (Egypt, Iran, Palestine, and Turkey).

TABLE 2.1

Mean TIMSS scores of eighth grade students, the MENA countries, 1999–2011. The world average in 1995 was 500.

| | Mathematics | | | | | | | | Science | | | | | | | |
| | Boy | | | | Girl | | | | Boy | | | | Girl | | | |
	1999	2003	2007	2011	1999	2003	2007	2011	1999	2003	2007	2011	1999	2003	2007	2011
Algeria	—	—	389.4	—	—	—	384.1	—	—	—	407.8	—	—	—	408.4	—
Bahrain	—	385.8	383.3	396.9	—	417.4	415.4	434.7	—	423.9	437.4	430.1	—	452.2	499.5	483.8
Dubai	—	—	395.5	453.7	—	—	410.6	475.3	—	—	436.5	453.5	—	—	448.5	487.1
Egypt	—	415.8	405.5	—	—	415.5	403.8	—	—	432.5	411.1	—	—	432.4	423.3	—
Iran	432.1	410.1	401.6	421.9	408.9	418.6	407.4	415.8	461.2	454.8	454.8	475.5	430.8	455.7	465.9	481.4
Jordan	413.7	409	413.2	394.2	421.1	438	436.4	421.2	431.3	460.8	463.6	430.1	451.2	487.8	499.1	472.7
Kuwait	—	—	345.4	—	—	—	364	—	—	—	395.5	—	—	—	441.1	—
Lebanon	—	442	461.9	464.7	—	435	446.3	451.6	—	399.7	425	417.9	—	400.3	413.6	413.3
Morocco	345.8	398.7	389.7	377.2	327.9	383.8	378.5	376.7	334.2	407	404.4	379.9	315.5	397.2	404.9	382.9
Oman	—	—	350	342.4	—	—	402.1	399.3	—	—	396.4	384.7	—	—	455.3	457.4
Palestine	—	392.1	355.7	399.5	—	398.3	388.3	415.2	—	434.7	394.9	414.1	—	445.3	426.6	435.7
Qatar	—	—	279.9	410.5	—	—	317.3	423.3	—	—	274.1	413.8	—	—	332	441.7
Saudi Arabia	—	337.8	317.2	384.6	—	324.6	339.4	401.8	—	393	383	421.9	—	407.3	423.8	449.9
Syria	—	360.9	409.9	386.3	—	354.4	391.1	372.1	—	418.6	464.1	429.9	—	405.4	431.7	421.3
Tunisia	460.5	424	434.4	426.6	436.3	399.7	411.8	413.5	442.7	417.4	458.2	441.2	417.3	393.4	437	428.1
Turkey	429.5	—	434.7	445.2	427.8	—	433	452.2	434.8	—	454.3	471.7	431.7	—	457.5	486.4
UAE	—	—	—	442.9	—	—	—	463.2	—	—	—	446	—	—	—	475.1

Source: Author's calculations using TIMSS data files, 1999–2011, available at http://timssandpirls.bc.edu/timss2011/international-database.html.

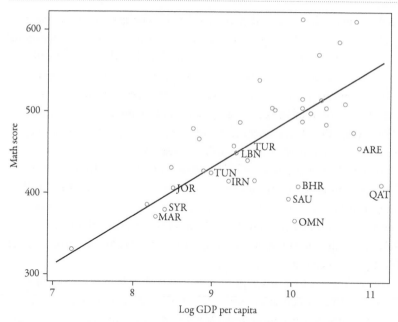

FIGURE 2.3 Average math scores and per capita GDP, the MENA countries, 2011.
Source: Author's calculations using TIMSS 2011 data files, available at http://timssandpirls.bc.edu/timss2011/international-database.html.

A striking feature of the data for the MENA counties is the low correspondence between the level of public resources devoted to education and average student scores. In fact, in 2007 Qatar, which spends more than Europe per pupil and is only second to Kuwait in terms of total per pupil education expenditures, had the lowest average scores in both math and science in the region and the second lowest globally.[2] Figure 2.3 depicts average math scores against GDP per capita for the 13 MENA countries that participated in the tests in 2011. All the MENA countries fall below the positively sloped fitted regression line, indicating that their average scores were too low, given their level of income. Oil-rich countries that can pay for first-rate infrastructure in education appear to have difficulty in generating the incentives for students, especially boys, to supply the necessary effort. The fact that in these conservative and male-dominated countries boys do worse than girls in math and science indicates the important role of incentives (Salehi-Isfahani et al. 2013).

Inequality of Opportunity in Education

It is no secret that success in education is to a large extent determined before children set foot in school. Even after entering school, parental resources—income and education—continue to influence educational success (Acemoglu and Pischke 2001) and act as the main channel through which inequality is passed from one generation to the next. "Inequality of opportunity" (IOp) refers to the extent to which children's educational outcomes depend on circumstances beyond their control, such as the type of family and community in which they grow up (de Barros et al. 2009; Ferreira and Gignoux 2011, 2014; Ferreira, Gignoux, and Aran 2011). Recent advances in the measurement of IOp enable us to estimate the contribution of family background and community characteristics to the inequality of educational attainment and achievement. The general methodology is to decompose the variation in the total inequality of years of schooling (attainment) or scores in standardized international tests (achievement) into the part that is explained by the variation in circumstances and the residual, which can be attributed to student effort, innate ability, or luck. This is done both parametrically using regressions or nonparametrically by analysis of variance. Available estimates using these methods show a disturbing level of inequality of educational opportunities in the MENA countries, though there is a fair degree of heterogeneity among them.

Assaad (2010) estimates that in Egypt the chance of a boy from a privileged background getting a university education is 97 percent, whereas a disadvantaged boy has only a 9 percent chance. Since in most of the MENA countries the bulk of the rewards of schooling lie at the university level (Salehi-Isfahani, Tunali, and Assaad 2009), this level of inequality in access to the biggest prize in education is quite significant. Region-wide estimates of IOp in attainment are available from Assaad and colleagues (2014), who study the inequality of the probability of ever attending school and reaching secondary school using available survey data from seven MENA countries. Salehi-Isfahani and colleagues (2013) analyze inequality of achievement using TIMSS scores. Assaad and colleagues (2014) find "alarming levels" of inequality of opportunity both in entering school and in reaching the secondary level in several of the countries in their study. In all the countries they study, a child growing up in an advantaged setting (parents with university education, living in an urban area, and in the top quintile of household wealth) has a nearly perfect (100 percent) chance of entering school and reaching the secondary level. The variation between the countries in the outcomes for the least advantaged child (illiterate parents, rural setting, and in the lowest quintile of household wealth) is quite large. In this respect, Iraq, Yemen, and Syria are particularly bad while Jordan and Tunisia seem more equal. In Iraq, the country that performs worst, the most advantaged boy or girl from a well-off family and with educated parents is 12 times as likely to reach secondary school as the most vulnerable child; in Syria the odds are 5.4.

Recent evidence suggests that the MENA education systems also yield high levels of inequality of opportunity in achievement. Salehi-Isfahani and colleagues (2013) report high levels of IOp for several MENA countries, notably Iran, Jordan, Lebanon, Qatar, Tunisia, and Turkey, using TIMSS scores. Their study employs a wider set of circumstances than that of Assaad and colleagues (2014), including the quality of teachers and schools in the community. The differences in findings regarding IOp in the two types of outcome are interesting and informative. Whereas gender is not an important contributor to inequality in achievement (test scores), it is in attainment (level of schooling), especially in Iraq and Yemen. In these two countries girls have a significantly lower chance of ever attending school. In contrast, in achievement (test scores), being a girl is an advantage in several countries. These differences are consistent with the hypothesis advanced earlier in this chapter that families play a greater role in education quality and governments do more for the quantity of education. Although the two sets of countries included in the two studies are not the same, in general the countries that do worse in IOp in attainment are not the same as those that perform badly in IOp in achievement. For example, Tunisia, which offers boys and girls relatively equal chances to attend school and advance to the secondary level, has a relatively high level of IOp in achievement (see Table 2.2). This is also consistent with the differential roles of the state and the family in different types of education outcome.

Table 2.2 shows estimates of the IOp for the two most recent rounds of TIMSS, in 2007 and 2011.[3] The estimates are the share of circumstances (the characteristics of the child's family and community) in the total inequality of scores for math and science. The IOp reported here is simply the R-squared for the regression of students' scores on their characteristics, that is, the share of the variation in scores that is explained by circum-

TABLE 2.2

Share of inequality of TIMSS scores of eighth grade boys attributable to circumstances, the MENA countries, 2007 and 2011.

Country	2007		2011	
	Math	Science	Math	Science
Algeria	0.070	0.072	—	—
Bahrain	0.253	0.301	0.402	0.413
Egypt	0.333	0.311	—	—
Iran	0.333	0.351	0.384	0.352
Kuwait	0.230	0.271	—	—
Jordan	0.254	0.304	0.284	0.360
Lebanon	0.370	0.431	0.348	0.347
Morocco	0.205	0.166	0.283	0.248
Oman	0.272	0.303	0.380	0.403
Palestine	0.253	0.252	0.228	0.243
Qatar	0.323	0.469	0.453	0.415
Saudi Arabia	0.280	0.303	0.259	0.286
Tunisia	0.262	0.209	0.265	0.230
Turkey	0.388	0.365	0.301	0.318

Source: Author's calculations using TIMSS 2007 and 2011 data files, available at http://timssandpirls.bc.edu/timss2011/international-database.html.

stances. There is a wide variation in IOp between countries, from a very low level for Algeria to very high levels in Bahrain, Lebanon, and Qatar. In several countries this share exceeds 30 percent, which is nearly twice as high as comparable estimates of IOp for western Europe and higher or about the same as those for Latin America, a region known for its high overall inequality.[4]

Research on inequality of education in the region is still in a preliminary stage. Much more work is needed before we can claim to understand what causes the high levels of IOp in certain countries or why it changes from one period to the next. But, as discussed, a better understanding of the behavior of the roles of the family and the state in education is a good starting point. With respect to equality of opportunity, the two appear to be playing complementary roles to *increase* inequality. In several countries, especially in Egypt, Iran, Jordan, Lebanon, Tunisia, and Turkey, where private schools and private tutoring are important, families are certainly busy pushing in the wrong direction. For their part, the governments are doing too little to undo or reverse the inequity-increasing effects of private resources. In fact, the way they allocate their meager expenditures for education, they exacerbate inequality of education opportunities.

Conclusion

The MENA countries receive a mixed grade in progress in education in the last few decades. While they have generally succeeded in increasing their citizens' average level of schooling—the quantity of education—they have failed to do as well in terms of education quality, as measured, for example, by average performance in international standardized tests. More important, they have failed to provide equal opportunities for all their citizens in attainment and achievement. This chapter has emphasized the distinction between the roles of the family and the state in the investment in education because designing policies to improve the efficiency and equity of human capital formation in the MENA countries requires understanding these separate roles.

In the past, states have played a critical role in promoting education in at least three ways: by building schools and making them freely available, by offering graduates well-paid and secure jobs, and by building the health infrastructure that has enabled families to raise more healthy children and to control their fertility so that they can invest better in their children's education. By their nature, states have a comparative advantage in investing in education quantity and a disadvantage in producing education quality. They can motivate students to learn, but only to the extent that they have control over how the labor market compensates education quality. Accountability and monitoring problems limit the state's ability to enforce education quality standards. Families on the other hand have a comparative advantage in the production of education quality because they can monitor it better. The lack of a relationship between public resources spent on education and average learning of math and science as revealed by TIMSS test scores is suggestive of the state's comparative disadvantage in the production of education quality. There is also a difference between families and the state in terms of purpose and impact. Families invest in education in order to ensure their own children's success in a competitive education system, which naturally preserves and amplifies the existing inequalities in income and education. The state on the other hand can and should invest in such a way as to preserve and advance equity in these outcomes.

The course of human capital accumulation in the MENA region is heavily influenced by the rising importance of families relative to states in investment in education. Public resources for education have shrunk, while competition for good places in universities—those that actually lead to decent jobs—has intensified. As families take greater responsibility for the education of their children, inequality of incomes and education transmits from one generation to the next. The available evidence on inequality of opportunity reviewed in this chapter shows that this may be particularly true of education quality, in which families have the comparative advantage.

A second trend affecting the role of the state in education also matters for the course of human capital accumulation in the Middle East. In the past, because most graduates aimed for a public sector job, the content of education was heavily influenced by what public employers could reward, which was mainly educational credentials (Salehi-Isfahani 2012). As bureaucracies have expanded beyond their useful size and state resources to hire more graduates have declined, there is room for a third actor, the private sector, to play its part in shaping the course of human capital accumulation in the region (Assaad 2014). The private sector, which offers more formal employment and has more discretion in determining the reward structure for skills, is in a position to redirect the educational system to focus more on the production of productive skills and less on handing out credentials.

REFERENCES

Acemoglu, D., and J. S. Pischke. 2001. Changes in the wage structure, family income, and children's education. *European Economic Review* 45(4): 890–904.

Assaad, R. 2010. Equality for all? Egypt's free public higher education policy breeds inequality of opportunity. Policy Perspective Economic Research Forum no. 2. http://www.erf.org.eg/CMS/uploads/pdf/ERF_PP_No2.pdf.

Assaad, R. 2014. Making sense of Arab labor markets: The enduring legacy of dualism. *IZA Journal of Labor and Development* 3(6): 1–25.

Assaad, R., D. Salehi-Isfahani, and R. Hendy. 2014. Inequality of opportunity in educational attainment in Middle East and North Africa: Evidence from household surveys. Economic Research Forum working paper series. Cairo: Economic Research Forum.

Barro, R., and J. W. Lee. 2013. A new data set of educational attainment in the world, 1950–2010. *Journal of Development Economics* 140 (September): 184–198.

Becker, G. S. 1975. *Human capital: A theoretical and empirical analysis, with special reference to education.* 2nd ed. New York: Columbia University Press.

Becker, G. S. 1992. Fertility and the economy. *Journal of Population Economics* 5(3): 185–201.

Becker, G. S., K. M. Murphy, and R. Tamura. 1990. Human capital, fertility, and economic growth. *Journal of Political Economy* 98(5): S12–S26.

Carneiro, P., and J. Heckman. 2005. Human capital policy. In *Inequality in America: What role for human capital policies?*, ed. J. Heckman and A. Krueger, 77–240. Cambridge, MA: MIT Press.

de Barros, R. P., F. H. G. Ferreira, J. R. M. Vega, J. S. Chanduvi, M. de Carvallo, S. Franco, S. Freije-Rodriguez, and J. Gignoux. 2009. *Measuring Inequality of Opportunities in Latin America and the Caribbean*. Washington, DC: World Bank.

Dhillon, N., and T. Yousef, eds. 2009. *Generation in Waiting: The Unfulfilled Promise of Young People in the Middle East*. Washington, DC: Brookings Institution Press.

Drèze, J., and M. Murthi. 2001. Fertility, education, and development: Evidence from India. *Population and Development Review* 27(1): 33–63.

Ferreira, F. H. G., and J. Gignoux. 2011. The measurement of inequality of opportunity: Theory and an application to Latin America. *Review of Income and Wealth* 57(4): 622–657.

Ferreira, F. H. G., and J. Gignoux. 2014. The measurement of educational inequality: Achievement and opportunity. *World Bank Economic Review* 28(2): 210–246.

Ferreira, F. H. G., J. Gignoux, and M. Aran. 2011. The measurement of inequality of opportunity with imperfect data: The case of Turkey. *Journal of Economic Inequality* 9(4): 651–680.

Heckman, J. J. 2011. The American family in black and white: A post-racial strategy for improving skills to promote equality. *Daedalus* 140(2): 70–89.

Houtenville, A. J., and K. S. Conway. 2008. Parental effort, school resources, and student achievement. *Journal of Human Resources* 43(2): 437–457

Lucas, R. E. 2002. *Lectures on economic growth*. Cambridge, MA: Harvard University Press.

Pop-Eleches, C., and M. Urquiola. 2013. Going to a better school: Effects and behavioral responses. *American Economic Review* 103(4): 1289–1324.

Preston, S. H. 1978. *The effects of infant and child mortality on fertility*. New York: Academic Press.

Roemer, J. E. 1998. *Equality of opportunity*. Cambridge, MA: Harvard University Press.

Salehi-Isfahani, D. 2012. Education, jobs, and equity in the Middle East and North Africa. *Comparative Economic Studies* 54(4): 843–861.

Salehi-Isfahani, D. 2013. Rethinking human development in the Middle East and North Africa: The missing dimensions. *Journal of Human Development and Capabilities* 4(13): 341–370.

Salehi-Isfahani, D., M. J. Abbasi, and M. Hosseini-Chavoshi. 2010. Family planning and fertility decline in rural Iran: The impact of rural health clinics. *Health Economics* 19(S1): 159–180.

Salehi-Isfahani, D., N. Belhaj-Hassine, and R. Assaad. 2013. Equality of opportunity in education achievement in the Middle East and North Africa. *Journal of Economic Inequality* 12(4): 489–515.

Salehi-Isfahani, D., I. Tunali, and R. Assaad. 2009. A comparative study of returns to education in Egypt, Iran and Turkey. *Middle East Development Journal* 1(2) (December): 145–187.

United Nations. 2003. Arab human development report 2003: Building a knowledge society. New York: United Nations Development Programme.

World Bank. 2008. *The road not traveled: Education reform in the MENA region*. Washington, DC: World Bank.

World Bank. 2014. World Development Indicators. http://data.worldbank.org/data-catalog/world-development-indicators.

NOTES

1. Population-weighted averages using the Barro and Lee (2013) data.

2. Qatari students performed much better in TIMSS 2011, but again later in the 2012 in Programme for International Student Assessment (PISA) tests Qatar ranked sixty-third out of 65 cou ntries.

3. In order to keep a common set of circumstances between 2007 and 2011, the sets of circumstances used in this table and in Salehi-Isfahani (2013) are slightly different, so the estimates for 2007 in this table may differ somewhat from those in Salehi-Isfahani (2013).

4. See de Barros et al. (2009). The estimates for other regions are not strictly speaking comparable to those reported here for the MENA countries because they may use different sets of circumstances and may use a different standardized test (PISA).

3 Arab Youth Employment in the Wake of the Global Financial Crisis
Mona Said

AS THE WORLD economy continues its recovery from the 2008–2009 global financial crisis, the ramifications of this downturn continue to reverberate around the world. One primary result of the crisis has been to increase the numbers of unemployed, working poor, and underemployed, especially among the youth. This issue continues to be of particular interest in the Middle East and North Africa (MENA) region, as the financial crisis directly preceded the Arab Spring protests, which were often swollen with the ranks of the young unemployed and underemployed. This chapter focuses on the situation in Arab labor markets on the eve of the Arab Spring.

The International Labour Organization (2010a) estimates that unemployment rates increased significantly throughout the world as a result of the crisis. By 2010, the number of people globally unemployed reached 205 million, an increase of 27.6 million from 2007, with the majority of this increase, 22 million, occurring in 2009. In addition to increasing unemployment and decreasing employment-to-population rates, labor productivity also decreased in 2009, raising concerns about future economic well-being (ILO 2010b). Even in countries where economic growth continued during the crisis period, the relative inexperience of youth left them more vulnerable to being unemployed or employed under disadvantageous terms.

Prior to the financial crisis and especially from 2002 to 2008 (which was a period of strong growth for the region) youth were routinely excluded from labor markets in the MENA region, as was evidenced by substantial gaps in adult-youth unemployment rates.

Despite this time of economic growth, North Africa (in particular) continued to see increases in youth unemployment throughout the 2000s as the economic boom appeared to largely bypass them (Dhillon et al. 2009).

Throughout the MENA region, high levels of youth unemployment can be seen across all educational levels. This is the result of poor education quality and a lack of desirable labor market skills. Private sector employers, who became more important during this time because the public sector had slowed its hiring, needed workers with critical thinking and problem solving skills. These skills were largely lacking in workers who had been trained in an educational system designed to expand the middle class by offering credentials rather than skills. While the mainstay of job growth from the 1950s to the 1970s was the public sector, government hiring began to slow in the 1980s, and this trend accelerated in the 1990s with economic reforms that attempted to curb government expenditures. With a growing and increasingly educated young population (see chapter 1 here), the private sector has not been willing to step in and provide jobs for these young people, as they often lack the necessary skills. Also compounding the problem of unemployed youth are the following factors: the lack of intermediate institutions such as employment services; cultural barriers and laws that prevent women from having access to all employment possibilities; and employees' high expectations for high wages and ideal working conditions. Due to this combination of factors, youth who are employed often have poor-quality jobs and informal employment, resulting in a lack of job security and social protection (see chapter 9 here). As a result, the full transition to adulthood has been postponed for many MENA youth, as marriage has been delayed due to lack of financial security required to start a family and set up independent housing (see Assaad and Barsoum, 2007; Dhillon and Yousef 2009).

This chapter investigates the effects of the financial crisis on the labor markets in the MENA region, with specific attention to the impact on youth and youth employment. The effects on the employment of youth, a precarious labor market segment before the crisis, are of utmost concern to researchers as the youth represent such a large segment of the global population and an even larger segment of the MENA population. This chapter presents a regional overview of the phenomenon of youth exclusion and an assessment of the ramifications of the financial crisis for youth labor markets in the MENA region. That analysis is followed by country-specific profiles of Algeria, Egypt, Jordan, Syria, Morocco, Tunisia, and the UAE. The chapter then summarizes the economic policies that were pursued in order to ameliorate the impact of the crisis prior to the advent of the Arab Spring.

Regional Overview

Before the Global Financial Crisis

Even before the financial crisis, high levels of youth unemployment, due in large part to a demographic bubble, plagued the MENA region. The proportion of youth in the population reached a peak between 2005 and 2010. The regional working-age population increased by 34.2 percent between 1998 and 2008 as young people entered the labor market in record numbers (Schmidt 2009). Unfortunately, most countries have thus far been unable to generate the rate of job creation required to absorb the new entrants; hence a high level of youth unemployment is a common stylized fact across the region.

Exacerbating the situation is a preference for public sector jobs at a time when economic conditions have been putting pressure on governments to reduce their employment levels. Despite attempts to shrink public sector payrolls, the preference for government jobs has not diminished, and people are willing to wait 10–15 years for jobs in the government or in state-owned enterprises. While some characteristics of public sector jobs are preferable to those in the private sector, the queueing for these jobs increases unemployment rates as individuals are willing to wait exceedingly long periods of time or insist on staying off of the private sector employment rolls (see chapter 9) in order to not lose their place in line for a public sector job. In some cases, such as Egypt, this queuing leads to university degree holders being the most highly unemployed of all educational groups (see Assaad and Barsoum 2007). In general, the region is hampered by arcane teaching methodologies and curricula that lead to skills mismatches in the private sector, where the quantitative expansion of education has not also meant an increase in quality (see chapter 2 here).

Another serious issue that the MENA region faced prior to the financial crisis, and that has been impacted by the crisis, is the participation of women in the labor market. As of 2008, only 25 percent of women were actively engaged in the labor market, as opposed to 75 percent of men (Schmidt 2009). The rates varied between the Middle East and North Africa, with North Africa experiencing slightly higher participation rates for both men and women and the Middle East experiencing the lowest female participation rates in the world. Despite historic low female participation rates, female labor force attachment increased during the 2000s for most of the MENA region; the largest increases were in Algeria, Qatar, and the UAE (see chapter 4 here for more details).

The Crisis and Postcrisis Periods

While the effects of the financial crisis spread globally, a combination of factors influences each individual country's experience. Among these factors are the initial labor market conditions in the country when the downturn began and the way three major channels were affected within each country: the depth of the financial sector; the impact of oil on the domestic economy; and the balance of payments, taking into account trade, remittances, foreign direct investment, and official development assistance flows (World Bank 2010a).

Youth unemployment rates in the MENA region are the highest in the world. In 2008 the MENA region's youth unemployment rate was 25.3 percent, and this unfortunate distinction continued in 2009 with an unemployment rate of 25.5 percent, rising further to 27.4 percent in 2010 (ILO 2014).[1] In North Africa, youth unemployment increased slightly from 2008 to 2009 (from 20.3 to 20.4), followed by a slight fall (to 20.1) in 2010. In a global comparison, while the MENA region's youth unemployment rate is the highest in the world, other regions saw larger increases in unemployment rates between 2008 and 2010. This increase was witnessed by both developed and developing economies, with the European Union witnessing a staggering 4.8 percentage point increase in the unemployment rate between 2008 and 2010 (from 13.3 to 18.1 percent). East Asia was the only region that experienced a decrease in youth unemployment rates during the same period. Over the 2008–2010 crisis period, youth unemployment rates increased for the whole world by 0.8 percentage points.

Figure 3.1 shows the ratio of the youth (15–24) unemployment rates to the total unemployment rates in seven MENA countries from 1991 to 2012. This includes three countries where conflicts/revolutions erupted (Egypt, Tunisia, and Syria); three with significant protests that were eventually placated and quelled (Algeria, Morocco, and Jordan); and Lebanon, which saw relatively few protests. The values in figure 3.1 show the degree to which the labor market outcomes differed between young participants and those with a few years of experience.[2] The pattern that emerges from this figure is that for at least some MENA countries, the relative labor market outcomes deteriorated for young people

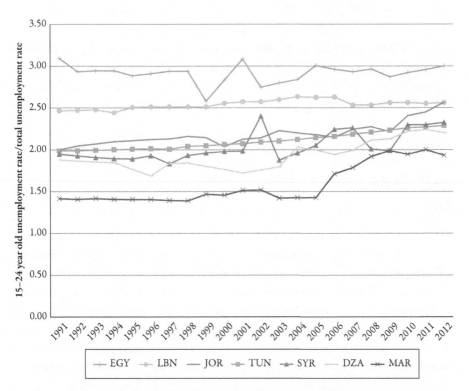

FIGURE 3.1 Ratio of youth (15–24) unemployment rate to total unemployment rate in selected MENA countries, 1991–2012.

Source: Author's calculations and ILO (2014).

during the 2000s. For example, in Morocco (MAR in the figure), the ratio of youth to total unemployment rose from 1.51 to 2.00 from 2001 to 2010. In Tunisia it rose from 2.07 to 2.30 over this decade. In Algeria (DZA in the figure) the increase was more dramatic than in Tunisia and rose from 1.72 to 2.22 from 2001 to 2010. Outside North Africa, some Middle Eastern countries had a similar experience of deteriorating conditions. In Jordan the ratio rose from 2.13 in 2001 to 2.41 in 2010. Despite the trends in these four countries, not all countries shared this experience. For example, in Lebanon the ratio began the decade at around 2.5 and stayed there for the entirety of the 2000s. Likewise, in Egypt the ratio was at 3.00 in 2001, fell to 2.75 in 2002, and rose back to 3.00 by 2005, remaining approximately at that value for most of the rest of the decade.

Two results emerge from examining the data in figure 3.1. First, on average, labor market conditions became relatively worse for young people during the 2000s. The average ratio of unemployment rates for these seven countries rose from 1.98 in 2001 to 2.29 in 2010, with the increase between 2009 and 2010 being the biggest between any two years during the decade. Thus, there appears to have been some relative deterioration of labor market conditions for young people in the MENA countries, as local factors combined with the global economic downturn to worsen labor market conditions for young people compared to older workers. Second, and just as important, these worsening conditions do not appear to predict which countries revolted or in which countries these revolutions were successful. Egypt's experience is particularly noteworthy. While Egypt had the highest average ratio of youth to total unemployment during this time, that ratio did not have a particularly sharp increase in the late 2000s. Despite the absence of worsening conditions, Egypt's youth were some of the most vocal, helping to lead the vanguard of the demonstrations and eventual overthrow of the Mubarak regime.

The Effects of the Crisis on Individual Countries

Egypt

The Egyptian economy did not contract as sharply as many of the economies in the region or throughout the world. However, national accounts data indicate that there was a slowing of economic growth toward the end of the first decade of the century and that this slowdown happened in an environment where youth were already being economically excluded. By 2006, Egyptian youth constituted fully 80 percent of the total number of unemployed (Assaad and Barsoum 2009). Most of this unemployment was occurring when youth were making the transition from school to work, as 95 percent of the unemployed youth had at least a secondary degree. The situation for women was even worse than for men. For example, the average wait time between schooling and work for young men in 2006 was two years, while even after 15 years of waiting, no more than a quarter of women had found jobs (Assaad and Barsoum 2009).

TABLE 3.1

Unemployment rate by sex, age, education status, and urban/rural location, Egypt, 2006–2010.

	2006				2007				2008				2009				2010			
	Q1	Q2	Q3	Q4	Q1	Q2	Q3	Q4	Q1	Q2	Q3	Q4	Q1	Q2	Q3	Q4	Q1	Q2	Q3	Q4
Males																				
No education/primary	1.2	1.4	1.4	1.4	1.6	1	1.1	1.6	0.9	1.4	1	1.5	0.9	0.9	1	0.9				
Secondary	13.3	12	12.3	9.8	14.2	10.4	11.3	10.5	10	8.7	9.4	8.2	7.6	7.8	7.6	7.4				
Tertiary	13.4	13.6	13.8	11.9	13.3	12.3	14.5	14.1	12	10.5	12.5	12.1	11.6	11.4	12.1	12.0				
Youth (15–24)	23.4	20.7	22.1	16.4	24.6	18.9	19.7	20.1	17.9	15.7	17.2	17.5	15.3	15.2	15.7	16.8				
Younger adults (25–44)	4.2	4.2	4	4.7	5.2	4.3	5.1	4.3	3.8	3.8	3.7	3.3	3.8	3.9	3.3	3.0				
Older adults (45–64)	0.1	0.4	0.3	0.4	0.3	0.3	0.1	0.3	0.2	0.2	0.3	0.1	0.1	0.2	0.2	0.2				
All	7.3	6.9	7.2	6	8.1	6.4	7	7	6.1	5.5	5.9	5.7	5.3	5.3	5.4	5.4	5.2	4.9	4.7	4.7
Females																				
No education/primary	0.8	0.8	1.5	2	2.8	1.8	1.8	1.1	1.3	1.6	1.7	1.6	6.4	9.1	5.1	2.2				
Secondary	48.2	42.5	37.9	32.1	42.9	37.8	38.3	37.1	39.7	34.8	33.4	36.1	38.1	37.4	36	36.3				
Tertiary	28.7	27.1	26.4	26.3	28.1	26.6	32.3	31.5	28	23.5	24.3	26.4	30.3	28.2	31.7	32.8				
Youth (15–24)	64.5	53.9	54	45.9	60.3	55.9	55.7	54.1	56.2	52.2	53	56.5	50.7	60.1	56.2	57.7				
Younger adults (25–44)	16.2	16.2	17.1	14.2	17.7	15.4	16.2	14.8	14.3	12.4	10.4	11.4	14.7	13.5	14.1	17.7				
Older adults (45–64)	0.1	0.2	0.1	0	0.5	0.4	0.2	0.3	0.3	0.4	0.2	0.1	14.4	6.8	7.5	2.7				
All	27	24.9	25.6	18.8	25.4	22	23.9	22.1	21.6	19	18.4	20	23.1	23.3	23	23.1	22.0	22.2	23.4	22.7

Source: Central Agency for Public Mobilization and Statistics (CAPMAS), February 2006 to December 2010.

Economic reforms were introduced in the early 2000s, and Egyptian economic growth was highly variable throughout the decade. Economic growth peaked at a rate of 7.0 percent per annum in 2007 but declined to 4.1 percent in 2009. This slowdown was coupled with a rising inflation rate, which more than doubled from 8.4 percent in 2007 to 18 percent in 2008, and a high fiscal deficit measuring 7.9 percent of GDP in 2009 (ETF 2010a). Downsizing of the public sector, limited growth within the private sector, and the international economic downturn (with the resulting increase in return migration) further complicated the economic situation in Egypt at the time.

Further evidence on the impact of the financial crisis on youth in Egypt can be seen in table 3.1.[3] The table demonstrates the pre- and postcrisis change in the unemployment rate by gender, educational attainment, and age. The table presents figures from the period preceding the crisis (starting in 2006) up to the postcrisis year 2009. Aggregate figures for 2010 are also included. Table 3.1 shows that the unemployment rate was unstable during the 2006–2010 period. Yet, on average, it increased from about 8.5 percent in the second quarter of 2008 to 9.6 percent in 2009. Considering only the youth (15–24) cohort, unemployment rates remained stable at around 16 percent for males, with an uptick in the fourth quarter of 2009. However, for female youth, unemployment increased substantially from its characteristically high level of 52 percent in the second quarter of 2008 to 56.2 in 2009. Results not shown in table 3.1 but consistent with data from Egypt's central statistical bureau, the Central Agency for Public Mobilization and Statistics (CAPMAS), indicate that youth unemployment fell slightly in 2010, falling from 56.7 percent to 54.6 percent for female youth and from 15.1 percent to 14.8 percent for male youth (World Bank, 2014).

In sum, the foregoing analysis provides evidence that while it seems that there was not a substantial crisis-related impact on the Egyptian labor market, some subgroups of workers were more vulnerable than others during the crisis. This is consistent with historical experience in Egypt, which suggests that young, unskilled, and female workers are more likely to bear the brunt of an economic downturn (Roushdy and Gadallah 2011). It is worth emphasizing that even before the crisis, female youth unemployment was a substantial 3.5 times greater than that of male youth (Assaad and Barsoum 2009). Female youth appear to have been strongly negatively affected by the crisis, as their unemployment increased more rapidly than that of other groups.

Jordan

While the economic impact of the financial crisis for many countries was negative, Jordan fared moderately well. This lack of impact was due in part to Jordan's low market capitalization (Behrendt, Haq, and Kamel 2009). As in the experience in Egypt, the Jordanian economy continued to grow during the crisis, but the rate of growth slowed toward the end of the 2000s. Jordan's GDP growth rate was 7.2 percent in 2008, slowed to 5.5 percent in 2009, and slowed further to 2.3 percent in 2010 (World Bank 2014).[4]

TABLE 3.2

Unemployment rates by sex and age group, Jordan, 2006–2010.

	2006				2007				2008				2009				2010			
	Q1	Q2	Q3	Q4	Q1	Q2	Q3	Q4	Q1	Q2	Q3	Q4	Q1	Q2	Q3	Q4	Q1	Q2	Q3	Q4
All males	12.7	11.8	12.6	11.2	11.9	9.1	10.4	10.2	11.6	9.7	9.7	9.9	9.9	10.4	10.8	10.6	10.2	10.7	9.2	10.0
Youth (15–24)	27.2	25.2	25.5	23.4	26.7	21.7	23.5	22.5	24.9	20.1	22.4	23.3	22.5	20.3	23.6	24.1	23.6	22.4	23.7	18.2
Younger adult (25–44)	8.3	8	8.8	8.1	7.7	6.1	6.9	6.9	8.2	7.1	6.5	6.5	7	7.2	7.4	7	6.4	7.3	5.3	7.9
Older adult (45–64)	4.2	5	6	5.2	4.9	3.2	4.4	4.6	4.8	4.6	3.3	3.1	3.3	7.5	5	4.9				
All females	24.9	21.3	31.4	22.5	25.4	19.3	30.9	26	26	25.5	23.7	22.1	23.3	24.3	28.1	20.3	22	19	26	19.8
Youth (15–24)	47.2	41	55.8	37.6	46.9	39	55	48	47.2	49.5	49.9	48.9	44.6	44.2	52.7	41.3	46.8	40.6	56.6	42.5
Younger adult (25–44)	17.7	16.8	23.2	17.8	20.5	14.2	23.9	20.2	20.8	15.3	20	18.2	14.8	17.5	19.8	22.1	14.7	13.1	17.1	13.3
Older adult (45–64)	1.5	3.9	11.9	6.8	4	3.5	7.7	7	4.5	3.4	1.4	2.3	3.9	8.2	7.8	1.8				

Source: Murian and Salamat (2010) and author's calculations.

Unemployment rates fluctuated during the crisis; youth (both males and females age 15–24) experienced higher rates than their older counterparts across all years (see table 3.2). Education did not decrease the likelihood of unemployment, as males with tertiary levels of education experienced higher levels of unemployment than their less educated male counterparts (not shown). Being younger, however, was negatively associated with unemployment. Youth (15–24) had much higher rates of unemployment than younger adults (25–44), and older adults (45–64) had lower rates of unemployment than younger adults. During the crisis, female unemployment remained roughly the same as before the crisis (2006–2007) across all age groups, with a fair degree of cyclical volatility each year. Younger women (youth and younger adults) had significantly higher rates of unemployment than older adult women, who generally had unemployment rates lower than 10 percent during this time.

In sum, the foregoing evidence highlights that in Jordan, male unemployment rates remained largely unchanged when comparing the rates before the crisis with the rates after it. For females, unemployment rates also remained the same, but evidence presented in Murian and Salamat (2010) shows that female participation rates decreased over this time. When comparing age, older males saw a slight increase in their unemployment rates in early 2009 compared to early 2008 and thus appear to have been more affected by the financial crisis than their younger counterparts. However, for females the younger adult age group (25–44) was more greatly affected by the crisis, as unemployment rates increased for them. This pattern is supported by the evidence presented in figure 3.1, which shows that the ratio of youth to overall unemployment rates decreased in 2009 before continuing its upward trend in 2010.

Syria

The financial crisis affected several aspects of the Syrian economy. Starting in 2009 the value of exports, foreign direct investment, tourism, and remittances all declined, largely as a result of a slowdown in the world (and regional) economy and a decrease in the price of oil. The country experienced decreases in agricultural and hydrocarbon prices, lower export revenue, and reductions in remittances due to return migration from labor-receiving countries in the Gulf Cooperation Council (GCC), which were also impacted by the crisis. All of these factors were compounded by a three-year drought, reducing agriculture output and creating a domestic supply shock. Between 2008 and 2009, the country's GDP growth rate decreased from 3.7 percent to 2.5 percent, mirroring the trend for the entire MENA region (Kouame 2009).[5] This represented a significant departure from the average GDP growth rate of 5 percent the country experienced between 2004 and 2008.

Prior to the crisis and during the period of GDP growth, unemployment rates were shown to have decreased from 12.3 percent in 2004 to 8.3 percent in 2006. Reductions in inflation also coincided with the improving economy (Araujo 2009). Moreover, the country's current account deficit measured 2.7 percent in 2008 and was expected to worsen as a result of the crisis, making it necessary for the country to find new sources to fund its deficit (Saif and Choucair 2009).

The unemployment rates indicate a worsening of the country's conditions in the wake of the financial downturn. According to 2001 and 2002 labor force surveys, unemployment rates among male youth (age 15–29) were the highest for vocational and intermediate institute degree holders, at 22 percent, and were highest for female youth, at 53 percent for vocational degree holders (Kabbani and Kamel 2007).

Syria faces a demographic situation like Egypt's: more than 70 percent of the population is under age 30. Syria was somewhat insulated from the global financial downturn, in large part due to the country's lack of global integration. However, as a result of weakness in global demand for oil and as a result of the effect the financial situation has had on the GCC, Syria was impacted by a decrease in remittances and foreign aid. The continued arrival of Iraqi refugees into 2010 complicated the labor market further (ETF 2010c). Since that time, the refugee flow has reversed, as the Syrian civil war has become one of the biggest humanitarian disasters in recent history.

As in many MENA countries, there is a strong preference in Syria for public sector employment (which incorporates about 30 percent of all employment) with its higher wages and better nonwage benefits. The rate of new jobs opening up is slow, resulting in many young workers queuing for jobs because they would rather wait and remain unemployed than take jobs in the private sector. One reason for the preference for public sector employment among young Syrians is the state of education, which prepares students for national exams that provide a good basis for public sector employment but ignores training in the skills demanded by the private sector (see chapter 2 here). Precrisis data indicate that over 80 percent of young Syrians desired to work in the public sector and that over 60 percent of them pursued employment there exclusively. While young females have a higher desire for public sector employment, at 90 percent, research suggests that family necessity and societal norms encourage young men to seek employment outside the public sector if they cannot secure jobs within it (Kabbani 2009).

Morocco

While Morocco's key economic indicators showed strong improvement in the years leading to the crisis, a more thorough investigation reveals a more complicated and worrisome situation. Morocco's GDP grew 5.6 percent in 2008, and unemployment was at a 35-year low, less than 10 percent as of 2007. In addition, labor force participation for young people decreased, indicating that youth were choosing to stay in school longer. Though more education for youth can be counterproductive, as educated youth are more at risk to be unemployed, the higher unemployment rates are largely due to queuing for formal sector jobs: wages are still positively correlated with education for those who are employed.

During the financial crisis and the resulting economic fallout, Morocco fared better than both Egypt and Jordan. The first wave of financial shocks had little impact on the country; the second round hit harder. The country's phosphate export trade was credited with cushioning the impact; despite Morocco's dependence on energy imports (and the subsequent value fluctuations) phosphate exports tripled in value in 2008, which was enough to cover the oil deficit. Meanwhile, the most pressing threats to the country's financial stability were the decline in the textile and garment industry, declines in remittances, reductions in tourism revenue, and decreases in external investment. Increased return migration and the loss of remittances are important financial and economic issues in Morocco. The loss of remittances created a major source of insecurity among Moroccans in the areas of health, education, and employment needs, as Moroccans had become dependent on the cash flow from abroad. Likewise, the Moroccan government found it difficult to replace these losses through additional expenditures (ODI 2009).

The relatively minor impact of the financial crisis can be seen in both the change in macroeconomic activity and the health of the labor market. GDP growth fell from 5.6 percent in 2008 to 4.8 percent in 2009 and fell further to 3.6 percent in 2010. However, these growth rates are close to the mean for the decade, so Morocco was largely sheltered from the worst of the impacts of the crisis. The overall unemployment rate stayed below 10 percent for 2008–2010 and even fell from 9.7 percent in 2007 to 9.1 percent during these years. Youth did not fare as well; their unemployment rates increased from 17.3 percent to 18.1 percent from 2007 to 2009. However, by 2010, even the youth unemployment rate was falling again; it settled at 17.7 percent and remained below 18 percent for 2011 and 2012 (ILO 2014).

There has been a delayed response in Morocco to address the effects of the crisis. In 2009 the Moroccan government implemented an emergency response plan that addressed only very minor segments of the nation's economy. Under the plan, the government aimed to maintain 2008 levels of employment and social coverage. The plan consisted of addressing the automotive industry and the textile and leather industries. These measures failed to address the needs of the majority of the population and had little impact on youth employment and the problems of other vulnerable groups. The problem of youth exclusion continues unabated as a result of the plan's failure to address the issue of employment generation.

Algeria

Prior to the financial crisis Algeria's economy was growing, but it was not growing as quickly as other regional economies. In 2007, Algeria experienced a GDP growth rate of 3.4 percent. This was an increase from the 1.7 percent growth in 2006 but was down from the annual average for the 2001–2005 period, which was over 5.0 percent (World Bank 2014). The total number of youth employed rose from 1.19 million in 2003 to 1.58 million in 2007, marking an increase of 32 percent for the period. The unemployment rate for 15- to 24-year-olds in 2007 was estimated to be 25 percent for males and 40 percent for females, also indicating a decrease from the 2000 rates of 74 percent and

48 percent, respectively.[6] While the outcomes for young men continued to improve, as their unemployment rate fell from 21.9 percent to 19.1 percent from 2008 to 2010, young women failed to continue to make gains. The unemployment rate for young Algerian women was 35 percent in 2008 but rose to 38 percent in 2010.

Tunisia

Tunisia was particularly vulnerable to external financial and economic shocks due to its greater integration in the world economy and its dependence on imports. Furthermore, exports, foreign direct investment, remittances, and tourism are key national economic sectors and major sources of job creation for Tunisia. However, because declining growth rates were being experienced in all sectors and the government was unable to start investment projects to overhaul the economy, the country faced continued challenges during the crisis. Before the Arab Spring, tourism had been responsible for 450,000 jobs in Tunisia, and for the year 2007, remittances had been responsible for 5 percent of GDP, or $1.7 billion. Between 2005 and 2006 the country experienced a threefold increase in foreign direct investment (Drine 2009). Economic growth rates fell, as they did throughout the MENA region, during the financial crisis; economic growth had been 5.7 percent in 2007 but fell to 4.7 percent in 2008 and 3.6 percent in 2009. The economy continued to slow down into 2010; growth declined to 3.2 percent. Thus Tunisia, unlike several other countries in the region, continued to weaken as the crisis dragged on into 2010. However, like many countries in the region, Tunisia during the crisis did not suffer the sharp contraction that afflicted the United States and Europe but, instead, experienced a slowdown of growth. However, Tunisia did undergo a sharp contraction after the eruption of the Arab Spring, when GDP growth became negative in 2011, falling to -0.5 percent.

Like many other MENA countries, Tunisia has been experiencing a youth bulge, and this has led to substantially higher rates of unemployment for those aged 15–29 than for older workers (see table 3.3). This trend was especially noticeable during the 2000s. From 2005 to 2010 the unemployment rate declined for older workers and increased for youth. For example, the unemployment rate for 35- to 39-year-olds fell from 6.3 percent in 2005 to 5.3 percent in 2010. At the same time, the unemployment rate for 20- to 24-year-olds increased from 28.4 percent to 32.0 percent. This pattern held for nearly all youth/adult comparisons over this time. As seen in Haouas, Sayre, and Yagoubi (2013) these high rates of unemployment are especially a problem for young educated women. For youth aged 15–24 with tertiary schooling (very recent graduates), the unemployment rate for men was over 50 percent and for women over 60 percent.

Part of the reason for the severity of the problem of educated youth unemployment in Tunisia was that in comparison to other MENA countries Tunisia had experienced the demographic transition earlier and had been more effective in educating young women. While Tunisia before independence had a history of high birthrates, government programs that began in the 1960s helped reduce the birthrate to a replacement level of

TABLE 3.3

Unemployment rate by age, Tunisia, 2005–2010.

Age	2005	2006	2007	2008	2009
15–19	27.7	27.9	29.3	29.6	33.6
20–24	28.4	27.6	27.3	27.9	29.9
25–29	21.6	21.1	21.8	22.9	25.7
30–34	11.6	11.1	11.6	11.5	11.4
35–39	6.3	6.6	5.8	5.4	5.6
40–44	4.8	4.4	3.9	3.3	4.3
45–49	3.8	3.9	3	2.9	3.9
50–59	3.2	3.5	2.5	2.6	3.2
60+	1.2	2.2	2.4	1.8	1.2
Total	12.9	12.5	12.4	12.4	13.3

Source: Ministry of Vocational Training and Employment (2010).

2.1 children per woman. As mentioned in chapter 1 here, Tunisia was only one of two MENA countries (the other was Lebanon) that experienced fertility rates falling below replacement rates. These rates decreased dramatically from levels that had been higher than most current fertility rates in Africa when these programs of female education, family planning, and legal reform began (World Bank 2008b). The employment-to-population ratio for youth aged 15–24 decreased slightly from 22.8 in 2006 to 22.3 in 2008. The female youth employment-to-population ratio remained constant at 15.4 percent during the same period; the level for male youth decreased from 29.7 percent in 2006 to 28.9 percent in 2008 (World Bank 2010a).

Due to the growing number of graduates from the higher education system in Tunisia, more and more individuals have become unemployed. The number of young unemployed graduates nearly doubled in 10 years, from 121,800 in 1996–1997 to 336,000 in 2006–2007 (World Bank, 2008a). Unemployment remains a serious problem among young graduates, notably those who graduate with a postsecondary degree. The problem has been most severe for graduates with two-year technical degrees and master's degrees, both of which have an unemployment rate of 50 percent.

The United Arab Emirates

The UAE, and the Emirate of Dubai in particular, struggled more as a result of the financial crisis than other GCC countries. By the end of 2009, the UAE stock market had dropped sharply, growth had plummeted, and the rest of the GCC had experienced higher volatility in economic outcomes. For most of the 2000s, the UAE was the fastest growing country in the region; growth rates averaged over 6.0 percent and reached

9.8 percent in 2006. In 2007 and 2008 the economy of the UAE softened, and growth shrank to 3.2 percent for each year. Much of Dubai's growth during the decade was fueled by a construction boom financed by the same easy money practices that had led to the global crisis. When global financial markets began to freeze in 2008, the contagion only took a few months to hit Dubai, and by February 2009 the economy was in free fall. As already mentioned, the financial crisis affected world oil prices because as worldwide growth shrank, so did the demand for hydrocarbons. However, it was the finance- and trade-dependent economy of Dubai that was most severely affected by the financial shocks. Much of the impact from Dubai's woes did not spill over to the rest of the MENA region. Loans funded by Abu Dhabi to Dubai were instrumental in helping to curb further problems in Dubai by increasing investor confidence. In addition to the loans by Abu Dhabi, the UAE Central Bank and the Finance Ministry provided more than $32 billion in bailout funds (Saif and Choucair 2009). Public debts of this magnitude had substantial effect on job creation, as companies cut back expenses in an effort to stay financially afloat.

Despite the UAE's heavy dependence on foreign workers, national unemployment rates have remained relatively stable, due to initiatives to introduce government quotas of nationals employed in the private sector. (See chapter 5 here for a detailed analysis of Gulf labor markets.) These trends are currently being challenged, and the government's employees are now holding the government responsible for securing their employment. (See below here for the government's responses.) As a result of the unemployment threat to national workers, working conditions for foreign workers have worsened.

While the UAE has fared better than most of the MENA region in terms of youth exclusion, the country still faces a significant gender imbalance in the workforce, with difference between male and female participation rates among Emirati youth of 34 percentage points. Significantly, female youth face higher unemployment rates than their male counterparts, despite the fact that their tertiary enrollment is double that of their male counterparts, at 36 percent (compared to 17 percent for males) (Brookings Institution 2010). The higher female tertiary enrollment, however, could help to explain the lower female youth labor force participation rate, as they are delaying entrance into the market while they complete their degrees. Despite the gender differences in participation, these gender gaps in labor force participation are still smaller than those in many other MENA countries.

Policies to Address Youth Unemployment and the Financial Crisis

This section discusses initiatives that were implemented in the MENA region in the wake of the global financial crisis to address the problems of economic downturn and youth unemployment. As Saif and Choucair (2009) succinctly explain, developing effective policies to mitigate the impact of the crisis was not always a straightforward process, especially given the interconnectedness of the world economy. As such, Saif and Choucair point to several main drivers that influence responses to the crisis: different economic drivers, such as remittances, foreign direct investment, and trade; the political atmosphere of the country; the fiscal context; the institutional structure of lobbying bodies and agencies; the ability for public and private entities to act efficiently; and the deficiencies of social safety nets prior to the crisis (Saif and Choucair 2009). While some programs predate the crisis and specifically aim to protect and promote youth employment, many programs either have fallen short of the intended success or have been counterproductive. These measures can be classified into three main categories: macroeconomic and financial initiatives that have an impact on youth labor demand; direct labor market and skill development initiatives; and policies related to regulating labor migration.

Macroeconomic and Financial Initiatives

Egypt took a variety of steps to help curb the impact of the economic and financial crisis. According to the country's European Training Foundation (ETF) report (ETF is an EU agency), three major steps were taken. First, a stimulus program was implemented that included infrastructure and local development projects, including water, sewage and roads. Second was a program of reforms and strategic development through strengthening key economic sectors, particularly agriculture and tourism. Third, the government supported the development of new international partnerships, particularly with India and China, in the hope that new markets and outsourcing possibilities would be accessed in an effort to maintain sufficient levels of foreign direct investment (ETF 2010a).

The GCC countries, and Saudi Arabia in particular, responded quickly to the financial crisis and implemented policies similar to those of the United States, European Union, and eastern Europe, with the main objective of maintaining financial sector stability. General policies that were introduced included the government guarantees on deposits and debt, capital injections, asset purchases, and monetary easing. Saudi Arabia also introduced fiscal stimulus packages to ensure both short- and long-term growth. The Saudi government spent over $200 billion after the crisis began and was credited with contributing to the global recovery process because Saudi Arabia has such a large import ratio (World Bank 2010a). Jordan focused its policy responses on deposit guarantees and monetary easing; Tunisia and Morocco offered liquidity support. Tunisia supplemented this policy with further support for small and micro enterprise; similar policies were offered in Bahrain, Egypt, Jordan, Morocco, and the UAE (Tzannatos 2009). Tunisia also implemented support for youth employment, and Morocco supplemented the aforementioned policies with working capital loan guarantees, debt rescheduling, and easing of regulation (World Bank 2010b).

All these measures mainly relied on government spending and financial sector interventions to cushion the crisis's impact on economic activity and prevent further drops in growth rates. However, to have more specific youth impacts, these measures needed to be better targeted to sectors that disproportionately employ young and new entrants to the labor market.

Labor Market Interventions

Several initiatives were introduced in Arab countries to cushion the negative impact of the crisis on youth employment. These included training and skills development initiatives in Egypt, Jordan, and Syria; employment subsidies and coverage of social security contributions in Tunisia, Algeria, and the UAE; and multidimensional programs, including financial and nonfinancial services, to promote youth entrepreneurship and income-generating projects targeting youth in Egypt, Jordan, Morocco, and Tunisia. In addition, Algeria, Lebanon, Libya, Morocco, and Tunisia implemented wage increases for civil servants (Tzannatos 2009). These measures, while they may have alleviated immediate income concerns and helped to counter some of the crisis's effects, may also have exacerbated the problem of queues for public sector jobs, which were already of serious concern in parts of the region. (See chapter 5 here for more details on these policies in the Gulf.) Similarly, minimum wage and civil servant salary increases have also been introduced in a number of countries, including Algeria, Jordan, Lebanon, Morocco, Qatar, and Tunisia. New forms of unemployment insurance and assistance have been implemented in Bahrain, Jordan, and Syria. Egypt has also offered greater support for income-generating projects. Tunisia introduced early retirement options in an effort to reduce unemployment by opening new positions through retirement. Subsidies for small and medium-sized enterprises have also been introduced in Bahrain, Egypt, Jordan, Morocco, Tunisia, and the UAE (Tzannatos 2009).

Country-Specific Interventions

Egypt

In the wake of the crisis, the Egyptian government increased financial support for training institutions to expand the participation of youth in these programs (ILO 2010b). During 2009, an initiative for the design of a specific strategy for reform of technical and vocational education and training (TVET) was also launched, with an action plan for short-, medium-, and long-term implementation (ETF 2010a). Although the strategy provided an integrated policy umbrella for existing programs (e.g., the EU's TVET reform program and the World Bank's Skills Development Project), its short-term measures can be thought of as part of response mechanisms to address the continued exclusion of youth in an environment of economic slowdown. Several multidimensional projects were also put in place following the crisis. Besides the announced $3 billion spent on a fiscal stimulus package, the Egyptian government also spent some $2.6 billion on labor-intensive projects (which the government calls social solidarity measures) to combat unemployment.

Jordan

In the wake of the crisis, Jordan implemented a multicomponent initiative that addressed training, employment in both the public and private sectors, and income subsidies. Furthermore, the initiative aimed at providing specialized vocational training for labor-intensive sectors of the economy and to provide secure employment for at least one year after training, social security, medical insurance, and transportation to work (ILO 2010b). Education reform was further highlighted as a priority, with curriculum reform, governance, and quality assurance in keeping with the Bologna Process, and with the 2008 Jordan Employer Driven Skill Development (a program to harmonize TVET programs with employer needs). Together these projects total $8.8 million commitment to reform (ETF 2010b). Although started in the precrisis period, the program was enhanced and strengthened in the crisis's wake.

Algeria

Realizing the precarious situation of youth in the country, in the wake of the crisis the Algerian government took steps to both promote job creation and preserve existing jobs. The National Commission for the Promotion of Employment included funding of an emergency program for youth employment and job preservation. In addition, to address the issues of employment and unemployment, proposals were submitted with the goals of preservation of current employment and boosting the overall level of employment. Furthermore, policies aimed at medium- and long-term employment promotion and measures related to social protection and solidarity were introduced (ILO 2009). These measures indicated the government's awareness of the importance of not only immediate youth inclusion but also long-term sustainability in programs targeting employment and labor market reforms.

Tunisia

The Ben Ali government of Tunisia took an active role in trying to preserve and promote youth employment in the country. In this regard, in addition to the aforementioned promotion of business incubators, the country's response to the crisis included implementing a series of programs to further promote and boost youth employment. First, 18 million dinars was allocated for incentives to businesses who hired university graduates. Second, the government created a call center to provide real-time information for job seekers. Third, the government established programs in universities to help build skills and vocational training to bolster youth employment by providing recent graduates and new job seekers with employer-demanded skills. Fourth, the government attempted to increase the capacity of existing vocational training within the country and to increase the emphasis on youth-oriented training programs. Fifth, the government increased the power of regional councils to help promote, design, and implement employment schemes for the region (ILO 2009). These policies indicated an acknowledgment on the part of the government of the importance of youth's role in the economy. However, as the events of December 2010 and January 2011 demonstrated, many of these policies were too short-sighted and did not address the issues at a fundamental level.

The United Arab Emirates

A policy that the UAE implemented in 2009, in an effort to protect Emirati jobs, was to prohibit the dismissal of national employees except in the case of "serious misconduct." Securing national employment is a serious concern for this Gulf country, which mostly employs foreigners in the private sector, while the national labor force is primarily engaged in the public sector. Such policies are highly controversial and may prove to be counterproductive. They may especially discourage Emirati workers' productivity, since employment will be guaranteed despite productivity, and will discourage the hiring of national workers in the first place because foreign workers are exempt from the employment protection laws (Dhillon et al. 2010). This could disproportionately affect younger Emirati workers who lack the experience and skills of their older national counterparts and exclude them further from being hired. As seen in chapter 10 here, protections that prevent firing of certain workers can have the adverse effect of making them less desirable to be hired in the first place, since any hiring decision becomes a risky, permanent one.

Policies Relating to Regulating Labor Migration

The foregoing country analyses show that unemployment rates among youth either remained at their high precrisis levels or worsened during the crisis. The increasing number of excluded youth, aside from engaging in low-wage employment outlets in the informal sector, also intensified their search efforts to seek employment outside their countries of origin. Traditionally, the policies enacted by countries in the region, which are all net recipients of labor migration, have generally attempted to protect national workers at the expense of expatriate workers. For example, Kuwait and Saudi Arabia both reduced the number of migrant workers in an effort to protect national jobs. Kuwait's plan included reducing the number of expatriates working in the public sector and deporting approximately 15 percent of the country's population (about half a million foreign workers, who either lacked skills, were unemployed, or were residing illegally in the country). Similarly, Saudi Arabia planned to reduce its migrant population from 9 to 2 million people over eight years (Tzannatos 2009).

Interestingly, the crisis triggered many other labor-receiving countries also to try to adopt more flexible approaches and introduce much-needed reforms to their migrant worker policies. Some receiving countries have tried to reform their migrant labor standards to improve standards for expatriate workers. In Lebanon, the new policies of unified contracts and improved employment oversight are targeted at domestic workers, a typically exploited and neglected foreign worker contingency in Lebanon and the GCC countries. Jordan passed important antitrafficking legislation in 2009; additional measures addressing protections for migrant workers were also considered. Jordan has also introduced an initiative to protect its own migrant workers abroad—particularly in the GCC countries, Egypt, and Libya—to cover the costs of dispute resolution should a case be lost. Bahrain has implemented the most expansive policies of all the labor-receiving countries, including greater freedom for migrant workers to change jobs, higher levels of inspection of labor recruitment offices, new arbitration policies for migrant workers (including domestic workers), wage protection, unemployment insurance eligibility during job transitions, increased fees for work visas, and enforcement of a previously implemented law that prohibits working in the sun from 12 to 4 o'clock in the afternoon during July and August (Tzannatos 2009).

After the financial crisis and before the Arab Spring, these new laws had the potential to attract additional migrant workers from the region as job stability and employment conditions became more attractive there, especially given the alternative in some of these workers' originating countries. With expanded opportunities to work in some MENA countries, the draw for migrants from countries like Egypt, where the waiting time for public sector jobs is exceedingly long, becomes appealing. Unfortunately, these policies were not in place long enough before the Arab Spring uprisings, which then led to a complete revision of migration policies in response to the increased supply of potential migrants from Egypt, Tunisia, Syria, Libya, and elsewhere.

Conclusion

Globally, the economic downturn hit youth hard, with increases in unemployment and decreases in the labor force participation rate among this vulnerable age group. Even when jobs are being created, the inexperience and lack of market-oriented skills of youth pose major concerns and barriers to employment. These factors combine to create an expansion in the informal sector and perpetuation of youth exclusion. When the preexisting problems for youth are then combined with a sharply deteriorating labor market, the youth are likely to take the brunt of any economic downturn, suffering worse than the rest of the labor market.

The specific country data analyses for Egypt, Jordan, Morocco, Algeria, Tunisia, Syria, and the UAE indicate that the labor market effects of the crisis were delayed in some countries. These delays resulted from the fact that only the countries that had developed the fastest growth (UAE) and were the most dependent on remittances and oil rents (Tunisia and Syria) were vulnerable to sudden reversals due to the financial crisis. Thus, the effects of the crisis have varied throughout the region. However, generally speaking, most countries did experience worsening conditions for youth as a result of the financial crisis and global economic downturn, though these impacts may have been relatively minor in some countries.

The crisis highlighted the need for long-term alternatives that will address the causes of youth exclusion to help bring them into the labor market as productive and efficient workers. However, immediately following the crisis the region witnessed the Arab Spring, which led to a sharp contraction in growth for many countries (Tunisia, Syria, Egypt, and Yemen) in 2011, followed by slow growth for all countries, with the exception of Syria. Thus, long-term responses to the weaknesses highlighted by the financial crisis had to take a back seat to the immediate concerns of the post–Arab Spring regimes. The policy challenge for these regimes is highlighted in the conclusion of this book; they now need to meet both short-term societal goals and the long term-challenges presented by the existence of historically excluded groups, including, women, young people, and the poor.

REFERENCES

Achy, L. 2009. Government response to international crisis: The case of Morocco. Carnegie Middle East Center. http://carnegieendowment.org/2009/03/24/government-response-to-international-crisis-case-of-morocco/6pq.

Araujo, J. 2009. Short and medium-term growth prospects: Challenges and opportunities. In *Development Horizons: The Financial Crisis: Impact on the Middle East*, 22–27 Washington, DC: World Bank.

Assaad, R., and G. Barsoum. 2007. Youth exclusion in Egypt: In search of "second chances." Middle East Youth Initiative working paper. Washington, DC: Wolfensohn Center for Development, Brookings Institution.

Assaad, R., and G. Barsoum. 2009. Rising expectations and diminishing opportunities for Egypt's young. In *Generation in waiting: The unfulfilled promise of young people in the Middle East*, ed. N. Dhillon and T. Yousef, 67–94. Washington, DC: Brookings Institution.

Behrendt, C., T. Haq, and H. Kamel. 2009. The impact of the financial and economic crisis on Arab states: Considerations on employment and social protection policy responses. Beirut: ILO Regional Office for Arab States.

Brookings Institution. 2010. Understanding the generation in waiting in the Middle East. http://www.brookings.edu/research/articles/2010/06/middle-east-youth.

Central Agency for Public Mobilization and Statistics (CAPMAS). 2010. Labor Force Survey. http://www.capmas.gov.eg/.

Chaaban, J. 2008. The costs of youth exclusion in the Middle East. Middle East Youth Initiative working paper. http://www.meyi.org/publication-the-costs-of-youth-exclusion-in-the-middle-east.html.

Dhillon, N. D. Salehi-Isfahani, P. Dyer, T. Yousef, A. Fahmy, and M. Kraetsch. 2010. Missed by the boom, hurt by the bust: Making markets work for young people in the Middle East. Middle East Youth Initiative. http://www.meyi.org/publication-missed-by-the-boom-hurt-by-the-bust.html.

Dhillon, N., and T. Yousef, eds. 2009. *Generation in waiting: The unfulfilled promise of young people in the Middle East*. Washington, DC: Brookings Institution.

Drine, I. 2009. Impact of the global economic crisis on the Arab region. World Institute for Development Economics Research. http://www.wider.unu.edu/publications/newsletter/articles/en_GB/05-06-2009/.

European Training Foundation (ETF). 2010a. ETF Country Information Note 2010: Egypt. Turin: European Training Foundation.

European Training Foundation (ETF). 2010b. ETF Country Information Note 2010: Jordan. Turin: European Training Foundation.

European Training Foundation (ETF). 2010c. ETF Country Information Note 2010: Syria. Turin: European Training Foundation.

Haouas, I., E. Sayre, M. Yagoubi. 2013. Youth unemployment in Tunisia: Underlying trends and an evaluation of policy responses. *International Research Journal of Finance and Economics* 115 (October): 95–107.

International Labour Organization (ILO). 2009. *Youth Employment in Algeria.* Algiers: International Labour Organization.

International Labour Organization (ILO). 2010a. Global Employment Trends. Geneva: International Labour Organization.

International Labour Organization (ILO). 2010b. "Global Employment Trends for Youth. Geneva: International Labour Organization.

International Labour Organization (ILO). 2014. ILOSTAT database. http://www.ilo.org/ ilostat/faces/home/statisticaldata/bulk-download?_adf.ctrl-state=kjpnknfqw_185&clean= true&_afrLoop=2014206648837215.

Kabbani, N. 2009. Why young Syrians prefer public sector jobs. Middle East Youth Initiative policy outlook no. 2. Washington, DC: Wolfensohn Center for Development, Brookings Institution.

Kabbani, N., and N. Kamel. 2007. Youth exclusion in Syria: Social economic and institutional dimensions. Middle East Youth Initiative working paper no. 4. Washington, DC: Wolfensohn Center for Development, Brookings Institution.

Kouame, A. T. 2009. The financial crisis: Impact on the Middle East. In *Development Horizons: The Financial Crisis: Impact on the Middle East, 6–12.* Washington, DC: World Bank.

Ministry of Vocational Training and Employment. 2010. *Employment Statistics.* http://www .emploi.gov.tn/en/.

Murian, N., and M. Salamat. 2010. *The impact of the world financial crisis on the labor market in Jordan* Cairo: Population Council WANA regional office.

National Institute of Statistics-Tunisia (INS). 2011. *National Employment Survey* http://www.ins .nat.tn/indexen.php.

Office of National Statistics. 2010. *Employment and Unemployment: 4th Quarter 2010.* Algiers: Office of National Statistics.

Overseas Development Institute (ODI). 2009, November. Impact of the economic crisis and food and fuel price volatility on children and women in the MENA region. Working paper 310. London: Overseas Development Institute.

Roushdy, R. and M. Gadallah. 2011. Labor Market adjustment to the world financial crisis: Evidence from Egypt. Economic Research Forum working paper 643. Cairo: Economic Research Forum.

Saif, I., and F. Choucair. 2009. Arab countries stumble in the face of growing economic crisis. Carnegie Endowment for International Peace. http://carnegieendowment.org/files/economic_ crisis_wc_english.pdf.

Schmidt, D. 2009. Youth employment and regional international experiences. Geneva: International Labour Organization.

Tzannatos, Zafiris. 2009, October 19–21. The global financial, economic and social crisis and the Arab countries: A review of the evidence and policies for employment creation and social protection. Presentation at Arab Employment Forum, Beirut.

World Bank. 2008a. For a better integration into the labor market in Tunisia. http://web .worldbank.org/WBSITE/EXTERNAL/COUNTRIES/MENAEXT/TUNISIAEXTN/ 0,,contentMDK:21671683~pagePK:1497618~piPK:217854~theSitePK:310015,00.html.

World Bank. 2008b. Africa's population set to double by 2036. World Bank. http://web .worldbank.org/WBSITE/EXTERNAL/COUNTRIES/AFRICAEXT/0,,contentMDK: 21709116~menuPK:258659~pagePK:2865106~piPK:2865128~theSitePK:258644,00.html.

World Bank. 2010a. Recovering from the crisis. World Bank Middle East and North Africa Region—a regional economic update. Washington, DC: World Bank.

World Bank. 2010b, August 3. Morocco fights poverty through "human development" approach. http://web.worldbank.org/WBSITE/EXTERNAL/PROJECTS/0,,contentMDK:22665028~ menuPK:64282137~pagePK:41367~piPK:279616~theSitePK:40941,00.html.

World Bank. 2014. World Development Indicators. http://data.worldbank.org/data-catalog/ world-development-indicators.

NOTES

1. These data and all data from the International Labour Organization (ILO) sources referring to youth unemployment define "youth" as 15–24 years old.

2. Please note that these data from the World Bank did not include the information for only older participants (25–54), which would be better to use in these calculations, as therefore the ratio would truly represent the relative disparity. With the current calculation, the youth are included as part of the total in the denominator, and therefore, depending on the relative size of the youth cohort, the values in this figure may underestimate the relative difference between youth and adults.

3. Table 3.1 focuses on market work, i.e., economic activity engaged in for the purpose of market exchange, using the broad definition of unemployment. Previous studies also use the standard definition of unemployment. Both the standard and broad definitions require that the individual has not worked or been attached to a job during the week prior to the interview and has desired work and been available for it. The standard definition also requires that the individual has actively searched for work in the three months prior to the interview. The broad definition loosens the search requirement to include the discouraged unemployed, i.e., those who are no longer actively searching for a job.

4. Except when noted, this chapter will use the World Bank (2014) World Development Indicators for growth rates, available at http://data.worldbank.org/indicator/NY.GDP.MKTP.KD.ZG.

5. The latest World Bank Development Indicators available GDP figures for Syria are from 2007.

6. There is some difference between the numbers reported by the Office of National Statistics (2010) and the ILO estimates. These numbers reflect the ILO estimates.

4 The Effects of Education and Marriage on Young Women's Labor Force Participation in the Middle East and North Africa

Edward A. Sayre and Rana Hendy

ECONOMIC DEVELOPMENT AND women's opportunities are intrinsically linked. If a society limits women's ability to contribute outside the home, economic growth is restrained. If women are not able to go to school or to work outside the home because of cultural, legal, or other institutional barriers, then a country will not be using all of its resources effectively. In the Middle East and North Africa (MENA) region this is a particular problem in that women's labor force participation rates there are the lowest in the world.

This region, although it still lags behind others in women's labor force participation, has made substantial improvements in closing the gender gaps in literacy and educational attainment. For example, in 1986 in Egypt the youth literacy rate was 17 percent higher for boys than for girls, but by 2010 this gap had shrunk to 7 percent (World Bank 2013). In addition, women have been increasing their educational attainment at a much faster rate than men in the Middle East. In many MENA countries women now have higher schooling rates than men (especially at the tertiary level); 25 years ago this was not the case for a single country.

As Middle Eastern women have become more educated, their willingness to seek out careers and enter the labor force has also increased. Much of the increase in labor force participation has resulted from higher levels of education. The discouraging part of this trend is that educated women have less labor force attachment today compared to a generation ago (Assaad et al. 2012). Women with university degrees 20 years ago were more likely to seek work than they are today. Even more disappointing is that such women are even less likely to find employment now than they were 20 years ago, as unemployment rates for university educated women are the highest of any educational category.

Overall, the region has a female labor force participation rate of 21 percent, but individual country rates vary significantly, ranging from a high of 52 percent in Qatar to a low of 13 percent in Syria. While Syria has the lowest participation rate, it is not an outlier; most MENA countries outside the Gulf have female participation rates in the teens or low twenties, and the countries in the world with the five lowest participation rates are all found in the MENA region. Thus, nearly all countries in the region have much lower participation rates than those outside the Middle East, especially when accounting for differences in education level and the level of economic development.

The failure of women's labor force participation rates to rise is connected to their limited job prospects. Young women with university degrees have the highest unemployment rates among any age/education demographic group. For example, in Tunisia 30 percent of adult women with more than a secondary education are unemployed, more than double the rate for any other educational level. For women under the age of 30, more than half of those with university educations are unemployed. This is due to both supply and demand factors. As education levels have risen, there has not been sufficient job creation in the economy to absorb these newly educated women. However, the "lack of jobs" story is only partly true. In addition, as these women (along with most young people) have a strong preference toward working in the public sector, the decline in the role of the public sector in the economy has hit them worse than other groups.

Low female labor force participation has delayed transitions from youth to adulthood for young people. The two main transitions youth make are the transition from schooling to work and from dependency in their parents' households to forming their own families. In the welfare life course that was prevalent in the MENA region, schooling was acquired as a credential for employment in the public sector (Dhillon et al. 2009). Women acquired higher levels of schooling, both to be able to work in "acceptable" jobs in the public sector and to find better husbands. Women with higher levels of education tend to marry men with higher levels of education, and the university serves as a place to meet potential partners. Thus, education for women is an investment toward both direct earnings and finding a partner with better job opportunities.

This chapter demonstrates how the institutional features of the labor market lower women's labor force participation in the MENA region and the deleterious effects these low participation rates can have on young women and on the economies and societies throughout the region. In the next section we compare the participation rates of women from the MENA region with rates for women in other regions. We then focus on current rates of labor force participation in different countries in the region. Finally, we compare the three cases of Jordan, Tunisia, and Egypt to show how differences in labor market institutions have led to different behavior by women in the workforce. The analysis shows that private sector wage work is still largely not an option for married women and that the role of the informal sector determines whether women stay in the labor force or drop out when they marry.

Female Labor Force Participation in the Global Context

Women in the MENA region, compared to those in every other region of the world, are less likely to work outside the home. This is true for women of all education levels and of all ages, though there are clear differences between countries in the MENA region and between groups within countries. This section examines the former; the next section will begin to look at the latter.

Figure 4.1 shows female labor force participation rates for developing regions of the world from 1990 to 2010. These data come from the World Bank and use consistent definitions of labor force participation from the International Labour Organization. The data include women aged 15 and older, and data are excluded for countries such as Iraq that do not have accessible data for the entire time period.

Figure 4.1 shows that women in the MENA region participate in the labor force at less than half the rate of those in the rest of the world. The average rate over the 21 years was lower than 20 percent; the average for the world was 48 percent. The only region whose rate was not double that of the MENA region was South Asia, at 35 percent.

Labor force participation rates for women have increased in many regions, though the world average has remained flat. In the MENA region, participation rates have increased

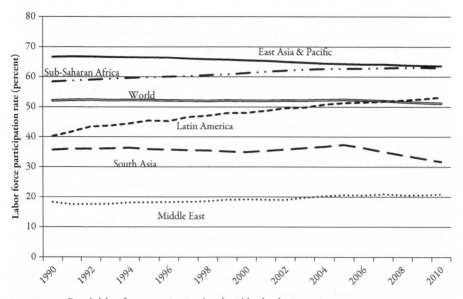

FIGURE 4.1 Female labor force participation (aged 15+) by developing region, 1990–2010.
Source: World Bank Development Indicators, World Bank, http://data.worldbank.org/indicator/SL.TLF.CACT
.FE.ZS/countries/1W-ZQ.

from 18 percent to 21 percent, but the pace of this growth has been slower than in most other regions. Participation rates in Sub-Saharan Africa increased from 58 percent to 63 percent, and rates in Latin American rose from 40 percent to 53 percent. Not all regions improved. Participation rates in East Asia and South Asia actually decreased over this time, but the regions that did improve did so more rapidly than the MENA region.

Despite the nature of the MENA region as an outlier, it is important to avoid oversimplifying explanations for these regional differences. Explanations for these differences that are based on cultural factors are usually off the mark. Islam in particular has received the most attention. Because of Islamic theology's relegation of women to a subordinate position outside the home, some observers blame low workforce participation rates on Islam (The rights of Muslim women 1997). However convenient this explanation, Islam is not the source of the gender gap (Moghadam 1993). Outside the MENA region, Muslims tend to have labor force patterns more similar to their regions of residence. For example, in the United States, Muslim women who are daughters of immigrants and who have been raised in the United States have work patterns similar to those of other American women (Read 2004). Instead, economic and institutional factors, such as work opportunities for men in high-wage countries and social pressure for women to stay at home with children, are seen by most scholars as much more salient explanations (Shafik 2001). Cross-country studies that find significance in the role of religion also tend to find that the most important factor is education, an area where, up until recently, women in the MENA region also lagged far behind (Psacharopoulos and Tzannatos 1989).

Differences between MENA Countries

Despite the overall low levels of women's labor participation for the entire region, there are large differences between countries. This section offers some preliminary explanations of these differences by focusing on characteristics of countries that have similar participation rates. One way to organize the countries in the region is by relative wealth. Figure 4.2 shows a scatter plot of female labor force participation rates and gross national income per capita for 15 MENA countries for 2010. Figure 4.2 uses a logarithmic scale, and units on the horizontal axis are in hundreds of US dollars per person. Labor force participation rates range from a high for 52 percent in Qatar and 44 percent in the UAE to a low of 13 percent in Syria.

There are natural groupings of countries on this graph. The clearest difference between countries occurs between the Gulf and the rest of the MENA region. Kuwait, Qatar, and the UAE have female participation rates over 40 percent; the non-Gulf countries have rates lower than 30 percent. While these labor force participation rates are inflated by the presence of expatriates, the labor force participation rate of nationals is still very high. For example, the World Bank data for Qatar indicate a rate of 52 percent for all women aged

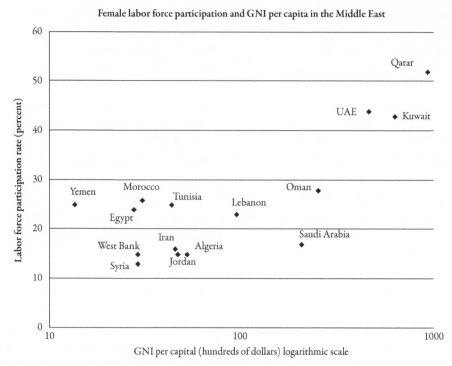

FIGURE 4.2 Labor force participation and GNI per capita, Middle East, 2010.

Source: World Bank Development Indicators, 2010 data, http://data.worldbank.org/indicator/SL.TLF.CACT.FE
.ZS/countries/1W-ZQ?display=graph.

15 and over, while Qatari national statistics indicate that the rate is 31 percent for female Qatari nationals (QSA 2011). Although the rate in Qatar is lower for female nationals than for female expatriates, the rate for all Qatari women is still higher than the averages seen in other countries in the region, outside the Gulf.

On the logarithmic scale used in figure 4.2, one can see the positive correlation between female labor force participation rates and average income. Among the countries not in the Gulf Cooperation Council (GCC), Yemen is an outlier largely because it is the poorest country in the region. While most countries outside the Gulf are "middle income" according to the World Bank, this is not the case in Yemen. Yemen fits expectations due to the historical "U-shaped" curve when plotting female labor force participation and income (Goldin 1995). When countries are relatively poor, labor force participation rates are high, as many women work in the agricultural sector. In rich Western developed countries, participation rates are also high, due to lower fertility rates, high female education rates, and abundant opportunities for work outside the home. It is mostly as countries pass through the intermediate stage of economic development (middle income) that participation rates for women are the lowest. As we will show, the tendency for labor participation rates to be lowest for middle-income individuals occurs within countries and is not just an explanation of between-country differences.

A second natural grouping includes those countries in the Mashreq plus Iran. Iran, Jordan, West Bank and Gaza, and Syria all have a gross national income per capita between $3,000 and $5,000 and have female labor force participation rates below 20 percent. These countries not only represent the lowest levels of female labor force participation in the region but, with the addition of Algeria, are also the five lowest in the world. As mentioned in chapter 1, Algeria, Iran, and Syria are high-population, oil-producing countries with slow fertility transitions. Thus, it is not surprising that they, along with the remittance dependent economies of the West Bank and Gaza and Jordan, share a similar pattern of labor force participation, given their dependence on rents. The next natural grouping includes three North African countries, including two that are featured in this chapter: Tunisia, Egypt, and Morocco. These countries' gross national income is between $2,500 and $4,500, and their labor force participation rates are between 20 percent and 30 percent.

What accounts for these differences? Largely, it is the relative sizes of the public sectors and levels of education. The Gulf states are wealthy enough to be able to absorb most women who want to work into the education, health, and public administration sectors, and this wealth allows women to work in an acceptable environment that is often gender segregated. Culturally appropriate jobs for women are at a premium, and most of these jobs are found in the public sector. For example, in Qatar many female workers are employed in companies like Qtel, the public telephone utility, which allow them to work in an environment that is both female-only and largely Qatari-only. This gives them the privilege of both gender segregation and the ability to avoid encountering expatriate workers, who are often met with suspicion. In countries with small and shrinking health and education sectors, like Jordan, culturally appropriate job opportunities for educated women have been shrinking (Assaad et al. 2012).

Each country also has specific historical and institutional factors that affect the labor force participation rate. In Tunisia, Habib Bourguiba promulgated the Code of Personal Status when he was prime minister in 1956. This radical law gave women greater equality, instituting women's ability to initiate divorce, more favorable inheritance laws, and the abolition of polygamy. These changes also influenced the literacy and education gap, as women were given the legal right to education and the right to work (Murphy 2003). In addition, the legalization of abortion in the 1960s and limitations of family allowance benefits to only four children led Tunisia to become one of the first countries in the region to see its fertility rates decline (Lecomte and Marcoux 1976). With the rise in women's education and the decline in fertility, an increase in women's labor force participation followed. However, in order to get a better sense of the determinants of women's labor force participation, it is useful to examine the subject using the available microdata, to which we now turn.

Determinants of Labor Force Participation in Tunisia, Jordan, and Egypt

In this section we examine three case studies—Egypt, Tunisia and Jordan—in order to understand the relationships between age, marriage, education, and fertility in determining labor force participation for Arab women. We examine the roles of these different factors in each individual country.

The Egyptian and Jordanian labor market panel surveys (ELMPS and JLMPS) are unique data sets collected on behalf of the Economic Research Forum for the purpose of making consistent labor force data between different Arab countries. The ELMPS has been collected in four rounds (1988, 1998, 2006, 2012); the most recent data available for this study are from the 2006 round. The JLMPS's first round was collected in 2010, and those data are available for this study.

Table 4.1 describes labor force participation by age, education, and marital status for Egyptian women in the 2006 ELMPS. These data show the basic pattern of labor force participation by women that is found throughout the MENA region. Three of the most important determining factors in women's labor force participation are age, education, and marital status. There is a life-cycle effect in that women begin with relatively low levels of labor force participation, as many are still acquiring their schooling. As schooling ends, there is a significant rise in participation, but this rise is transitory, and participation begins to fall as women age. In Egypt, for unmarried women, the ages of peak labor force participation are between 30 and 34. After this time, women slowly begin to drop out of the labor force. For married women the pattern is slightly different, as they tend to keep low levels of participation throughout their twenties and into their thirties, until they slowly decrease participation in their forties. This is particularly true of women with at least secondary educations. For women with only basic educations, participation levels begin to decline in their late thirties.

The next important factor is education. Education levels are broken down into four categories: Illiterate, below secondary education, secondary education only, and above secondary education. Education tends to increase labor force participation but not monotonically. Women in Egypt with below secondary education tend to participate less than illiterate women, but women with secondary education or above participate more. For married women and for unmarried women, the highest participation rates are found for those with above secondary education. Unmarried women with above secondary education have the highest participation rates, as approximately three-quarters of those in their thirties participate in the labor force.

Marriage has the perhaps the most significant impact on participation rates. Women aged 25–29 who are married participate in the labor force at half of the rate of women who are not married. However, this effect diminishes for women in their thirties, as many of those with above secondary education enter the workforce at this age. This is likely due to the effect of the limited number of children (more educated women have fewer children) going to school, allowing educated women to then enter the workforce. Despite this increase in participation for some married women, unmarried women tend to have more labor force attachment at all education levels and ages.

The impact of marriage on labor supply is negative for all women, but it has a particularly large effect for women in their twenties who have secondary or below education.

TABLE 4.1

Labor force participation by women by age, education, and marital status, Egypt, 2006.

Age	Never married					Ever married				
	Illiterate	Below sec	Secondary	Above sec	All	Illiterate	Below sec	Secondary	Above sec	All
15–19	22.0	5.3	9.3	18.2	8.3	20.0	8.5	7.7	*	11.7
20–24	22.1	19.4	17.4	30.9	21.7	15.9	8.0	9.8	15.9	12.0
25–29	19.5	36.4	34.9	53.8	39.8	24.8	9.6	12.9	30.3	19.4
30–34	28.6	16.7	69.7	77.8	54.3	28.5	17.0	17.8	46.1	27.0
35–39	43.7	37.5	42.1	76.5	51.7	25.7	15.2	41.8	54.7	32.9

Source: Authors' calculations based on 2006 Egyptian Labor Market Panel Survey.

For women aged 25–29, their labor force participation rate decreases from 56 percent when single to 20 percent when married. For those with less schooling the effect is equally large. Women aged 20–24 with below secondary schooling who are single have a participation rate of 40 percent; those who are married only have a 13 percent participation rate.

Participation rates in Jordan by age and marital status are similar to those found in Egypt. Jordanian women between the ages of 20 and 24 who have never been married have a participation rate of more than 15 percent; those who are married only have a participation rate of 5 percent. For women aged 25–29 and 30–34, the impact of marriage on labor force participation is even greater. Unmarried Jordanian women in their late twenties and into their thirties have a participation rate twice that of married women the same age (42 percent compared to 16 percent for 25- to 29-year-olds). These differences are even more dramatic for women with more schooling. While unmarried women with more than secondary degrees have a participation rate of 80 percent, married well-educated women only have a participation rate of 40 percent. So young Jordanian women, like the same cohort in Egypt, increase their labor force participation as they get into their later twenties and early thirties. However, for married Jordanian women, the participation rate only increases from 5.5 percent to 17.3 percent. Thus, the effect of marriage is to lower young women's labor force participation by two-thirds. For older women the effect is even more dramatic; participation rates for women between the ages of 35 and 44 are 36 percent for single and 16 percent for married women.

The Tunisian data come from the Tunisian Labor Force Survey of 2010. This is a representative household survey collected to show basic household labor force trends on an annual basis. As in the case of Jordan and Egypt, the three most important factors determining women's labor force participation are age, education, and marital status. Unlike the Jordanian and Egyptian cases, education in Tunisia tends to increase participation for all marriage status and age groups. Recall that in Egypt, women—especially married women—with below secondary education work less than illiterate women. In Tunisia, unmarried women with above secondary schooling who are between 30 and 34 years old attain participation rates that are three times those of women who are illiterate. The same is true for unmarried women aged 25–29 and 35–39. While 90 percent of single women in their thirties with advanced education are in the labor force, only 30 percent of single illiterate women in their thirties are.

For married women the difference is even more striking. While married women have lower participation rates overall, it is much more likely that a woman will continue to be in the workforce if she is educated than if she is not. Labor force participation rates for married illiterate women range from the single digits for women in their teens to 17–19 percent for women in their thirties. For women with schooling beyond the secondary level, these rates increase from 72 percent for married women aged 25–29 to 86 percent for married women aged 35–39. Thus, educated married women are four times more likely to be in the workforce than women who are illiterate.

Marriage and Young Women's Labor Force Participation

From the foregoing description of how education, marriage, and age impact labor force participation, it is clear that between ages 15 and 29, women undertake several critical decisions that impact their overall life courses. It is during this time that the decisions about education are made. The decision about whether or not to enter the formal workplace is made at the same time as the education decision, since choosing a particular education path also influences the possibility of future employment (Psacharopoulos and Tzannatos 1989). Finally, it is still in these years that decisions about children are made. Based on the earlier discussion, a decision to increase education will have the effect of increasing labor force participation once a woman finishes school, though more education decreases participation during the schooling years. In addition, the decision to have more education may delay marriage (which also tends to decrease participation). However, many women still drop out of the labor force at marriage, and in this section we examine how marriage decisions affect participation decisions in Egypt, Jordan, and Tunisia.

Women in Jordan work far less than women in Egypt and Tunisia. This may be due largely to the impact of marriage on labor force participation in Jordan being more significant than in Egypt or Tunisia. For example, among women aged 25–29 with a secondary education in Jordan, only 6 percent are in the workforce. In Egypt this level is 13 percent (still not high); in Tunisia it is 20 percent. Thus, in order to understand why participation rates in countries like Jordan and Algeria are so low, it is useful to understand why so many more women drop out of the labor force at marriage, compared to women in other countries (in this case, Egypt).

The Egyptian and Jordanian data sets are particularly useful, as they have work history data. These panel surveys are structured in such a way that the enumerator collects a retrospective work history for each respondent. This allows us to be able to describe here a longitudinal work history for each respondent. This longitudinal nature of the data is particularly useful in describing transitions within an individual's work history, which is not possible to do with standard labor market surveys (including the Tunisian Labor Market Survey).

By analyzing the work histories, one can see the direct effect marriage has on the type of work one holds (and whether or not one is in the labor force). In the Egyptian data set, for example, there are 2,030 married women with complete work histories. Women are categorized as being in one of four employment states: public sector work, private sector wage work, private sector nonwage work (for example, working for a family-owned business), or inactive. In general, women working in the public sector one year before marriage remain in the public sector after marriage. Fully 94 percent of women who were in the public sector before marriage stayed employed in the public sector after marriage. The rest of the women in the sample moved from public sector work to becoming inactive in the labor market.

However, women in the private wage sector did not remain at their jobs after marriage as women in the public sector did. Only 56 percent of women who had been employed in the private wage sector one year before marriage remained there after getting married. Most of these women who changed their employment states went to inactivity (40 percent of the total who started in private wage work); the rest went into private sector nonwage work.

Women in Jordan have fairly similar transition patterns to those in Egypt, at least for those who start off in the public sector. As in Egypt, for those working in the public sector before marriage (about 40 percent of the survey respondents), nearly all (93 percent) stayed in public sector work after they got married. The benefits and work environment of the public sector are conducive to being married for women, so there is little need to transition away from the public sector.

Also similarly to the case of Egypt, another 35 percent of women were employed in the private sector as wage workers in Jordan one year before marriage. Of these women in the private sector, only 59 percent stayed on as private sector wage workers after marriage. Nearly all of those who left the private sector after marriage went into inactivity.

The differences between Egypt and Jordan are seen when comparing women who have not been active in the labor force before. Of the Jordanian women who were inactive before marriage, 98 percent were still inactive at marriage. In Egypt on the other hand 44 percent of those inactive before marriage transitioned to private nonwage work after marriage. Thus, in Egypt nonwage work (for example, working in family-owned businesses) allows women who have been inactive before marriage to contribute to the family in a way that is not available to women in Jordan. The trade-off is that while 23 percent of Jordanian married women work in the private sector for a wage during their year of marriage, only 9 percent of Egyptian women do. Both Jordanian and Egyptian women are equally likely to leave the private wage sector on marriage, but the size of the sector in Jordan means that more women remain there after they get married.

This pattern is seen even more distinctly in figure 4.3, which shows work histories for all of the ever married women in the Egyptian sample. As women approach their marriages, more and more of them leave inactivity as they are leaving schooling and entering the workforce. Many of these are entering the public sector (overwhelmingly the case for those with secondary and above schooling), but they are also entering private wage work and private nonwage work. At marriage, however, women leave private wage work, and the proportion of women in private nonwage work increases dramatically.

For Jordanian women the pattern is different (fig. 4.4). While inactivity rates continue to decrease into the year of marriage for Egyptian women, Jordanian women see a spike in inactivity during the marriage year. This is largely because of the transition from private wage work into inactivity at marriage. While Egyptian women also transition between private wage work to inactivity, they also transition to private nonwage work, and the relative size of the Jordanian private wage sector means that this transition at marriage has a much larger quantitative impact on the averages for all women. Thus, the key

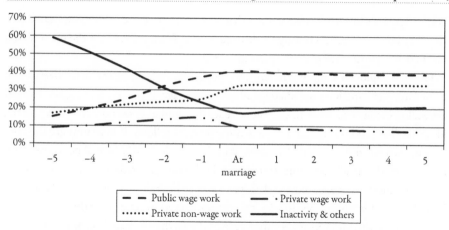

FIGURE 4.3 Marriage and labor market dynamics by employment sector for ever-married females, Egypt, 2006.
Source: Authors' calculations based on 2006 Egyptian Labor Market Panel Survey.

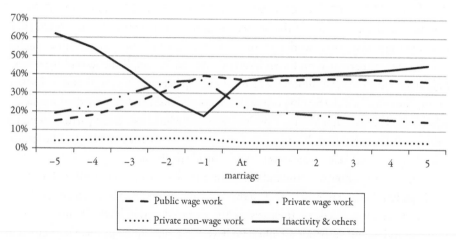

FIGURE 4.4 Marriage and labor market dynamics by employment sector for ever-married females, Jordan, 2010.
Source: Authors' calculations based on 2010 Jordanian Labor Market Panel Survey.

difference in understanding married women's lower participation rates in Jordan is that women transition into inactivity there while in Egypt they are more likely to transition into the informal sector.

In Tunisia, despite the high level of participation relative to other countries, labor force attachment for women is still lower than what one might predict given the country's high education levels and low fertility rates. Low participation levels could result from large nonwage income (for example, remittances from Europe allow families to consume more without women having to work) or from cultural norms. According to cultural explanations, Islam plays a role in stifling women's ability to work outside the home, especially in a work environment that is not sex segregated. Though, as stated previously, rigorous empirical testing tends to show that Islam is likely not the main reason for these low participation rates (Spierings 2014).

Here we explore a slightly different interpretation. Because of the sharp decrease in labor force participation immediately following marriage, Fargues (2012) argues that "society allows women to work in the public space, but husbands do not." We interpret the idea that "husbands do not allow women to work" as follows. If husbands are the constraint, then the more educated a husband is, then the less likely he will be to constrain his wife's work outside the home. If traditional values are generally associated with lower levels of education, we would see that wives whose husbands are less well educated to have the lowest levels of labor force participation, everything else being the same.

We will test this idea versus a competing hypothesis: that women drop out of the workforce when they become married due to time constraints. Specifically, this hypothesis sees the issue as a matter of specialization in the household, such that while husbands focus on earning income outside the home, wives focus on household production. The key variables here will be the relative impact on female labor force participation of the husband's education and the structure of the household. If the first hypothesis is supported (husbands prevent wives from working), then more male education should lead to higher wife labor force participation for all levels of wife's education. If the second hypothesis holds true, then the most important factor is the gap between husband's and wife's education. Specifically, if the first hypothesis holds true, if husband has more than secondary schooling, then this should have a positive effect of wife's labor force participation, regardless of her schooling. If the second hypothesis holds true, the bigger the gap in schooling, the less likely a woman is to work outside the home.

Table 4.2 shows how the husband's education level is related to the wife's labor force participation. In this table, the values across the column are given by the husbands' education levels; the values down the rows are the wives' education levels. Women who are illiterate and whose husbands are illiterate have a 12.6 percent labor force participation

TABLE 4.2

Relationship between husband's education and wife's labor force participation, Tunisia, 2010.

Wife's education	Husband's education			
	Illiterate	Less than secondary	Secondary	More than secondary
Illiterate	12.6	14.2	11.0	9.5
Less than secondary	15.4	13.4	10.5	7.0
Secondary	19.5	21.2	26.8	28.9
More than secondary	—	64.2	74.6	80.4

Source: Authors' calculations based on 2010 Tunisian Labor Force Survey.

rate. Illiterate women who are married to men with below secondary education work more than those whose husbands are illiterate. However, this is the exception to the following overall trend: for women with below secondary schooling, the more education their husbands have, the less likely they are to work.

This result seems to support the second hypothesis discussed above but is also related to the first. When the husband has more schooling he is better able to provide for his family, and there is less need for the wife to work. Since the wife has only a low level of education, the jobs available to her are not likely to be deemed appropriate. However, a second explanation (whose evidence is indistinguishable from the evidence for the second hypothesis above) is that the more educated the husband is relative to the wife, the less power the wife has in the household decisionmaking, including whether or not she will work, so the wife stays at home due to her lack of power.

Examining the differences for women with at least secondary education gives further insight into distinguishing between the two hypotheses. For those with secondary education or more, the higher the level of education the husband has, the more likely the wife is to work. Thus, there is support for the first hypothesis regarding whether or not husbands determine wives' labor force participation. In households where education levels are roughly equal (both with at least a secondary education), there is little difference between a husband with a secondary degree and a husband with more schooling, but it is still true that if the husband is more educated, then the wife is more likely to work. Women with secondary schooling, however, are more likely to work in the public sector, and it may be the sector of employment that determines these more educated women's different labor market behaviors. Since nearly half of them work in the government, there is no stigma to a wife working in these culturally appropriate jobs. Thus, for women with less than secondary schooling, the relationship between marriage and work may largely be due to specialization in the household. However, once women have more education, their husbands are more important in determining their labor force participation, and the more education the husband has, the more likely the wife is to work.

Conclusion

Women in the MENA region work less than women in any other part of the world. This is largely due to institutional factors that include cultural attitudes about what constitutes appropriate work for women and attitudes about mixed-sex workplaces. The critical circumstances that affect the ability of women to work occur during their youth, when decisions about education, marriage, and family formation are made.

Women in Jordan, West Bank and Gaza, Syria, and Algeria work far less than women in Egypt, Morocco, and Tunisia. Using microdata from Egypt, Jordan, and Tunisia, we are better able to understand the underlying causes of these differences, which are seen in country-wide averages. One of the most important factors in explaining participation rates is what happens at marriage. In Jordan, the impact of marriage on labor force participation is much more significant than in Egypt. These differences are driven in Jordan by women dropping out of the private sector when getting married; nearly 40 percent of women are employed in the private sector for wages a year before they marry. After marriage, only 20 percent are so employed. Because the Egyptian private wage sector is smaller, women do not move from private wage work to inactivity. Instead, they move from private wage work to private nonwage work, either working informally or as an unpaid family member. In both countries, women who work for the public sector tend to keep their jobs after marriage much more frequently. With the shrinking importance of the public sector, the option of female employment after marriage is also likely to shrink.

The rise in the level of schooling and the lack of public sector jobs for the current generation of young men mean delayed marriage and further social changes. Through tradition, women are more likely to marry men who are both older and at least as well educated as they are. Since there is a larger percentage of women who stay in school beyond the secondary level, these women may leave school only to find that there are relatively few suitable matches in terms of both employment and education level. Thus, the rapid rise of female schooling in the region means that women are more likely to either not marry or marry men who are less educated than they are. This shift has been most apparent in Iran because their quickly rising and then falling birthrate has led to a mismatch between prime marriage-age men and women. The result has been a decline in the age gap between men and women at first marriage (Amin et al. 2012).

The public sector has an appeal to both men and women for several reasons. Specifically, it offers shorter work days, better benefits in terms of pension and retirement, and more job security. In addition, for women, the public sector offers a host of special protections and considerations once they get married and achieve motherhood. Generous leave policies for maternity, special benefits for nursing mothers, and additional days off to attend to family needs are part of the package of benefits that governments provide to women. Private sector jobs are either not required to provide such benefits or, if they do, private sector employers choose not to hire women due to the increased cost and absenteeism that are likely when hiring someone who may become a mother. The failures of both the MENA countries' economies and of their economic policies to stimulate job growth means that without significant regulatory changes, women's high unemployment and low labor force participation will continue for years to come.

REFERENCES

Amin, M., R. Assaad, N. al-Baharna, K. Dervis, R. M. Desai, N. S. Dhillon, A. Galal, H. Ghanem, C. Graham, and D. Kaufmann. 2012. Opportunities for young people. In *After the spring: Economic transitions in the Arab world*, 54–79. New York: Oxford University Press.
Assaad, R., R. Hendy, and C. Yassine. 2012. Gender and the Jordanian labor market. Economic Research Forum working paper series no. 701. Giza, Egypt: Economic Research Forum.

Dhillon, N., P. Dyer, and T. Yousef. 2009. Generation in waiting: An overview of school to work and family formation transitions. In *Generation in waiting: The unfulfilled promise of young people in the Middle East*, ed. N. Dhillon and T. Yousef, 11–38. Washington, DC: Brookings Institution Press.

Fargues, P. 2012. Demography, migration and revolt in the Southern Mediterranean. In *Arab society in revolt: The West's Mediterranean challenge*, ed. C. Merlini and O. Roy, 17–46. Washington, DC: Brookings Institution Press.

Goldin, C. 1995. The u-shaped female labor force function in economic development and economic history. In *Investment in women's human capital*, ed. T. P. Schultz, 61–90. Chicago: University of Chicago Press.

Isfahani, D. S., and D. Egel. 2009. Beyond statism: Toward a new social contract for Iranian youth. In *Generation in waiting: The unfulfilled promise of young people in the Middle East*, ed. N. Dhillon and T. Yousef, 39–66. Washington, DC: Brookings Institution Press.

Lecomte, J., and A. Marcoux. 1976. Contraception and fertility in Morocco and Tunisia. *Studies in Family Planning* 7(7): 182–187.

Moghadam, V. 1993. *Modernizing women: Gender and social change in the Middle East*. Boulder, CO: Lynne Rienner Press.

Murphy, E. C. 2003. Women in Tunisia: Between state feminism and economic reform. In *Women and globalization in the Arab Middle East: Gender, economy, and society*, ed. E. A. Doumato and M. P. Posusney, 172. Boulder, CO: Lynne Rienner Press.

Psacharopoulos, G., and Z. Tzannatos. 1989. Female labor force participation: An international perspective. *World Bank Research Observer* 4(2): 187–201.

Qatar Statistical Authority (QSA). 2011. *Bulletin: Labor force statistics*. Doha, Qatar: Qatar Statistical Authority.

Read, J. G. 2004. Cultural influences on immigrant women's labor force participation: The Arab-American case. *International Migration Review* 38(1): 52–77.

Shafik, N. 2001. Closing the gender gap in the Middle East. In *The economics of women and work in the Middle East and North Africa*, ed. E. Mine Cinar, 12–31. Amsterdam: Elsevier.

Spierings, N. 2014. How Islam influences women's paid non-farm employment: Evidence from 26 Indonesian and 37 Nigerian provinces. *Review of Religious Research* 56(3): 399–431.

The rights of Muslim women. 1997. *Middle East Quarterly* 4(4): 83–84.

World Bank. 2013. *World Bank development indicators*. http://data.worldbank.org/indicator/SL.TLF.CACT.FE.ZS/countries/1W-ZQ?display=graph.

5 Gulf Youth and the Labor Market
Paul Dyer and Samer Kherfi

AMONG THE WORLD'S largest producers of oil and natural gas, the six countries of the GCC—Bahrain, Kuwait, Oman, Qatar, Saudi Arabia, and the UAE—have experienced significant economic development since the first oil price boom some 40 years ago. While economic growth has fluctuated with international oil prices, these states have maintained relatively high average rates of economic growth over time, with citizens benefiting from massive public investments in infrastructure and the redistribution of natural resource wealth through public employment and subsidies. Over the decade preceding the Arab Spring, GCC economic growth averaged 5.4 percent a year, and Qatar's economy grew by nearly 13 percent a year (World Bank 2014), significantly higher than the global average of 2.6 percent a year. Over the same decade, according to the International Monetary Fund (2011), GCC economies created nearly 7.1 million jobs.

Even in this context of high growth and job creation, young nationals in the Gulf have experienced persistent employment challenges, particularly in securing jobs that meet their expectations in terms of job quality and salary. In the context of a wider Arab region wherein youth face considerable economic marginalization, it is tempting to dismiss concerns about unemployment, underemployment, and other poor labor market outcomes among Gulf youth as the objections of a privileged elite. Indeed, young nationals in the GCC have enjoyed educational and employment opportunities unimagined by youth in other Arab states, and for many Gulf youth, unemployment and underemployment are voluntary states as they wait for suitable openings, mainly in the public or semipublic sectors. However, their delayed engagement with the labor force comes at the cost of making needed investments in building careers and taking constructive steps toward adulthood.

In this regard, it is important to understand that the choices Gulf youth are making in the labor market are based on a set of institutional norms, the most important of which is the long-standing role of the public sector as the primary employer of Gulf nationals. For young nationals in the Gulf, the lure of public sector jobs, in terms of high wages and job security, is reflective of trends seen elsewhere in the Arab region; however, in the Gulf these preferences are strengthened by strong social pressures to secure employment in the government and the stark segmentation—both cultural and regulatory—between public and private sector along nationality lines. This leads Gulf youth to prepare and queue for public sector opportunities that are increasingly difficult to secure while viewing work in the private sector with uncertainty or disdain.

Efforts to increase employment of nationals in the private sector and to make private sector employment more attractive to young nationals have long been a priority for Gulf governments concerned with the social and security challenges associated with both the growing presence of foreign nationals and the unfulfilled aspirations of unemployed nationals. On the policy side, pressures have only increased as the public sector has neared saturation and as wages for the civil service have taken on an increasingly burdensome share of government expenditures. However, policy approaches to nationalizing the private sector have proven largely unproductive, working as they have against the dominant institutional drivers that shape the preferences of young nationals. In fact, in many cases, policy efforts have led to a further distortion of market signals.

Understanding the institutional and regulatory context and how it shapes the behavior of actors therein is important to comprehending the predicaments faced by Gulf youth and developing means by which to resolve them. Toward these ends, this chapter provides an analysis of the transition of young nationals to the labor market in all six GCC countries.[1] The first section reviews demographics and the related growing domestic labor supply issues among young nationals in the Gulf. The next section explores employment for Gulf youth and the institutional context in which Gulf youth are making employment choices. In turn, we explore reform efforts to which Gulf governments turned in the decade leading up to the Arab Spring and how policy responses to Arab Spring tensions have affected such efforts. The conclusion focuses on future policy requirements.

The Unique Demographics and Labor Supply Challenges of the Gulf

Few regions have experienced the population growth seen in the Gulf over the past four decades. Between 1970 and 2010, the GCC's total population grew more than fivefold, increasing from fewer than 8 million to nearly 45 million (United Nations 2013). The

Gulf's natural population growth has remained high (see chapter 1 here);[2] nonetheless, the real bulk of the region's population boom was driven by an influx of expatriate workers brought in to provide manpower both for infrastructure development and private sector growth, both of which were supported by the oil boom. In turn, and importantly for the region's labor market dynamics, GCC nationals have decreased as a share of the total population and the labor force; in countries like Qatar and the UAE, nationals represent striking minorities in their own countries; nationals are a majority of the populations of only Saudi Arabia and Oman (see table 5.1).

Given the large presence of expatriate workers in the GCC states, the overall age structure of the region is heavily weighted in favor of working-age adults. The age structures of the Gulf's national populations, however, are notably weighted toward the young. In Bahrain, for example, Bahraini nationals under 25 years of age made up 52 percent of all nationals in 2010, while in other GCC countries youth under 25 formed population shares closer to 60 percent (table 5.2). The national demographic transition has effected a notable youth bulge across the Gulf, with roughly 6.7 million nationals aged 15–29 forming nearly 30 percent of the region's population of nationals in 2010. Moreover, as the population shares of the GCC's child cohorts—those younger than age 15—remain larger than those of the youth populations, the youth bulge is yet to peak in the GCC, both in total amounts and as a share of total population.

As is the case in less affluent Arab nations, the expansion of the youth bulge in Gulf countries is exacerbating labor supply pressures in the Gulf as more young nationals enter the labor market. For example, the number of nationals in the Saudi labor market has grown by nearly 4.2 percent a year, nearly doubling over a 10-year period, even as participation rates for young Saudi men have declined (Saudi Arabian CDSI 1999, 2009). Given the lag with which the youth bulge has grown in most Gulf states in comparison with other MENA countries and the increased duration for which youth are now

TABLE 5.1

Population share of nationals, GCC countries, 2010.

Country	Nationals (% of total population)	Total population
Bahrain	46.0	1,234,571
Kuwait	36.2	2,933,268
Oman	70.6	2,773,479
Qatar	14.3	1,699,435
Saudi Arabia	68.8	27,563,432
UAE	11.5	8,264,070
GCC	53.4	44,468,255

Sources: Bahrain Central Informatics Organization (2011); Kuwait Central Statistical Bureau (2013); Oman National Center for Statistics and Information (2011); Gulf Research Center (2014); Saudi Arabian Central Department for Statistics and Information (2013); United Arab Emirates National Bureau of Statistics (2011).

TABLE 5.2

Youth Population as a shares of youth nationals, GCC countries, 2010/2011.

Country	Year	Age 0–14	Age 15–24	Age 15–29
Bahrain	2010	31.8	20.2	28.6
Kuwait	2011	37.2	20.5	28.4
Oman	2010	35.3	24.8	35.3
Qatar	2010	39.8	19.6	—
Saudi Arabia	2011	38.8	20.6	29.4
UAE	2010	38.0	25.6	35.3

Sources: Bahrain Central Informatics Organization (2011); Kuwait Central Statistical Bureau (2013); Oman National Center for Statistics and Information (2011); Gulf Research Center (2014); Saudi Arabian Central Department for Statistics and Information (2011); United Arab Emirates National Bureau of Statistics (2011).

staying in school, the resultant labor supply pressures have only recently started to reveal themselves.

Overall, labor force participation rates among Gulf nationals of working age (15–64) have remained fairly low, at least by international norms and in contrast to rates among expatriate residents. In Bahrain, for example, participation among working-age nationals at the turn of the decade was 51 percent; in Qatar and the UAE it was slightly lower, at 48 percent and 47 percent, respectively.[3] Among Saudi Arabian citizens of working age, only 39 percent are economically active. In contrast, labor force participation rates among working-age expatriates (around 80 percent) reflects the fact that most expatriates in the Gulf come under guest worker contracts and only remain in the Gulf as long as they are employed. Internationally, labor force participation rates average 69 percent of the working-age population (ILO 2011).

Low participation among the GCC's national populations reflects the influence of a number of factors, most important the low rates of women participating in the labor force. The rate of participation among Qatari women, at 36 percent, is the highest in the Gulf and compares favorably to the regional average of around 22 percent (ILO 2011). Labor force participation rates of Bahraini, Kuwaiti, and Emirati women are closer to the GCC average, at about 30 percent. In Saudi Arabia on the other hand, the participation rate among working-age national women is a regional low of 15 percent. The GCC female labor participation rates are considerably below the international average of over 50 percent. In contrast, rates of participation among male nationals across the GCC states have all exceeded 60 percent, while in Bahrain, the rate has reached 71 percent.

Particularly low rates for women below age 25 reflect the growing tendency for them to stay in school longer (fig. 5.1). In the UAE, for example, only 2.5 percent of women below age 20 were in the labor force in 2009, a figure that grew to 33 percent for the 20- to 24-year-old population. However, labor force participation peaks among women between

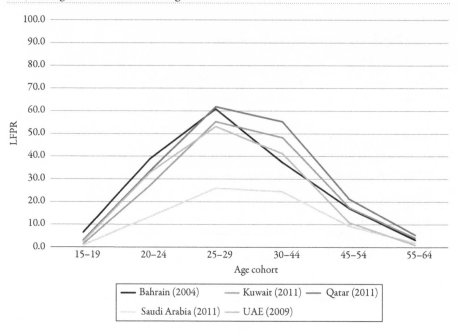

FIGURE 5.1 Female labor force participation rates (LFPRs) among Gulf nationals by age cohort, 2004–2013. (While more recent labor force data exist for Bahrain, it is not provided in a way that allows for age breakdown by relevant age cohorts.)

Sources: Bahrain Ministry of Labor and Bahrain Centre for Studies and Research 2004; Kuwait Central Statistical Bureau 2013; Qatar Statistics Agency 2011; Saudi Arabia Central Department for Statistics and Information 2011; United Arab Emirates National Bureau of Statistics 2009.

ages 25 and 29 across the GCC states. Nearly 53 percent of Emirati women between ages 25 and 29 were in the labor market in 2009, while in 2011 nearly 63 percent of these Qatari women were economically active. Similar patterns are found in Bahrain, although the participation rate drops rapidly for women after peaking in the 25- to 29-year-old age cohort. In Saudi Arabia, where female labor force participation rates are the lowest, nearly 25 percent of women aged 25–29 were working or seeking work in 2011.

The relatively high rates of participation among women nationals between ages 25 and 29 implies a strong link between educational attainment and the decision to enter the labor force, while suggesting a widely perceived generational shift in interest in working among Gulf women. At the same time, however, rates of participation decline steeply for women on marriage, suggesting that labor market participation for many young women is a temporary engagement between school and the taking up of household responsibilities with marriage. Labor force survey data from the UAE in 2009 support this view: among married women aged 25–29 the participation rate was 38.6 percent, while for those never married it was 79.6 percent. Nearly 92 percent of Emirati women not participating in the labor market reported being inactive due to household responsibilities.[4]

While it seems that most Gulf women stay out of the labor force in anticipation of marriage or exit the labor force when they get married, it is unclear whether this is by choice or due to familial pressure. As explained by Kherfi (2012), if seeking work is a joint decision in a household, men's attitudes toward female work—particularly in a conservative society like those seen in the Gulf—are expected to affect the participation rate among married women. At the same time, with young couples often living in multigenerational households, young married women in the Gulf would have access to child care support from family members, allowing them more time to take on employment. However, this strong extended-family relationship, notes Kherfi, gives older members of the family more say in decisions regarding work and fertility, tending to reduce participation.

Labor force participation rates for young men in the Gulf are also low, particularly when contrasted with those of middle-age male workers (fig. 5.2). Young men in the Gulf, like young women, are staying longer in school, although they show much higher rates of labor force participation than women at any age. In Qatar and the UAE, for example, the labor force participation rate of men younger than 20 stood at about 13 percent in 2009 and 2011, respectively. Rates jump up considerably for young men above 20. In the UAE, the rate rose to 71 percent for those between ages 20 and 24, and then to 93 percent for those between ages 25 and 29. In Saudi Arabia, only 4.4 percent of men aged 15–19 were economically active in 2011, a rate that rose to 42.8 percent among those aged 20–24 and 82.6 percent for those aged 25–29.

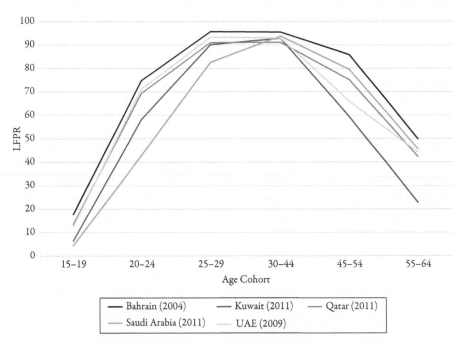

FIGURE 5.2 Male labor force participation rates (LFPRs) among Gulf Nationals by age cohort, 2004–2013. (While more recent labor force data exist for Bahrain, it is not provided in a way that allows for age breakdown by relevant age cohorts.)

Sources: Bahrain Ministry of Labor and Bahrain Centre for Studies and Research 2004; Kuwait Central Statistical Bureau 2013; Qatar Statistics Agency 2011; Saudi Arabia Central Department for Statistics and Information 2011; United Arab Emirates National Bureau of Statistics 2009.

Despite increased time in school for both young men and young women in the Gulf, educational attainment (on completion) has had a significant impact on the labor force participation of young women only. This is evident when comparing outcomes for those aged 25–29, a working-age cohort that assumes the completion of one's basic investments in secondary and tertiary education (UAE NBS 2009). Among Emirati women aged 25–29, 76 percent of those with more than a secondary degree were economically active in 2009, compared with 38 percent of those with a secondary degree only and 25 percent for those with less than a secondary degree. In contrast, for 25- to 29-year old Emirati men, rates of participation were nearly the same for those without secondary degrees (92.3 percent) and those with postsecondary degrees (94.5 percent).

While young men in the Gulf are staying in school longer than men in older generations, they are acquiring fewer years of education than younger women. In this regard, young men are drawn by employment and income opportunities available to them that are not open to (or attractive to) young women and that may not require tertiary degrees but are still considered respectable (Ridge 2014). These include some lower skill public sector jobs, self-employment, and, particularly, positions in the army or police. There is also evidence that high school dropouts are much more likely to be male than female. In contrast to young men, young women in the GCC seem to base choices in regard to labor force participation more on cultural norms, in addition to the perceived limits on opportunities available to them in the labor market.

Understanding Youth Employment Choices

According to the IMF, nearly three-quarters of the nearly 7.1 million jobs created in the GCC states over the period 2000–2010 went to expatriate workers (IMF 2011). While the bulk (78 percent) of those jobs that went to nationals were in the private sector, neither private nor public sector job creation efforts have kept up with the quantitative challenges of a growing pool of young national workers, particularly in the context of their expectations of job quality and type. As we will describe, the expectations among youth are driven largely by institutional constructs and norms in the Gulf, most notably the long-standing segmentation of the labor market by nationality along public and private sector lines, preferences for public employment among nationals, and the skewed set of incentives for both employers and employees that result from regulation of private sector employment.

The Continued Lure of the Public Sector

Across the Gulf there is a marked preference for public sector work among nationals, while nonnationals generally make up the majority of workers in the private sector. This segmentation of the labor market by nationality is evident in data from the UAE, where over 86 percent of employed Emiratis in 2009 worked in the government (federal or emirate level) while another 6 percent worked in quasi-governmental firms (UAE NBS 2009). This preference for public sector or semigovernmental work was shared equally by men (92.2 percent) and women (87.3 percent). In Bahrain, Oman, and Saudi Arabia, where the supply of public sector jobs for nationals is lower on a per capita basis, rates of public sector employment are still quite high. In Saudi Arabia, over 69 percent of the national workforce was employed in the public sector in 2009; in Oman, 48 percent of working nationals were in the public sector in 2010 (Saudi Arabian CDSI 2009; Oman NSI 2011). In Bahrain, in 2010, 34 percent of working nationals were in the public sector, down from an estimated 49 percent in 2004 (Bahrain CIO 2011; Bahrain BMOL and BCSR 2004).

The attraction to public sector work is founded largely on the wage and nonwage benefits found there. Wages in the public sector are generally higher than in the private sector. In the UAE in 2009, for example, median monthly salaries in the public sector for nationals were nearly two times those for nationals working in the private sector (UAE NBS 2009). Moreover, public sector workers can expect regular salary increases on the basis of education, training, and seniority, while they enjoy better benefits, more time off for public holidays, and shorter workdays. Importantly, while annual raises might not be as high as in the private sector, many public sector employees have benefited from periodic salary adjustments aimed at responding to the rising costs of living. For example, in 2008, federal government employees in the UAE, who make up nearly 46 percent of the Emirati workers, were given a 70 percent increase in basic salaries (see "UAE federal government employees" 2007). Similar periodic raises have been seen across the Gulf states, with each raise reinforcing preferences for public sector employment among new entrants to the labor force.

In this regard, it is important to highlight the impact of retirement and pension policies in the Gulf, where nationals working in the public sector are generally able to retire with full benefits after 20 years of service. This means that those who enter public service in their early twenties are able to retire on 80 percent of their final salary by their early forties. The resultant drop-off in labor force participation rates for those over 40 can be seen in figures 5.1 and 5.2. Labor force data from the UAE show that over 70 percent of economically inactive men are not working due to early retirement (UAE NBS 2009). While this does not have an immediate impact on youth, and may actually open employment opportunities in the public sector for more youth, prospects for early retirement do shape the initial behavior of youth, particularly young men, in the labor force, incentivizing them to enter the public sector and to do so earlier rather than later.

Aside from material benefits associated with public sector work, preferences for government work are reinforced by a range of social and cultural influences. In this regard, it is important to recognize that for many Gulf youth who are leaving the educational system and beginning their search for work, the private sector is a veritable unknown (Al-Waqfi and Forstenlechner 2012). With most working family members and friends employed in the public sector, these youth have little effective guidance or factual information about work in the private sector. Family members provide advice (if not pressure) to seek out public sector work, and personal connections used to secure work more often than not steer them in this direction. Moreover, aware as they are of negative stereotypes of nationals in the private sector, young nationals are drawn to opportunities in the public sector, where there is a stronger presence of nationals and the perception of a more enabling culture as they begin their careers.

With these factors in mind, for youth in the Gulf, securing a well-paying, predictable public sector position sends important signals about one's role and reputation in one's community. The respectability of careers in the public sector is particularly important for youth in the context of the Gulf's marriage market. Securing a public sector job becomes an important way for young men to signal their suitability as spouses to young women and their families. For young women, the public sector provides an opportunity to work in an environment that will be deemed appropriate in the socially conservative Gulf society, while private sector work is often viewed as being an unprotected space, exposing women to reputational concerns.[5]

The continued lure of public sector employment is reflected in youth preferences regarding future work across the Gulf, as is evident in recent surveys undertaken as part of the Silatech Index (Gallup 2010). Pollsters asked young nationals from across the Gulf region whether they would prefer to work in the public sector, in the private sector, for a nonprofit organization, or as an entrepreneur. In answering, 73 percent of Bahraini respondents favored the public sector. Among Kuwaiti youth the figure was 71 percent; among Emirati youth it was 66 percent; and among Saudi youth it was 60 percent. These figures are particularly noteworthy when one considers that pollsters specified in their question that the respondent was to consider the question on the assumption that "pay and work conditions are the same."

A Compression of Job Type Choices

Youth employment norms and preferences in the Gulf vary across age and between men and women. Generally, however, employment choices for both men and women reflect preferences for public sector work (as described above) and, if in the private sector, for more administrative or managerial positions. In Saudi Arabia, for example, nearly three-quarters of young working Saudi men were found in four areas of economic activity (Saudi Arabian CDSI 2011). They favor public administration (44 percent of employed Saudi males ages 15–29) and, to a lesser extent, wholesale trade (9.7 percent), education (9.9 percent), wholesale and retail trade (9.6 percent), and transportation (6.0 percent). No other area of economic activity attracted more than 5 percent of employed Saudi young men, a pattern that is reflective of choices of Saudi men in general.

For women nationals, those who are employed find themselves concentrated in fewer occupation groups and job types that are deemed culturally appropriate because they allow limited or no exposure to male coworkers and clients. Referring again to the Saudi

Arabian example, over 63 percent of all employed young women in 2011 were working in the education sector, while 20 percent were in health care and less than 4 percent were in public administration. In all, fewer than 13 percent of young working women were employed outside these three sectors.

While Saudi Arabia with its regulated segregation of the sexes in the public sphere may represent a polarized view of women's work in the Gulf, the compression of opportunities into a narrow range of job types is seen throughout the Gulf. Even in the UAE, where Dubai's reputation as a global hub for trade and services and relatively more open social norms suggest a more dynamic range of economic opportunities, working Emirati women are concentrated in specific areas. As of 2009, nearly 33 percent of working Emirati women were employed in public administration, 27 percent worked in the education sector, and 8 percent worked in the health sector (UAE NBS 2009). The UAE has been able to increase opportunities for national women in the financial sector with sector-specific quotas, and nearly 11 percent of working women are found in finance and banking. Similarly, 6.2 percent of working Emirati women are found in the transportation and logistics sector. Still, the concentration is fairly striking.

Obstacles to Private Sector Employment

The attractiveness of public sector employment in terms of wages and job security ensures that the limited number of Gulf youth interested in pursuing private sector employment come to the sector with wage and job expectations that are generally incommensurate with entry-level jobs in the private sector, or with skill sets that are often more in line with the needs of the public sector than those of the private sector. However, outcomes for youth in the private sector are also steered by the fact that the private sector itself is governed by two sets of regulations that apply differently to nationals and expatriates.

While the GCC states' labor laws stipulate specific rights and obligations of nonnational workers, much of the relationship between the employer and these employees is left to contractual agreement. More important, across the Gulf, employers generally serve as sponsors for residency permits for nonnational workers. Under the structure of the *kafala* (sponsorship) system, sponsors (employers) can revoke the residency permits of nonnational workers at any time and can effectively blacklist an employee by failing to submit a nonobjection letter should the employee decide to change employers. In this context, foreign workers have little bargaining power when contesting wages or ability to change jobs, leaving the bulk of the power in the employer-employee relationship in the hands of the employer. Moreover, to guard against workers "absconding" from their contractual obligations, many employers (albeit illegally) hold on to workers' passports while they are in country.

In contrast, national workers vying for private sector employment have more power, primarily because they can leave a position at will. Furthermore, private firms in the Gulf face legal barriers and high costs when seeking to dismiss nationals, whether due to a firm's need to downsize due to economic difficulties or to an employee's poor performance. These factors have been strengthened by the imposition of nationalization quotas on the private sector, which began being implemented across the Gulf in the mid-1990s (in the wake of international oil price declines and subsequent declines in GCC state budgets).

Oman initiated a sector-specific quota system in 1994 and implemented a 7 percent tax on wages paid to foreign workers as a means of incentivizing private employers to hire more Omani workers. Bahrain imposed a broad quota for all private sector hiring in 1995, requiring new businesses to demonstrate that 20 percent of their workforces were Bahraini and requiring all firms to increase the number of Bahraini employees by 5 percent a year. Similarly, Saudi Arabia began requiring firms with more than 20 employees to increase the number of Saudi employees by 5 percent a year. Kuwait, Qatar, and the UAE, which have smaller populations and higher per capita oil revenues than other Gulf states, followed with less stringent, often sector-specific targets for nationalization.

By and large, these nationalization quotas have served as blunt instruments. While they have provided policymakers with a way to signal that they were focused on job creation for nationals, they have been largely unenforced and unenforceable, subject to interpretation and confusion on the part of both officials and firms.[6] Still, even where adherence to quotas has not been effectively enforced or nationalization has been so far below targets that the quota has been moot, a firm's ability to show efforts to employ nationals has played well with policymakers, government procurement departments, and the public. This is particularly the case at the managerial level, where the right local hires by firms can open up national social networks that facilitate business generation.

By shifting hiring decisions to considerations of nationality rather than skills, nationalization quotas and protective regulations designed to make the private sector more attractive for young nationals have had important unintended consequences for both employees and firms. Understanding the need that firms have in meeting quotas and the weak means firms have to enforce productivity, young national employees are more difficult to incentivize toward higher productivity when compared with expatriate employees, reinforcing existing stereotypes and biases against nationals in the private sector. Similarly, young nationals are much more likely to change jobs with frequency in an effort to secure higher pay and better positions or to use a private sector position to wait for public sector work.

While firms have a long-term interest in hiring young nationals and training them where their skills fall short, concerns about short-term commitments by youth (whether due to job hopping, waiting for public sector opportunities, or, in the case of young women, the perceived likelihood of exit from the labor force on marriage) reduce firms' incentives to hire them in the first place and to invest in their career development. In this context, a considerable, if incalculable "gray market" has developed around private sector hiring in the Gulf. Nationalization efforts have facilitated an environment in which some firms pay nationals as "ghost workers," putting their names on the company's employment rolls for lower wages without the expectation that they will work.

Entrepreneurship as a Potential Solution for Youth

Entrepreneurship and family-owned businesses remain a potentially potent source of employment for Gulf youth, although their participation in firm ownership or in family-owned business activity is currently limited. In Bahrain, for example, nearly 9 percent of Bahraini workers worked for themselves or for family-owned businesses in 2010, with individuals in this category broken down fairly evenly between employers and the self-employed (Bahrain CIO 2011). On the other hand in the UAE, despite Dubai's reputation as a regional hub for entrepreneurial endeavors, only 3.1 percent of working nationals reported their primary means of employment either as an employer (2.6 percent) or as self-employed (0.5 percent) in 2009 (UAE NBS 2009).

Gulf youth do have an increasingly favorable view toward entrepreneurship and, according to Gallup (2010), maintain some of the highest intentions to start businesses in the Arab world. Among Bahraini youth (who were not already business owners) in 2009, 14 percent reported plans to start a business in 12 months, a low for the Arab region. Among Emirati youth in 2009, nearly 17 percent of those polled (who were not already business owners) reported plans to start a business in 12 months. Rates were somewhat higher in Qatar, Saudi Arabia, and Kuwait in 2009, at 24 percent, 25 percent, and 29 percent, respectively. The challenge in the Gulf states is translating these intentions into tangible action in a context where alternatives in public sector employment continue to have such allure. The reality is that pay and work conditions are superior in the public sector, as we have explained.

At the same time, there are opportunities for nationals to take advantage of the existing institutional structure that governs firm ownership in ways that work against their intent. For the most part, firm ownership in the Gulf is subject to a majority domestic ownership requirement. In many cases, a national will serve nominally as a local owner while exchanging profits from firm ownership for an annual fee. In essence, they secure rents based on their nationality rather than actively participating in a business. Similarly, a sizeable industry of "ghost firms" run by locals has developed in parallel with the formal private sector, wherein the firm imports foreign workers and provides them with residency sponsorship for a fee, while releasing them to work illegally in the economy.[7]

High Youth Unemployment in a High-Growth Environment

As noted, GCC countries experienced high rates of economic growth throughout the 2000s, and as a result job creation was significant. Moreover, throughout the Gulf region aggregate unemployment rates have been strikingly low. In Kuwait, for example, total unemployment was estimated at 3.6 percent in 2011 (Kuwaiti CSB 2013). Bahraini census data in 2010 placed unemployment there at 4.7 percent (Bahrain CIO 2011). In 2009 total unemployment in the UAE was estimated at 4.2 percent. Saudi Arabia's total unemployment in 2010 was estimated at 5.5 percent (Saudi Arabian CDSI 2011; UAE NBS 2009). In Qatar, total unemployment in 2010 was lower than 1 percent (QSA 2011). Importantly, however, these low rates of total unemployment are driven largely by the entry and exit of large number of expatriate workers in these countries and the low rates of unemployment evidenced among them given their legal status as guest workers.

By and large, expatriate residency is dependent on the ability of individuals either to secure an employer to sponsor them for residence or to be sponsored by working family members. With the exception of workers in a few fields or those holding higher degrees, expatriate workers must leave the country of residence within months of leaving their jobs and, in many cases, must leave the country (if only temporarily) on switching jobs. As such, during downturns in the business cycle unemployed expatriates also quit the labor force (and the country). Given these conditions, the aggregate or expatriate unemployment rates are not a reliable gauge of economic fluctuations, as Gulf states are able to export much of the cyclical unemployment to other countries.

On the other hand, unemployment rates among nationals have remained much higher than the aggregate, ranging from a low of 4.1 percent in Qatar (QSA 2011) to 14.4 percent in the UAE (UAE NBS 2009). The higher rates among nationals, and their persistence over time, indicate structural problems, particularly in relation to labor force penetration. With stringent regulations in place that effectively prevent or discourage the laying off of nationals (both in the public and private sector) during economic downturns, the unemployment rate among nationals is insensitive to business cycle conditions. It is also worth noting that unemployment measures in the Gulf tend to adopt a fairly relaxed "actively looking for work" criterion, such that job search can be demonstrated by a onetime registration with an employment office.

Given the institutional constraints we have explored, it is understandable that young nationals make up the bulk of the unemployed in the Gulf region, but the rates of unemployment faced by youth, particularly young women, are of concern, especially in view of the overall job creation record in these economies. In Qatar, which has experienced the lowest rates of total unemployment, nearly 6.6 percent of economically active youth (aged 15–29) were unemployed in 2010; for young women this rate was 12.5 percent. Importantly, Qatari youth made up 66 percent of unemployed nationals, and young Qatari women made up nearly 65 percent of unemployed national youth. Given the relatively low number of Qatari nationals and the rapid, natural-gas-fueled growth of its economy, the Qatari government is best placed among Gulf states to absorb its growing youth population into the labor force, even at the cost of overall productivity.

In contrast, the highest reported rate of unemployment among young Gulf nationals has been in Saudi Arabia.[8] The youth unemployment rate there in 2011 was nearly 27.4 percent, meaning that at the time nearly 450,000 Saudi youth were unemployed. The rate in Saudi Arabia was particularly high for younger youth: although their numbers were relatively low, with 15- to 19-year-olds making up less than 1 percent of the Saudi national labor force, they had an unemployment rate of nearly 43 percent, which was shared equally between young men and women. The unemployment rate for young Saudi men seems to decline with age, dropping to 12.7 percent for those aged 24–29. For young Saudi women, the unemployment rate increased to more than 71 percent for those aged 20–24 and returned to 45.5 percent for women aged 25–29. Overall, according to the most recent data, young women in Saudi Arabia face an unemployment rate of nearly 54.5 percent.

Unemployment rates among youth in Kuwait and Bahrain fall between those of Saudi Arabia and Qatar. In Kuwait, where unemployment among nationals was estimated at 7.1 percent in 2011, among Kuwaiti youth it was 13.1 percent. Youth unemployment data by gender is unavailable, but economically active Kuwaiti women overall had an unemployment rate of 8.5 percent compared with 5.9 percent among Kuwaiti men. In Bahrain, the official youth unemployment rate was estimated at 10.7 percent in 2010 while 2004 labor force survey data suggest an unemployment figure among Bahraini youth of 29.2 percent.

The availability of micro-level data from the UAE allows us to explore the dynamics of unemployment in more detail. Overall, in 2009 Emiratis maintained an unemployment rate of 14.4 percent, compared with 2.8 percent among nonnationals. At the same time, Emirati youth faced an unemployment rate of 21.4 percent and made up nearly 78 percent of all unemployed Emiratis. Young female Emiratis bore the heaviest burden in regard to unemployment, with an unemployment rate of 29 percent, compared with just 12 percent among young men. Even given the relative low rates of labor force participation among young Emirati women, they made up nearly 63 percent of unemployed youth in 2009. Importantly, among 25- to 29-year-old Emiratis, women made up nearly 76 percent of the unemployed.

There are strong links between labor market outcomes and education for Gulf youth, as evidenced by labor force data from the UAE. Among young Emirati women, the unemployment rate generally decreases with educational attainment, although young women from all educational backgrounds face fairly high rates of unemployment. For those women aged 15–29 without a secondary degree, the unemployment rate was 57 percent in 2009; for those with a secondary degree, it was 54 percent. The unemployment rate drops to 29.5 percent for those with more than a secondary degree, although it should be reiterated that these women have the highest rates of labor force participation. For those women aged 25–29, rates of unemployment by education were similar to the wider cohort, at 43 percent, 49 percent and 22 percent, respectively.

Among young men, unemployment also decreases as educational attainment rises. For 15- to 29-year-old Emirati men, the unemployment rate for those having completed less than a secondary degree was 20.5 percent in 2009, while the rate dropped to 9.3 percent for those with a secondary degree. For those with more than a secondary degree, the unemployment rate was 6.3 percent. Among 25- to 29-year-old men, the unemployment rates for each level of educational attainment were lower but followed the same trajectory at 12.9 percent, 3.4 percent, and 3.5 percent, respectively. Thus, the unemployment rates for young men seem to reflect a struggle in securing desired public sector opportunities that are increasingly scarce for those without secondary degrees.

Overall, unemployment among Gulf youth points to a structural problem around initial labor market penetration. In particular, while a significant number of private sector jobs are being created in these economies, most of these jobs are not aligned with the expectations that new national job seekers have for job security, salary, and work environment. As such, unemployment reflects a rational waiting among youth for public sector employment. For young women, these desires are further challenged by a narrower range of opportunities that would be perceived as appropriate work, as well as employers' resistance to hiring women they expect will leave the labor force on marriage.

Efforts to Reform the GCC States' Labor Markets

Efforts to increase employment of nationals in the private sector and make private sector employment more attractive to young Gulf nationals have long been a priority for Gulf governments concerned with youth unemployment and, increasingly, with the social and security-related challenges they perceive to be associated with the growing presence of foreign nationals. On the policy side pressures have only increased, as the public sector has neared saturation and as wages for the civil services have become an increasingly burdensome share of government expenditures.

Past efforts at creating private sector employment centered on the establishment of employment quotas, which largely failed due to their focus on achieving quantitative goals and their lack of effort toward realigning institutionally driven incentives for both employers and employees. In the aftermath of the global economic downturn of 2008, Gulf governments began experimenting with new ways to facilitate the placement of young nationals in the private sector. Instead of relying on the imposition of quotas, these "second-generation responses" focused more on improving the job skills of young nationals and realigning employer incentives (Forstenlechner and Rutledge 2010; Hertog 2014). With a better understanding of the limitations of quotas and their unintended consequences, policymakers hoped to invest in youth and make them a more attractive asset for private sector firms.

Educational Investments

Governments across the GCC countries have invested heavily in education over the past decade, particularly at the tertiary level. In the mid-2000s, these governments facilitated the expansion of schooling and university options by establishing new free zones for education and investing in branch campuses of internationally known universities. Moreover, the Gulf states have increased the number of public universities and their satellite campuses, while undertaking serious efforts to improve quality by making changes needed to secure accreditation by international bodies.

While these investments have opened up new opportunities for Gulf youth, particularly young women whose parents have been unwilling to allow them to travel abroad for university, such efforts have not been without challenges. Graduates of public secondary schools have arrived, in many cases, unprepared for the academic rigor of higher quality tertiary programs, forcing universities to adopt a bridge year for nationals coming from public secondary schools. These bridge year programs, designed to bring basic skills up to required levels for university entrants, have proven a costly and ineffective way of making up for years of poor-quality education at the secondary level ("Foundation year at UAE state universities to be scrapped from 2018" 2014).

In contrast to the significant changes observed at the university level, the quality of secondary schooling in the Gulf, particularly in the public school system, continues to suffer. In one way, this is evidenced by the poor showing of Gulf students, on average, on international examinations like the Trends in Mathematics and Sciences Study. Despite some evidence of progress over the period 2007–2011, youth in Gulf states continue to test below international mean scores on both the mathematics and sciences examinations (see chapter 2 here). Moreover, while there is a demonstrated gap in outcomes between girls and boys across the world on such examinations, in the Gulf girls outperform boys in mathematics and sciences to a degree that places the region among the highest in terms of the global gender gap ranking.

Ridge (2010) explores the differential in secondary school performance between Emirati boys and girls in detail. In summary, she finds that the relative success of girls in primary and secondary school is reflected in differences found in their school environments. In particular, instruction in girls' schools—where faculty are often Emirati women—is of better overall quality, driven by both better teacher quality and supportive relationships between teachers and students. In contrast, boys' schools rely heavily on foreign teachers, many poorly trained and with few incentives to improve their capacities.

Overall, even at the university level, it is important to reiterate the relationship between educational outcomes and labor market signals. Despite investments in pedagogical quality and efforts to create new educational opportunities, especially in the sciences and technology, Gulf youth continue to favor areas of study that are aligned with securing favorable public sector employment, ensuring that their personal investments in education are just enough to secure such jobs.[9] This is particularly relevant for boys who, as we have noted, have a wider range of socially and economically acceptable job opportunities that do not require the long-term investments needed for higher skills training at the tertiary level.

Targeted Changes in Labor Regulations

Gulf governments began experimenting with targeted approaches to labor policy and regulation reform in the early 2000s. For example, in 2006 Oman began eliminating the kafala sponsorship system for expatriate workers, allowing them to change employers without sponsor approval. The success of this change in leveling the wage expectation differential between nationals and nonnationals and reducing the segmentation of Oman's labor market may explain the upward shift in wages among foreign workers seen in subsequent years (Hertog 2014). In addition, Oman experienced a significant increase in employment among Omani nationals, which grew by an average 4.6 percent a year over the period 2003–2010.

Saudi Arabia's reform efforts have focused on modifying the traditional quota system in an effort to better align firm incentives with national goals of labor force nationalization. In 2011, Saudi Arabian authorities began implementing what is called the Nitaqat system. Rather than applying a general quota to all sectors, this system categorizes private firms by industry and company size. Within these subcategories firms are further categorized into bands (*nitaqat*) on the basis of their commitments to nationalizing their workforces. Highly committed companies are rewarded with more flexibility on hiring decisions; companies with low nationalization rates are penalized with restrictions on hiring foreign workers or securing new licenses (Hertog 2014). While generally lauded as a more balanced approach, early evidence suggests that the new scheme suffers from many of the same problems as the former quota system (Al-Bawaba 2014).

Kuwait and the UAE, which face less intensive labor market pressures and maintain higher per capita oil revenues, have also engaged in experimental reforms (Hertog 2014). Kuwait implemented a wage subsidy system in 2001, providing privately employed nationals with allowances that largely balance out the wage differentials between public sector and private sector work. In 2009 Kuwait also loosened kafala restrictions on some foreign workers. While the UAE has explored the possibility of wage subsidies, it has not taken steps to implement such a system. However, the UAE did remove restrictions on the ability of foreign workers in selected skilled occupations to shift sponsors or to start their own businesses in 2011 ("New rules bring flexibility to UAE's labour market" 2010). Qatar has not moved forward on any important reforms in recent years.

In contrast with other GCC states, Bahrain's efforts to improve employment outcomes for young Bahrainis have been more systemic and comprehensive. Faced with rapidly declining oil revenues and the government's inability to absorb additional workers, Bahraini authorities put forward a scheme in the early 2000s aimed at eliminating the wage expectation differential and skills gap between Bahrainis and expatriates in the private sector and making the hiring of Bahrainis a rational business decision (Dyer 2008; Hertog 2014). The plan included elimination of Bahrainization quotas and the kafala system, deregulation of hiring and firing procedures, increased regulation of working conditions standards, and allowing of labor union membership for both nationals and expatriates. Bahraini authorities also announced the establishment of an unemployment insurance and training scheme, supported by a 1 percent tax on the wages of Bahrainis and increased fees associated with securing foreign work visas. Processes associated with labor issues were to become more efficient with the establishment of a one-stop shop for employers under the newly established Labor Market Regulatory Authority.

Since the new system's launch in 2007 its implementation has proven difficult, as it has been challenged by the vested interests of a range of stakeholders. Private sector employers protested against the removal of the kafala system and the increased fees on foreign worker visas, leading to a significant reduction in planned fees. Bahraini workers voiced resistance to the levy on wages, viewing it as an income tax rather than a contribution to unemployment insurance. Foreign workers have been slow to take up union membership or to change employers in significant numbers. Still, by and large, Bahrain has been able to move forward on the body of its labor market reform effort, and evidence suggests that the effort has had a positive impact with regard to steering Bahraini youth into the private sector. As Hertog (2014) has noted, "not only is the proportion of private to public employment for nationals higher than in Saudi Arabia and Oman, but Bahrain's total employment rate of Bahrainis of working age is also higher." In this regard, the Bahraini attempt at reform serves as a model for more effective reform in the GCC states, even as it has proven to be difficult to implement.

Gulf States and the Arab Spring

Despite a history of relative political security and social cohesion, the Gulf states were not immune to the general unrest that swept the Arab world during 2011. Popular protests, while short-lived in most cases, broke out in a number of Gulf countries, most notably Bahrain and Oman. In part, these protests were driven by youth frustrated with a lack of desirable employment, the rising cost of living, and perceptions of a growing inequality of economic opportunities. These frustrations have been reinforced by the coexistence of (and frequent clash between) traditional social values, and new cultural norms that have been brought about by rapid economic development and the influx of foreign workers, leaving young people to navigate increasingly complex norms as they transition to adulthood.

While the unrest in the Gulf in 2011 was met with a widely documented security response, the more telling governmental reaction was fiscal in nature. In the early months of 2011, governments across the Gulf announced large raises for nationals working in the public sector, increased government hiring, and the provision of allowances to families that were designed to reduce the burden associated with the rising cost of living in the Gulf. Minimum wages for nationals were put in place in Oman and the UAE, and unemployment insurance benefits were either put in place or raised, with monthly unemployment benefits generally equal to half of the average national salary. In order to aid Bahrain and Oman in covering the costs associated with these responses, other GCC governments agreed to provide each of these two countries with US$10 billion in aid over the subsequent decade.

While such initiatives did much to alleviate the economic concerns of nationals and youth unrest, they have served to reinforce long-held perceptions regarding the economic role of the state in terms of citizen welfare and direct job creation. No matter what progress individual states had made toward labor market reforms, governments' responses to the Arab Spring have undermined states' ability to steer more youth to the private sector and have bolstered market signals that encourage youth to wait out opportunities in the public sector at the expense of making early investments in careers in the private sector. This point was evidenced dramatically in the case of Oman, where significant employment growth among nationals in the private sector over the first decade of the 2000s halted abruptly in 2011 after the government announced the creation of new government jobs. Hertog (2014) reports that with the announcement, some 37,000 Omanis quit their private sector jobs to apply for public employment, while some 60,000 Omanis quit their private sector jobs after the announcement of an unemployment benefit.

Conclusion

While economic conditions in the Gulf region contrast starkly with those found in most other Arab countries, job creation for young nationals remains a persistent public policy challenge. Despite high rates of economic growth, Gulf states have continued to struggle with efforts to foster the creation of economic opportunities for a growing youth population. Moreover, they face an additional challenge of enabling an increasingly educated young female population to find work that puts the investments made in their education to productive economic use. These issues are particularly important when viewed in the context of efforts in the Gulf to diversify these economies away from dependence on oil and cheap labor through private sector development and the promotion of high-skill and high-productivity sectors.

The lack of job creation for youth in the Gulf has not been a quantitative challenge, as is evidenced by the high rate of overall job creation in these high-growth economies. Rather, the challenge is one of matching opportunities with young nationals' aspirations and skills as they enter the labor market. In this regard, unemployment, underemployment, and other poor labor market outcomes are reflections of rational choices by young people responding to market signals. These signals are driven by long-standing institutions—both formal and informal—that govern behavior, particularly the public-private and foreign-national segmentations of the labor market. Because the signals are distorted, they serve to steer youth toward behaviors that work against their long-term interests, if not the long-term interests of the economic development of the Gulf countries.

Over the past decade, governments across the region have tried increasingly to better align the expectations of youth with opportunities in the private sector, investing in educational reforms aimed at enhancing the skills Gulf youth bring to the labor market and reforming labor market regulations in a way that better incentivizes the private sector to hire nationals over nonnationals. While these efforts have shown some success, they have fallen short of their goals because they have failed to address the core institutional context and market signals facing youth as they enter the labor force. For youth, public sector employment remains worth the wait, while for employers, cost and productivity differentials between nationals and nonnationals still favor nonnationals. Importantly, policy reactions to Arab Spring unrest by Gulf governments have served to reinforce these incentives in a dramatic fashion.

Finding solutions for this bind remains a pressing public policy challenge in every Gulf state, as declining oil revenues are putting significant pressures on the state's ability to provide traditional services to a growing generation. The increasing youth bulge, rising educational attainment among Gulf youth, and an expectation of growing labor force participation ensure that in the long term the current model for employment generation for youth in the Gulf is untenable.

In this regard, Gulf governments have a strategic choice to either continue with policy tweaks that do little to alter the incentive structure for economic actors or to move forward with systemic reforms in the labor market. By continuing to invest in training and education among young nationals and giving more bargaining power to nonnational workers, while providing balanced protections for both national and nonnational workers, Gulf governments can effect changes that effectively rebalance the equation in the private sector and stimulate job creation for national youth. Such efforts will prove politically difficult, as Bahrain's own experience has demonstrated, but are essential for the realization of sustainable job creation for the region's growing youth population.

REFERENCES

Al-Bawaba. 2014, January 27. Say what? GCC failed nationalization schemes creating "ghosts." *Al-Bawaba.* http://www.albawaba.com/business/saudi-nitaqat-nationalization-550103.
Al-Waqfi, M., and I. Forstenlechner. 2012. Of private sector fear and prejudice: The case of young citizens in an oil-rich Arabian Gulf economy. *Personnel Review* 41(5): 609–629.
Bahrain Central Informatics Organization (Bahrain CIO). 2011. Results of census 2010. http://www.cio.gov.bh/cio_eng/SubDetailed.aspx?subcatid=256.
Bahrain Ministry of Labor and Bahrain Centre for Studies and Research (Bahrain BMOL and BCSR). 2004. Labour Force Survey, November 2004. Manama, Bahrain: Bahrain Centre for Studies and Research.
Dyer, P. 2008. Human capital and the labor market in Bahrain. In *Bahrain country profile: The road ahead for Bahrain.* Cairo: Economic Research Forum.
Forstenlechner, I., and E. Rutledge. 2010. Unemployment in the Gulf: Time to update the "social contract." *Middle East Policy* 17(2): 38–48.
Foundation year at UAE state universities to be scrapped from 2018. 2014, February 4. *The National.* http://www.thenational.ae/uae/education/foundation-year-at-uae-state-universities-to-be-scrapped-from-2018.
Gallup. 2010. *The Silatech Index: Voices of Young Arabs.* Doha, Qatar: Silatech.
Gulf Research Center. 2014. Gulf Labor Markets and Migration Database. http://gulfmigration.eu/glmm-database/demographic-and-economic-module/.

Hertog, S. 2010. The sociology of the Gulf rentier systems: Societies of intermediaries. *Comparative Studies in Society and History* 52(2): 282–318.

Hertog, S. 2014. Arab Gulf states: An assessment of nationalisation policies. Gulf Labour Markets and Migration Programme research paper no. 1. http://cadmus.eui.eu/bitstream/handle/1814/32156/GLMM%20ResearchPaper_01-2014.pdf?sequence=1.

International Labour Organization (ILO). 2011, October. Economically active population, estimates and projections. 6th ed. http://laborsta.ilo.org/applv8/data/EAPEP/eapep_E.html.

International Monetary Fund (IMF). 2011. *Gulf cooperation council countries: Enhancing economic outcomes in an uncertain global economy.* Washington, DC: International Monetary Fund.

Kherfi, S. 2012. Unemployment and labor market participation of UAE youth. Discussion paper for workshop "Social-Economic Situation of Middle East Youth on the Eve of the Arab Spring." Youth Policy Press & Youth Policy Labs. http://www.youthpolicy.org/wp-content/uploads/library/2012_Unemployment_UAE_Eng.pdf.

Kuwait Central Statistical Bureau (Kuwait CSB). 2013. Annual statistics abstract 2012. http://www.csb.gov.kw/Socan_Statistic_EN.aspx?ID=18.

New rules bring flexibility to UAE's labour market. 2010, December 30. *Khaleej Times.* http://www.khaleejtimes.com/DisplayArticle09.asp?xfile=data/theuae/2010/December/theuae_December799.xml&section=theuae.

Oman National Center for Statistics and Information (Oman NSI). 2011. Census 2010: Final results. General Census of Population Housing and Establishments 2010. http://www.ncsi.gov.om/NCSI_website/documents/Census_2010.pdf.

Qatar Ministry of Development Planning and Statistics. 2012. Annual abstract 2012. http://www.qsa.gov.qa/eng/GeneralStatistics.htmhttp://www.qsa.gov.qa/eng/GeneralStatistics.htm.

Qatar Statistics Agency (QSA). 2011. Annual bulletin of labor force sample survey. http://www.qix.gov.qa/portal/page/portal/QIXPOC/Documents/QIX%20Knowledge%20Base/Publication/Labor%20Force%20Researches/labor%20force%20sample%20survey/Source_QSA/Labour_Force_QSA_AnBu_AE_2011.pdf.

Ridge, N. 2010. Teacher quality, gender and nationality in the United Arab Emirates: A crisis for boys. Dubai School of Government working paper no. 10-06. Dubai: Dubai School of Government.

Ridge, N. 2014. *Education and the reverse gender divide in the Gulf States: Embracing the global, ignoring the local.* New York: Teachers College Press.

Salahi-Isfahani, D., and N. Dhillon. 2008. Stalled youth transitions in the Middle East: A framework for policy reform. Middle East Youth Initiative working paper no. 8. Washington, DC: Wolfensohn Center for Development, Brookings Institution.

Saudi Arabian Central Department for Statistics and Information (Saudi Arabian CDSI). 1999. Labor force survey 1999. http://www.cdsi.gov.sa/english/index.php?option=com_docman&task=cat_view&gid=49&Itemid=162.

Saudi Arabian Central Department for Statistics and Information (Saudi Arabian CDSI). 2010. Statistical yearbook 2009. Labor force survey 2009. http://www.cdsi.gov.sa/english/index.php?option=com_docman&task=cat_view&gid=207&Itemid=162.

Saudi Arabian Central Department for Statistics and Information (Saudi Arabian CDSI). 2011. Detailed results of the General Census of Population and Housing 2010. http://www.cdsi.gov.sa/english/index.php?option=com_docman&task=cat_view&gid=271&Itemid=113.

Saudi Arabian Central Department for Statistics and Information (Saudi Arabian CDSI). 2011. Labor force survey results 2011. http://www.cdsi.gov.sa/english/index.php?option=com_docman&task=cat_view&gid=86&Itemid=113.

UAE federal government employees get 70 per cent pay hike. 2007, November 20. *Gulf News*. http://gulfnews.com/news/uae/government/uae-federal-government-employees-get-70-per-cent-pay-hike-1.213243.

United Arab Emirates National Bureau of Statistics (UAE NBS). 2009. Labor force survey 2009.

United Arab Emirates National Bureau of Statistics (UAE NBS). 2011. UAE in figures 2010. http://www.uaestatistics.gov.ae/EnglishHome/ReportDetailsEnglish/tabid/121/Default.asp x?ItemId=1925&PTID=187&MenuId=2http://www.uaestatistics.gov.ae/EnglishHome/ ReportDetailsEnglish/tabid/121/Default.aspx?ItemId=1925&PTID=187&MenuId=2.

United Nations, Economic and Social Affairs, Population Division. 2013. World population prospects: The 2012 revision. DVD ed.

World Bank. 2014. World development indicators. http://data.worldbank.org/data-catalog/ world-development-indicators.

NOTES

1. In doing so, the authors must depend largely on aggregate indicators and cross-tabulations published by the statistical authorities in each of the Gulf states due to the lack of availability of micro-level data sets. These analysis are supported by deeper analysis of available micro-level data from the 2009 Labor Force Survey in the UAE, which was carried out under the authority of the UAE National Bureau of Statistics.

2. See chapter 2 here for analysis of natural population growth and the rise of the youth bulge in the context of the GCC countries.

3. Reported labor force data are drawn from the following sources: Bahrain, Bahrain Central Informatics Organization (2011); Kuwait, Kuwait Central Statistical Bureau (2013); Qatar, Qatar Statistics Agency (2011); Saudi Arabia, Saudi Arabian Central Department for Statistics and Information (2011); and, United Arab Emirates National Bureau of Statistics (2009).

4. See chapter 4 here for more on the impact of marriage on female labor force participation elsewhere in the region.

5. For more on the interaction between work choices and the marriage market, see Salehi-Isfahani and Dhillon (2008).

6. Quota regulations in Saudi Arabia, for example, were whittled down in practice to sector-specific quotas over the course of the next 10 years. At the same time, the labor law of 2005 included a system-wide 75 percent nationalization quota, which did not include any structure for implementation, which was largely ignored.

7. For a deeper exploration of the scope of this issue, see Hertog (2010).

8. Unemployment rates for Omanis may be as high or higher; recent official rates of unemployment are not available.

9. For deeper analysis of the links between skills investment and public sector work, see Salahi-Isfahani and Dhillon (2008). See also Ridge (2014) for analysis on this issue in the case of the UAE.

6 The Role of Social Media in Mobilizing Political Protest

EVIDENCE FROM THE TUNISIAN REVOLUTION

Anita Breuer

THE POLITICAL ROLE of the Internet and digital social media has become a well-established topic of research on political communication and participation. The Internet's prominent role in the diffusion of popular protest across the Arab world and the ouster of authoritarian regimes in Tunisia and Egypt has reinvigorated the debate on the implications of social media for political mobilization and patterns of protest diffusion, as well as for influencing individual political engagement.

Prior research on these aspects of social media has largely been conducted in the context of consolidated Western democracies. The question that has clearly received most attention in political science literature is whether and how platforms for social networking, such as Twitter, YouTube, and Facebook, affect individuals' political behavior. While there is a widespread popular belief that the Internet will undermine authoritarian rule, the political implications of the Internet in the context of authoritarian or democratizing political systems remain underresearched. Inroads have been made by the case study series of Aday and colleagues (2010), but by and large, the literature on democratic transitions is still a long way from having established a clear understanding of a causal relationship between new media and protest mobilization under authoritarian rule. Under authoritarian rule the task of coordinating civil protest is significantly more difficult than in a democratic context. Ordinary citizens in authoritarian regimes do not control weapons, personnel, or other political resources. In explaining the breakdown of authoritarian regimes, the political economy literature has consequently focused mainly on the role of elites, such as the military or royal families, in challenging autocratic rulers. Drawing on the case of the Tunisian uprising that led to the ouster of President Zine el-Abidine Ben Ali in January 2011, this chapter seeks to test the ability of existing theoretical frameworks to explain popular protest under authoritarian rule.

One of the hallmarks of the Tunisian protest movement that ousted President Ben Ali in January 2011 was its broad social base. Regime support from conservative, risk-averse middle classes had long been considered one of the major obstacles to democratization in the region. Continued support for authoritarian rule by the middle classes, especially state employees and small to medium business entrepreneurs was seen as related to high levels of regional conflict, a perceived potential for democracy to lead to increased civil strife deriving from ethnic or religious cleavages, and fears regarding the potential empowerment of Islamist parties seeking to reverse economic liberalization (Greenwood 2008). In this respect, the perception of the Middle East and North Africa (MENA) region's middle classes resembled the Marxist conception of the "petite bourgeoisie"—that is, a class averse to social change because of its vested interest in protecting its financial assets and its standard of living (Solimano 2009). As one observer of the Tunisian political scene pointedly summed up Ben Ali's tacit bargain with the middle class: "Shut up and consume!" (Goldstein 2011).

Contrary to this notion, however, the Tunisian revolution was borne by a broad coalition of social forces that united an alienated intellectual elite with the rural poor and urban middle classes in opposition to the regime. It is a widely shared assumption that this joining of forces would not have been possible without modern communications technology and social media, which helped to bridge geographical and social distances. However, it is not clear how exactly social media interacted with other contextual factors to bring about a national protest movement of sufficient size to topple an extremely entrenched authoritarian regime. The aim of this chapter is to advance our understanding of this complex dynamic process.

Theoretical Approaches to Protest Mobilization and the Role of New Information and Communications Technology in Authoritarian Contexts

Psychological and Attitudinal Approaches

Traditional grievance models of political activism have focused on psychological factors that lead people to engage in contentious politics (e.g., Gurr 1970). As Müller and Jukam (1983) posit: "people who take part in acts of civil disobedience or political violence are discontented about something." The psychological mechanism at work is that unfulfilled expectations cause frustration, which manifests itself in an individual propensity to protest. The traditional approach emphasized the primacy of material motives; more recent studies have shifted the focus of attention toward emotions. For instance, people may be motivated to engage in protest out of a sense of moral indignation in the face of injustice (van Laer 2011).

While grievances provide an abundance of motives under authoritarian rule, civil society's ability to channel these motives into collective action is thwarted by the fact that the public sphere is sealed: the national narrative is controlled by a government that usually resorts to a mix of censorship and intimidation to suppress information that could negatively reflect on itself. Here, the Internet poses an existential threat to government control (Kuebler 2011). Web-based communications technology makes it possible to disseminate narratives that diverge from the "official" government-supported narrative to a wide public. Once such information is leaked, it can push people into protest action. Furthermore, information that is prone to produce negative emotions has a high potential to "go viral," that is, quickly diffuse on the Internet and virtually spiral out of governmental control.

It can thus be hypothesized that the Internet provided an element of emotional mobilization in the Tunisian uprising by helping to break the grip of state censorship and by making information on corruption in the regime and its human rights violations available to a large segment of the population.

Rational Choice Approaches

The "grievance approach" has been seriously challenged by the "rational choice" approach. Tullock (1971) and Olson (1965) argued that grievances are essentially irrelevant to a self-interested individual's decision regarding participation in collective political action such as protest. Grievances typically represent a desire for outcomes that satisfy the definition of a public good. The so-called free rider problem consists in the fact that individual members of a large group lack incentives to endure the high transaction costs related to protest participation, since they will enjoy the public good in any case—if others provide it. Yet individual ethical principles such as personal honor or patriotic duty may induce persons to participate in the provision of public goods.

Given that the public sphere is sealed, under authoritarianism the mobilization of protest faces a serious challenge: citizens are incompletely informed about their fellow citizens' attitudes toward the regime and disposition to rebel. Citizens can also expect to pay a high personal cost (arrest, incarceration, death on streets) if they participate in unsuccessful protests. Therefore, they will turn out to do so only if they are convinced that the government's ability to crush the protest will be undermined by the magnitude of the protest (Hendrix, Haggard, and Magaloni 2009).

Rational choice models of collective action in networks also posit that individuals' willingness to assume the risks related to protest action depends on the expected participation of others (Granovetter 1978). This information is primarily conveyed through social networks. In this context, the Internet can influence individuals' decisions in two ways. First, online content that documents participation in past protest events may trigger informational cascades that lead to mass civil uprisings. Second, the event management features offered by some social networking sites (e.g., "Facebook group events") inform users about the prospective turnout in upcoming events.

In this sense, this chapter hypothesizes that the Internet helped individual Tunisian citizens to overcome the rational choice dilemma of collective action, by providing them with information about the magnitude of past and upcoming protest events.

Resource Mobilization Approaches

Resource mobilization theory claims that open and affluent societies provide more favorable conditions for contention to thrive, thus making protest more common (Dalton and van Sickle 2005). According to this theory, the extensive existence of NGOs and other civil society groups allows citizens to engage freely in a variety of voluntary associations and to develop the social and organizational skills required for promoting their interests (Coleman 1988; Putnam 2000). At first sight, then, the occurrence of protest in closed authoritarian societies runs counter to this theory's basic premises. This phenomenon can only be explained by the broader assumption that even closed societies may create resources suited to the stimulation of collective action once they reach a certain degree of socioeconomic development.

As nations progress economically, they produce denser communication infrastructures. The Internet may then become a key factor in facilitating protest where civic activism is systematically suppressed. The availability of information communications technology (ICT) enables activist groups to communicate with potential constituencies over large distances. Thus, ICT constitutes an important resource for challenging the strategies of social isolation typically employed by authoritarian regimes.

Given the relatively high level of Tunisia's ICT infrastructure development, it is reasonable to conjecture that the Internet provided an alternative communication realm that enabled political activists to create networks despite heavy state control over the public sphere and the media.

The Structural or Network Account of Activism

Structural or network theories regard the causes of collective action as strongly influenced by network connections (Friedman and McAdam 1992). An essential element of the mobilization process is that potential participants are informed about an upcoming protest event. Hence, a person is more likely to become mobilized as his or her degree of embeddedness in social networks increases. Another important function of social networks is that they build a collective identity supporting protest action. Collective identities motivate protest participation by providing the potential participant with a sense of membership, and solidarity and an oppositional sense of "us" versus "them" (van Laer 2011).

Clearly, the Internet is conducive to an increased awareness about collective action events such as protests. One's likelihood of being mobilized increases with the number of one's memberships in different online networks and the number of social relations one maintains on these networks. Considering that the Tunisian uprising started from a local revolt in a marginalized provincial town and then very quickly expanded both geographically and socially, the country provides an important case of online social networks' contribution to the process of political mobilization across social and geographic boundaries.

Methodology of Data Collection

In December 2010, violent clashes between police and civilians in the provincial town of Sidi Bouzid developed into a full-scale national protest movement that led to the ouster of President Ben Ali in January 2011. This success prompted others across the Middle East and North Africa to emulate the Tunisian model and triggered the regional protest wave that came to be known as the Arab Spring. Despite its role-model status, however, the Tunisian case continues to be widely viewed as atypical: the protests succeeded under an authoritarian regime that held unusually tight control over the media (Patel and Bunce 2012). It is generally accepted that the mobilization of large-scale protests in Tunisia would not have been possible without the contribution of new digital communications technology; however, little is known about the precise nature of this contribution.

To address this research lacuna and to test the theoretical propositions presented in the previous section, I applied a two-step mixed methods design of data collection in the Tunisian case. The first and qualitative phase involved a field trip to Tunisia in October 2011 during which semistructured expert interviews were conducted with 16 Tunisian bloggers and Internet activists. The interview participants were asked to tell about their own online and offline protest activities prior to and during the uprising, to describe the nature of digital activist networks, to describe their own positions in these structures, to provide personal assessments of the contribution of ICT to the protest movement, and to help identify online content they regarded as having been particularly influential.

Sampling and the Socioeconomic Characteristics of the Sample Population

The German Development Institute conducted a web survey (titled "Internet and Politics in Tunisia") among Tunisian Facebook users between March 1 and May 31, 2012. The software used to administer the survey was SurveyMonkey. The survey contained a total of 34 questions and took about 12 minutes to complete. It was conducted in Arabic and was pilot-tested for comprehensiveness and ease of use among native Tunisian-Arabic speakers prior to its launch.

The sample was developed through the creation a Facebook group dedicated to a discussion of the role of social media in the Arab Spring; the activists interviewed during the field trip were invited to join this group. The group was then systematically enlarged, using the Facebook friendship suggestion algorithm whereby the network recommends new friends to its users on the basis of their existing friends. Once the survey was launched, members of this group were sent an invitation to participate using the Facebook group event organizing function. The invitation message contained the survey's URL, a brief description of its academic purpose, and the suggestion that one circulate the survey URL among friends, relatives, and colleagues. No monetary or other material incentive was offered to the respondents. The survey resulted in 608 responses.

When interpreting the survey results, it is therefore important to keep in mind that they refer to a population of more or less politically engaged Internet users and do not permit inferences about the behavior of individuals who are fully outside this set, that is, those who can be regarded as politically apathetic and/or were not connected to the Internet. Table 6.1 provides a basic illustration of the degree of political engagement of the sample population prior to and after the fall of the Ben Ali regime.

The results must be interpreted with care. For instance, while the high rate of electoral abstention (85.4 percent) would clearly indicate general political disaffection in the context of a democracy, here it can be viewed as an indicator of respondents' ideological opposition to the regime. The relatively high portion of respondents who participated in street protests once (8.7 percent) or several times (31.8 percent) seems to support this notion, as well as the fact that participation rates were practically reversed in the first postautocratic elections in October 2011.

The majority of respondents in the sample are medium- to high-frequency Internet users, with 28.3 percent reporting daily use of three to four hours and 43.6 percent reporting more than five hours. Network embeddedness among the respondents is high: 98.5 percent indicated Facebook as their most important online social network, and 65.4 percent reported having more than 200 friends on their most important network—well above the worldwide average of 130 friend connections on Facebook. A considerable number of respondents maintained profiles in more than one social network, with YouTube (46.3 percent) and Twitter (44.0 percent) coming second and third in importance. The vast majority reported informational rather than recreational use of the Internet, with 93.0 percent indicating "following the news" as their most important online activity.

The sample population was relatively young, with 24.0 percent of respondents born in the 1970s, 38.8 percent in the 1980s, and 10.1 percent in the 1990s. The sample population is predominantly male (77.8 percent male respondents) and relatively highly educated, with 49.8 percent of respondents holding bachelor's and 37.0 percent master's degrees. Compared to the population in general, 6.2 percent held university degrees in 2010 (Tunisie 2015 2015). Only 12.5 percent indicated secondary school as their highest completed educational level.

Regarding regime support, 55.4 percent assessed the Ben Ali regime's ability to create jobs as very bad, and 57.5 percent strongly agreed with the statement that it was impossible under his rule to get a job without family connections. Interestingly, however, 48.8 percent of the respondents were fully employed prior to the revolution, only 8.2 percent were unemployed, and a relatively large proportion (27.1 percent) were still studying. One possible interpretation for this apparent contradiction is that many of those still studying

TABLE 6.1

Citizens' political behavior before the revolution in Tunisia. Responses to the survey question "Prior to the revolution did you ever undertake or consider undertaking one of the following actions to influence the government or its policies?"

	I never considered this action	I thought about it but never did it	I engaged in such an action once	I engaged in such an action several times	Response count
Collecting signatures or signing petitions	58.8% (322)	20.1% (110)	4.6% (25)	16.6% (91)	548
Writing a letter to a newspaper or government officials	55.5% (303)	27.8% (152)	5.1% (28)	11.5% (63)	546
Working with or founding a citizen initiative	49.5% (271)	29.8% (163)	6.8% (37)	13.9% (76)	547
Organizing or participating in a street protest	35.2% (194)	24.3% (134)	8.7% (48)	31.8% (175)	551

Source: German Development Institute web survey "Internet and Politics in Tunisia," March 1–May 31, 2012.

had a rather gloomy view of their future job prospects given the high rate of youth unemployment. While 90 percent indicated Islam as their religious affiliation, the respondents predominantly subscribed to secular views: 55.9 percent strongly agreed with the statement that religious leaders should not influence government decisions.

The Role of Information and Communications Technology and Social Media in Protest Mobilization during the Tunisian Uprising

Information and Communications Technology Infrastructure Development in Tunisia

Government policymakers across the Muslim world adopted widely varying strategies during the 1990s in reaction to the opportunities and risks of ICT use. While established democracies allowed free competition for ICT services, the pace of ICT development in most autocratic countries was set by state-owned telecommunication providers who held a monopoly over ICT services. At the same time, these bodies also monitored and regulated online content and reported directly to the government (Howard 2011).

Tunisia was in the middle of this spectrum. In line with President Ben Ali's often-reiterated desire to develop the Internet in Tunisia, his government invested heavily in the telecom sector from the mid-1990s on. As a result, Tunisia had one of the most highly developed telecommunications infrastructures in North Africa by the mid-2000s, with 11 competing Internet service providers (Reporters Without Borders 2004). A total of 1.7 million of Tunisia's 10.2 million inhabitants were Internet users in 2008, and 9 out of 10 Tunisians owned a cell phone. Tunisians for whom personal computers remained prohibitively expensive had access to the Internet from one of 300 public Internet centers (*publinets*) set up by the authorities throughout the country, and the education sector reported a connectivity of 100 percent for universities, research labs, secondary schools, and primary schools (OI 2009).

Ben Ali's strategy of depicting himself as a democratizer of the Internet and a role model for the promotion of information and communications technology (ICT) in the developing world sold well internationally: In 2001, Tunisia was chosen to host the second stage of the 2005 UN World Summit on the Information Society. The summit's objective was to "develop and foster a clear statement of political will and take concrete steps to establish the foundations for an Information Society for all, reflecting all the different interests at stake" (ITU 2001).

The Tunisian Internet Agency's Censorship Activities

Retrospectively, it is difficult to understand why so much international approval was showered on a government which kept tight control over the public sphere and ruthlessly cracked down on free expression. The Ben Ali regime went to great lengths to dominate and protect the official political narrative, according to which the leader was the legitimate heir of Habib Bourguiba, the much-revered first president of independent Tunisia, whom Ben Ali removed in a palace coup in 1987. This narrative was complemented by a visual cult of personality and was accompanied by political programs intended to fashion regime-obedient citizens by proclaiming hypocritical messages about economic progress, liberty and plurality (Chomiak 2011; ICG 2011).[1]

In 1996, the Tunisian Ministry of Communications established the Tunisian Internet Agency (Agence Tunisienne d'Internet; ATI) to regulate the country's Internet activities. In 1998, a telecommunications law authorized the ATI to intercept and check the content of email messages under the pretext of preventing access to material contrary to public order and morality. Since the ATI was the gateway from which all of Tunisia's Internet service providers (ISPs) leased their bandwidths and all fixed-line Internet traffic passed through its facilities, the ATI was able to load content control and filtering software onto the ISP servers. Furthermore, downloads and additions of email attachments had to go through a central server (OI 2009). In contrast to other Internet regulation agencies in the Arab world (e.g., Saudi Arabia and UAE), who publish reports on their censoring activities and alert users who try to access a blocked page, the ATI purposefully hid its censorship activities from Internet users. Websites the ATI blocked in Tunisia appeared with a fake 404 "File not found" error message—a practice that gained the ATI the nickname "Ammar 404" (Censor 404) among Tunisian Internet users. In addition to technical surveillance, the ATI exercised control by obliging service providers such as Internet café owners and the *publinets* to register the ID numbers of Internet users and by holding them legally responsible for their customers' online activities.

All in all, the trajectory of online censorship in Tunisia exhibits the dynamics described by Howard (2011): government watchdogs initially monitor sexually explicit websites and then gradually expand their activities to cover political commentary online as officials become increasingly versed in the application of control software. While this "Big Brother" creep sometimes occurs slowly, it can also take an exponential leap in times of crisis that threaten national security. This occurred in Tunisia in 2008 as a response to strikes and demonstrations in the region of Gafsa against corruption and abysmal working conditions at the Compagnie Phosphate de Gafsa (Gafsa Phosphate Company). The protests turned violent when security forces opened fire on the protesters, killing one and injuring twenty-six (Pollock 2011; Schraeder and Redissi 2011). Following this escalation, the protests began to attract citizen support and developed into a loosely organized social movement across the Gafsa region, with weekly protests in the town of Reddeyef. While the state-controlled press remained silent, Internet activists began to cover the events on Facebook.

In order to prevent information about the protests from spreading, the ATI stepped up its censorship program: Facebook was blocked on August 18, 2008, at the request of Ben Ali, who cited national security violations by terrorists as the reason (Chomiak 2011; ICG 2011). In reaction to a massive wave of online protest, the government lifted the blockade on September 2 and switched to a strategy of covert surveillance and manipulation of social networks. According to the US State Department and the Committee to Protect Journalists, the government ordered Tunisian ISPs to intercept log-ins by Tunisian Facebook users and to relay the details to the ATI, which then used them to block accounts entirely or remove undesired contents (Tunisian protests fueled by social media networks 2011).

The government's censorship efforts went even further: As cyberactivist Yassine Ayari recalls: "In 2009, there was a wave of censorship never seen before. It was ridiculous. Everything was censored. Any website having the words *human* or *rights* in it would be blocked. YouTube, DaylyMotion, WordTV... all the video sharing platforms were shut down. If you had more than twenty visitors on your blog, no matter what the subject— even if you were blogging on cooking recipes, it would be blocked automatically"[2] Although the government succeeded for a while in 2008 in confining the protests regionally, its massive censorship strategy backlashed by prompting increased efforts by those who had long been campaigning for online free speech in Tunisia.

The Preparation Phase: 1998–2010

To understand the phenomenon of cyberactivism in the Tunisian revolution, it is important to keep in mind that it long predated the Arab Spring. As early as 1998, two activists with the pseudonyms "Foetus" and "Waterman" founded Takriz, a group they described as a "cyber-think and street resistance network."[3] From the beginning, the group targeted the country's politically alienated youth as its core audience, and its combination of aggressive street slang, radical messages, and irreverent mockery of the authorities soon caught the regime's attention. Takriz's website was blocked in Tunisia in August 2000, but others soon sprang up.

One of these was *TuneZine*, a satirical political web magazine. Under the pseudonym Ettounsi (The Tunisian) its founder, Zouhair Yahyaoui, published numerous columns and essays criticizing government corruption and the lack of rule of law. In 2002, Yahyaoui was arrested at a Tunis publinet. In 2003, he launched a hunger strike to protest the harsh conditions of his imprisonment and was awarded the Reporters without Borders Cyber-Freedom Prize.

Another example is the collective blog Nawaat (Core), cofounded in 2004 from European exile by Riadh Guerfali, a constitutional lawyer, and Sami Ben Gharbia, a political science student. The purpose of Nawaat was to provide a public platform for Tunisian dissident voices and to collect and publish information about the regime's corruption and human rights violations. The innovative and often humorous way the Nawaat bloggers combined citizen footage and data from other sources to get their message across soon became one of the group's most distinctive trademarks. In one of their most popular YouTube videos, produced in 2008, they combined pictures from plane spotter sites with a geotagging program to document the flight paths of Tunisia's presidential jet.

By reconstructing the plane's itinerary across Europe at times when the president was known to be in-country, the bloggers demonstrated that its main purpose was apparently to transport Ben Ali's wife to exclusive shopping destinations.

While the foregoing groups were political from the beginning, other activists started out with cultural or entertainment topics and became politicized along the way in reaction to the regime's increasing repression. Lina Ben Mhenni, a lecturer in linguistics at the University of Tunis, started out by reporting on the capital's club scene on her blog Nightclubbeuse, but beginning in 2009 she reported more and more frequently on social and political issues. This led the authorities to block her site in early 2010. In the relaunched version of her blog, A Tunisian Girl, she adopted a decidedly political tone that won her several journalist awards, as well as a Nobel Peace Prize nomination in 2011, for her courageous documentation of the regime's human rights violations.

Another example is that of Haythem El Mekki (@ByLasko on Twitter), now a popular political commentator on the Tunisian National TV channel El Watanya. A digital expert and student of communication sciences, El Mekki originally made a name for himself by commenting on Tunisia's independent music scene on Facebook and Twitter. By the late 2000s his fan community had grown to such an extent that any political comments posted on his website spread widely throughout the social networks, thus almost automatically turning him into a political cyberactivist.

Thus it is clear that a political culture of dissent existed prior to the events of December 2010. The Internet provided an alternative public sphere that was at least partially shielded from the government's unilateral oversight and control. Here, Tunisians were able to form a solidarity community with shared feelings of repression and humiliation and to formulate a collective alternative discourse made up of street wisdom, political satire, and irreverent mockery of the regime and its authorities (Chomiak 2011; ICG 2011).

Tunisia's cyber avant-garde, with some exceptions, was dominated in the beginning by affluent, well-educated, polyglot individuals with a high degree of cultural capital—a social profile that has been described as characteristic of early ICT adopters throughout the developing world (Norris 2001). However, it would be inaccurate to regard their network as a socially exclusive club. Inasmuch as the cost of accessing the net was considerably reduced by the early opening of the Tunisian telecom market to competition among service providers, economic factors did not have a limiting effect on Internet use (Howard 2011). On the other hand bloggers' efforts to convey their political messages to a critical mass of citizens were thwarted by the Ben Ali regime's tight controls over both traditional media and the Internet. According to Kuebler (2011), the limited impact of blogging in Tunisia from the late 1990s to 2010 can mainly be attributed to the fact that it lacked "the bridge from an elitist medium to the general public sphere."

In response to this, digital activists in Tunisia stepped up their efforts to connect with both international and domestic constituencies. Over the late 2000s, several of the anticensorship movement's core activists started to become active in international blogger communities, such as Global Voices, in order to increase their visibility abroad. Some of them received training in e-journalism and blog publication from programs sponsored by US embassies and funded through the Middle East Partnership Initiative, an organization that focused in 2005–2010 on training journalists throughout North Africa and the Middle East.[4]

The spring of 2010 saw a new wave of anticensorship protests both online and offline. One illustrative example was the initiative Tunisie en Blanc, in Arabic A'la A'mar (Day Against the Censor): in May 2010 the activists Slim Amamou and Yassine Ayari, joined later by Lina Ben Mhenni, called for a rally against Internet censorship in front of the Tunisian Ministry of Communication Technology on May 22. In preparation for the rally, the organizers announced that officially prescribed procedures for the organization of public demonstrations would be adhered to and proceeded to request legal authorization, which, unsurprisingly, was turned down. The bloggers accordingly documented each Kafkaesque step of their subsequent bureaucratic negotiations in a series of videocasts published on Vimeo and Facebook. When Amamou and Ayari were arrested for investigation and forced by the authorities to call the rally off, their online community called for Plan B: a May 22 turnout on the streets in white shirts in a symbolic protest against censorship. The initiative was only partly successful. While various online groups drew the support of roughly 19,000 protesters (Gharbia 2010) and hundreds of Tunisians living abroad assembled in front of their country's embassies and consulates in Bonn, Paris, Montreal, and New York to support the protest, only a few dozen young people dared to defy the security forces by participating in a flash mob in Tunis itself on the central Avenue Habib Bourguiba.

This episode shows that online activism alone was unable to provide sufficient impetus to mobilize a critical mass of regime challengers on the Tunisian streets. Notwithstanding this, the years between 1998 and 2010 can be regarded as an important preparatory phase during which activists used digital media to build national and international networks online and offline, to identify collective political goals, and to build solidarity regarding shared grievances (Chomiak 2011; Howard and Hussain 2011). These preparations proved to be valuable assets in the subsequent phase that culminated in the ouster of Ben Ali.

The Ignition Phase: December 17 to Late December 2010

The event that unraveled the ability of Ben Ali's security apparatus to control the public sphere occurred in the provincial town of Sidi Bouzid, 210 kilometers southwest of Tunis. The remote Sub-Saharan governorates of the interior, popularly labeled "areas of darkness," had been systematically neglected by the regime and were characterized by profound social and political isolation, rampant economic deprivation, and a youth unemployment rate nine times that of the capital (ICG 2011; Saidani 2012).

On December 17, 2010, the distress triggered by these socioeconomic, generational, and geographic disparities came to a head when Mohammed Bouazizi, a 26-year-old fruit seller, set himself on fire after a police officer confiscated his wares because he did not have a vendor's permit and publicly humiliated him by slapping him in the face. By committing his desperate act in front of the office of the regional governor, Bouazizi forced the regime to assume political and moral responsibility for his situation, thus turning him into a symbolic representative of millions of young Tunisians who lacked opportunities for socioeconomic advancement (Aday et al. 2010; Lynch 2012).

The same day, members of Bouazizi's family, accompanied by trade unionists, marched to the police headquarters to express their anger. The protests soon turned into violent clashes between the police forces and members of Bouazizi's extended family, along with neighbors and youths who identified with his plight. Within a week, the protests spilled over to the neighboring cities of Menzel Bouzaiane, al-Maknasi, and al-Mazuna and then to Argab, Bin Aoun, Jilma, Souq al-Jadid, Bi'r al-Hafi, and Sabala, all of which are dominated by the Hamama tribe, to which Bouazizi's family belongs. In contrast to the situation two years earlier in Gafsa, the regime failed to contain the uprising. By the time Bouazizi died in a hospital from his injuries on January 4, what had begun as a local, socioeconomic, and to some extent tribally motivated bread-and-butter protest had turned into a nationwide antiregime movement, with tens of thousands of Tunisians from all levels of society demanding Ben Ali's fall. Bouazizi's death provided the spark that ignited the antiregime movement and its spread beyond the boundaries of the Internet and onto Tunisian streets.

How did this information manage to filter through the state-controlled media and reach such a broad audience so quickly? The answer apparently lies in the way the previously developed online networks interacted with traditional international media outlets. The initial protests in Sidi Bouzid following Bouazizi's self-immolation were recorded by participants via cell phone videos and posted on personal Facebook profiles. On the eve of the revolution, Facebook penetration still hovered around a modest 17 percent in Tunisia (DSG 2011), and Tunisian users were wary of overtly accessing and sharing regime-critical content, given the government's omnipresent surveillance. Thus it is unlikely that this information would have reached a mass audience had it not been for a small elite of digital activists, many of them operating from exile, who acted as information brokers. Around the globe, these activists joined efforts to screen Facebook for protest-related posts, translate the material into other languages, and structure it into a coherent, chronological narrative:[5]

> When the revolution came I was in Belgium. At that time I was already known through the [Tunisia in white] demonstration and my blog. I had two thousand or three thousand friends on Facebook, which gave me a little bit of influence. So I took a vacation from my job and sat with three other friends, PCs, pizzas, and a telephone. We tried to use all the information we could handle: status updates, pictures, videos. When we heard that something happened in Kasserine or somewhere else, we'd pick up the phone, we'd know someone who knows someone, and we would find the information and post it.[6]

Networks like Global Voices and Nawaat began running special online features about the protests and spreading the word through their own social media channels on Facebook, Twitter, and YouTube.[7] Once the information had been made available in publishable form, international broadcasters picked it up and imported it to their respective countries, thus leapfrogging the blackout imposed by Tunisia's state media gatekeepers. Social media video footage about the Sidi Bouzid protests first appeared on Al Jazeera on December 20, 2010.[8]

It was only through this complex threefold interaction between individual, nonelite protesters, motivated and strategically oriented digital activists, and international broadcasters that the information about the death of Bouazizi and the ensuing protests were able to reach a larger portion of Tunisian society. During the first 10 days of protests, the regional administrative centers of the two middle-western governorates on the Algerian border, Sidi Bouzid and Kasserine, became the focal points of popular action (Saidani 2012). During this first period, Twitter, a site that allows the communication of telegraphic information instantaneously over a wide network of Internet users, began to play a significant role, with the emergence of the hashtag #sidibouzid.

The Escalation Phase: Late December 2010 to January 12, 2011

Over the second week of the conflict, the movement expanded geographically, socially, and politically. Protests reached the neighboring governorates, moving to Kef in the northwest, Kairouan in the center, and Kebili, Tozeur, and Ben Guerdene in the south. Unemployed young people, who had so far been the socially dominant group among the protesters, were joined by employed professionals and occupational groups, most notably elements of the trade unions and law professionals. The National Bar Association and the regional branches of the Union Générale Tunisienne du Travail emerged as poles of protest, giving the movement both structure and sustainability (ICG 2011; Lynch 2012; Saidani 2012). Politically, the movement became radicalized, with socioeconomic demands that rapidly became overt challenges to the regime, most clearly expressed by the slogan "Ben Ali dégage!" (Ben Ali get out!).

The regime responded with increased repression on the one hand and an almost complete breakdown in public communication on the other hand. Ben Ali finally addressed the nation in a televised speech on December 28, promising to respond to the protesters' demands. Thereafter, almost two weeks elapsed before he promised in a second speech on January 10, 2011, to create 300,000 jobs over the next two years while condemning the protests in the same breath as "terrorist acts" orchestrated by foreign interests. In the meantime, however, police violence increased between January 8 and 10, particularly in Kasserine, Thala, and Regueb, and resulted in the deaths of 21 protesters, according to official sources, and roughly 50, according to union and hospital sources (ICG 2011). These delayed and disconnected reactions on the part of the regime, in harsh contrast with a reality that had become visible for all to see, thanks to social media, contributed significantly to the transformation of a spontaneous and locally rooted movement into a determined national revolution.

Toward the end of December 2010, web activists from the capital began to travel to remote regions of the country to cover the events and transmit them on Facebook in the form of real-time videos. Although Al Jazeera's TV channel had only one correspondent based in the country and its Tunis office had been shut down (Lynch 2012), it could now draw on a wealth of footage from the web, which it then broadcast to Tunisian households, many of which had no Internet connection but were equipped with satellite dishes:

> I remember a video taken at somebody's funeral in Thala. People were carrying him on their shoulders and suddenly the police started shooting at them. So they were obliged to put the body on the ground and run. This was shocking because a funeral is a very sacred thing in our culture. You cannot harm somebody attending a funeral.... In another picture you could see a dead man lying on the street and beside him a packet of milk. He wasn't armed, he had just gone to buy milk. These pictures were important because until then the RCD [Rassemblement Constitutionnel Démocratique: Democratic Constitutional Rally] had been saying that police were only shooting at armed people, people trying to burn and loot. But now everybody could see that the president and the RCD were lying.[9]

One particularly unforgettable video, recorded by a medical student at the emergency ward of the Kasserine municipal hospital, showed the desperate attempts of medics to handle the flow of incoming injuries.[10]

> The Kasserine video was very graphic. You could see people had been killed, their heads blown up. There were also videos with mothers and women from Sidi Bouzid. One old woman had been beaten by the police, she was begging them: "You are our children, you have to protect us"; and they kept insulting her. Videos like this are very shocking, but that's what good about them. Because many Tunisians did not have a problem with Ben Ali. They said: "We're OK, we are not poor we have food, we have hotels, we have beaches...it's OK. Where is the problem!?" But when you show them stuff like this they radically change their point of view about the system.[11]

The results of the German Development Institute's survey strongly indicate that the Internet contributed to the emotional mobilization of Tunisian citizens by providing information about the atrocities of the regime in response to the protests (see fig. 6.1). Asked whether or not the pictures circulating on the Internet were disturbing, 57.3 percent of the survey's responders said that they "strongly agreed" that they were; 34.5 percent responded that they "agreed."

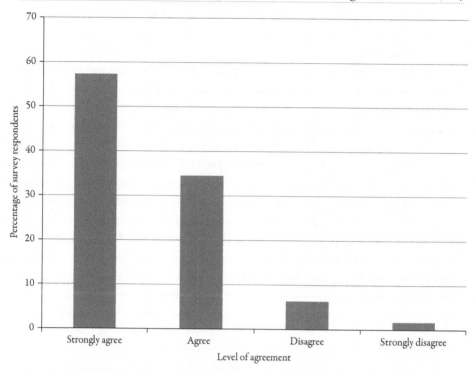

FIGURE 6.1 Results of survey of citizens' emotional response to regime repression, Tunisia: responses agreeing with the survey statement "Some of the pictures and videos circulating on the Internet during that time made me feel angry, frustrated or sad. They made me doubt the regime's legitimacy."
Source: German Development Institute web survey "Internet and Politics in Tunisia," March 1–May 31, 2012.

The Collapse of the Regime: January 12–14

During the last days of the uprising, an important function of the Internet was that it helped to overcome the inertia against collective action that is typical under authoritarian regimes. Reports about large-scale demonstrations spurred many Tunisians to overcome the fear that had previously prevented them from taking offline action. On January 12 the Union Générale Tunisienne du Travail called for a street rally in Sfax, and some 30,000 people responded—the largest demonstration before Ben Ali's fall, regarded by many observers as the revolution's point of no return: "Everyone who saw the video about the demonstration in Sfax said: if this has happened in Sfax then it can happen in Tunis. And if it happens in Tunis then it will be a success."[12] Social media not only showed the extent of previous demonstrations but also helped users to calculate the turnout of forthcoming protest events. Toward the end of December, activists increasingly began to use social media to organize further demonstrations. The event-planning feature of Facebook, which allows users to create an event online that other users can then sign up to attend, proved to be a particularly helpful tool for this purpose.

The findings of the German Development Institute's survey suggest that social media helped to overcome the free rider problem of detached sympathizers and to mobilize Internet users offline.

To begin with, the majority of users in the survey sample (79.0 percent) said they had been targeted at least once by a mobilization attempt carried out via the Internet. Equally important, many respondents (75.7 percent) reported having learned through the Internet that a protest event in their hometown would be attended by a large number of fellow citizens (fig. 6.2). Fully 80.5 percent of the respondents simply or strongly agreed that their belief that the protest movement would bring down the Ben Ali government came from what they had learned on the Internet. And although the majority simply or even strongly agreed that participation in a protest event was a risky endeavor in terms of their personal security (81.3 percent), 72.4 percent participated in street protests once or repeatedly.

In his last televised speech on January 13, Ben Ali announced that he would abstain from running as a presidential candidate in 2014 and offered to call for early parliamentary elections. It was too little, too late. According to Schraeder and Redissi (2011), students and young people under 30 in particular were reluctant to grant the regime a four-year reprieve during which it might craft the conditions for a transition. Many of them under-

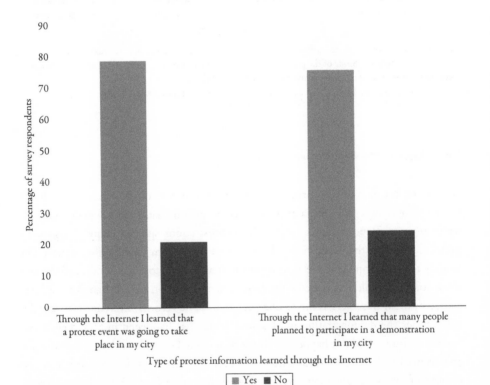

FIGURE 6.2 Results of survey of citizens' awareness of upcoming protest events and expected event turnouts in Tunisia.

Source: German Development Institute web survey "Internet and Politics in Tunisia," March 1–May 31, 2012.

stood the mass demonstrations scheduled for January 14 in the center of Tunis as a unique opportunity for their generation to break with a tradition of quiescent obedience; they regarded participation in these protests as a patriotic duty. Our survey results reflect this notion: 96.4 percent of respondents agreed or strongly agreed with the statement "What I learnt about the protest movement on the Internet filled me with hope and made me feel proud to be Tunisian," and 93.3 percent agreed or strongly agreed with the statement "I felt that, being Tunisian, I had to support the people protesting in the streets."

It also appears that social media were a crucial element in the politicization and mobilization of the young urban middle class and elites. Nadia Zouari, a Tunis-based plastic artist and feuilletonist, remembers the final days leading up to the regime's fall as follows: "During this period we spent white nights in front of the computer. Facebook connected us to the things that were going on, and it felt like we were living in a different country. Because in Tunis you could lead a normal life. But in Sidi Bouzid, Kasserine, and Kef it was totally different. And when we saw what was happening to people there we decided that we had to show solidarity with them."[13] Blogger Yassine Ayari has argued similarly:

> The first people to protest were the poor people in the street and the bloggers online. These are two groups that have nothing in common....But to put the middle class in the street you needed really strong things for them to see and feel what was happening. Because the middle class is selfish. They have their own concerns: they have their loans to pay and their consume [*sic*] problems. And there was no other way to touch them than through social media....So as the revolution progressed, middle-class people started to get interested. And in the end all of these groups overlapped....I strongly believe that if the revolution succeeded and spread it was because for the first time the middle class had an interest in this.[14]

Religious political actors seem to share this interpretation of the Internet's role. In an interview by the International Crisis Group, a member of the moderate Islamist party Ennahda stated: "The Internet caused the failure, to all of our surprise, of the regime's project of creating a consumerist and apolitical middle class."[15] It thus appears that another important role of Facebook and social media was to span a bridge between hitherto unrelated socioeconomic groups, thus providing the basis for intergroup collaboration that facilitated a large cycle of protest to develop.

On January 14, confronted with the largest antigovernment demonstration that Tunis had ever seen, Ben Ali and his family fled the country on a plane to Dubai.

Conclusions

A surprising element of the Tunisian uprising was its broad, cross-class support. As has been demonstrated, the Internet and social media significantly contributed by transcending geographical and socioeconomic boundaries and facilitating collaboration among the alienated intellectual elite, the rural poor, and the urban middle class. It thus helped to remove one of the central obstacles of collective action under authoritarianism: the lack of social interaction. The ways the Internet and social media contributed to this inter-group collaboration confirm various aspects of the different theoretical views of protest mobilization and can be summarized in three main categories.

Network Formation

During the preparatory phase from 1998 to 2010, the Internet facilitated the formation of personal networks of digital activists who challenged the regime's control of the public sphere and offered an alternative discourse to the official political narrative. In line with the arguments of resource mobilization theory, the Internet thus provided the resource of a partially uncontrolled space that undermined the regime's strategy of social isolation and fostered solidarity among Tunisians based on their shared feelings of repression. While the most proactive actors of this digital network typically came from the socioeconomic and cultural elite, the relatively high degree of Tunisia's ICT infrastructure development made their dissident discourse accessible to a larger portion of Tunisian society.

Information Transmission

During the ignition phase of the first two weeks following the self-immolation of Mohammed Bouazizi on December 17, 2011, social media allowed a digital elite of bloggers to circumvent the national media blackout by brokering information to the international mainstream media, most notably Al Jazeera. The breakdown of censorship barriers enabled Tunisians both with and without Internet access to mobilize collective action around the material and moral grievances symbolically represented by Bouazizi's fate. The nationwide availability of this information significantly contributed to the movement's geographical and social expansion. During the escalation phase, from late December to early January, the Internet became increasingly important as a conduit for information about the extent of the protests, which the state-controlled media tried desperately to conceal. By informing the public about the magnitude of past protest events and helping to calculate the extent of upcoming events, social media helped Tunisian citizens to overcome the "barrier of fear" associated with protest under authoritarianism. The function of the Internet as an information hub in the Tunisian case thus supports arguments of both relative deprivation and rational choice theories regarding protest mobilization.

Collective Identity Formation

Toward the final days of the revolution, social networking sites played an important role in politicizing the urban middle class. This supports the arguments brought forward by structural and networking accounts of collective action according to which overlapping membership in several networks leads to a spillover of information from activist networks to networks of less engaged citizens. It also illustrates the important function of social networks in building a collective identity supportive of protest action. By depicting the worst atrocities associated with the regime's response to the protests, social media led to the emotional mobilization of hitherto politically apathetic segments of Tunisian society. The Internet thus helped to connect impoverished rural street protesters, socioeconomically and culturally privileged and highly motivated digital activists, and the young urban middle class in the large cycle of protest that led to the final collapse of the Ben Ali regime on January 14, 2011.

REFERENCES

Aday, S., H. Farrell, M. Lynch, J. Sides, J. Kelly, and E. Zuckerman, eds. 2010. *Blogs and bullets: New media in contentious politics.* Peaceworks. Washington, DC: United States Institute of Peace.

Chomiak, L. 2011. The making of a revolution in Tunisia. Middle East Law and Governance 3: 68–83.

Coleman, J. 1988. Social capital in the creation of human capital. American Journal of Sociology 94: 95–120.

Dalton, R. J., and A. van Sickle. 2005. The resource, structural, and cultural bases of protest. Center for the Study of Democracy working paper. Irvine, CA: Center for the Study of Democracy, University of California, Irvine.

Dubai School of Government (DSG). 2011. Facebook usage: Factors and analysis. In *Arab social media report,* 1(1): 1–20. Dubai: Dubai School of Government.

Friedman, D., and D. McAdam. 1992. Collective identity and activism: Networks, choices and the life of a social movement. In Frontiers in social movement theory, ed. Aldo D. Morris and Carol McClurg Mueller, 156–172. New Haven, CT: Yale University Press.

Gharbia, Sami Ben. 2010, May 29. Anti-censorship movement in Tunisia: Creativity, courage and hope! Blog entry. http://nawaat.org/portail/2010/05/29/anti-censorship-movement-in -tunisia-creativity-courage-and-hope/.

Goldstein, E. 2011, January 18. A middle-class revolution. *Foreign Policy.* http://www.foreignpolicy .com/articles/2011/01/18/a_middle_class_revolution?hidecomments=yes.

Granovetter, M. 1978. Threshold models of collective behavior. American Journal of Sociology 83: 1420–1443.

Greenwood, S. 2008. Bad for business? Entrepreneurs and democracy in the Arab world. Comparative Politics 41(6): 837–860.

Gurr, T. R. 1970. Why men rebel. Princeton, NJ: Princeton University Press.

Hendrix, C., S. Haggard, and B. Magaloni. 2009, February 15– Grievance and opportunity: Food prices, political regime, and protest. Paper presented at the annual convention of the International Studies Association, New York.

Howard, P. N. 2011. The digital origins of dictatorship and democracy: Information technology and political Islam. Oxford: Oxford University Press.

Howard, P. N., and M. M. Hussain. 2011. The role of digital media. Journal of Democracy 22(3): 35–48.

International Crisis Group (ICG). 2011. Popular protest in North Africa and the Middle East (IV): Tunisia's way. Middle East/North Africa report no. 106. http://www.crisisgroup.org/en/regions/middle-east-north-africa/north-africa/tunisia/106-popular-protests-in-north-africa-and-the-middle-east-iv-tunisias-way.aspx.

International Telecommunication Union (ITU). 2001. World Summit on the Information Society. Geneva 2003–Tunis 2005. Geneva: International Telecommunication Union.

Kuebler, J. 2011. Overcoming the digital divide: The internet and political mobilization in Egypt and Tunisia. *CyberOrient* 5(1) http://www.cyberorient.net/article.do?articleId=6212.

Lynch, M. 2012. The Arab uprising: The unfinished revolutions of the new Middle East. New York: Public Affairs.

Muller, E. N., and T. O. Jukam. 1983. Discontent and aggressive political participation. British Journal of Political Science 13: 159–179.

Norris, P. 2001. Digital divide: Civic engagement, information poverty, and the internet worldwide. Cambridge: Cambridge University Press.

Olson, M. 1965. The logic of collective action: Public goods and the theory of groups. Cambridge, MA: Harvard University Press.

OpenNet Initiative (OI). 2009. Internet filtering in Tunisia, 2005. A country study. https://opennet.net/sites/opennet.net/files/ONI_Tunisia_Country_Study.pdf.

Patel, D., and V. Bunce. 2012, February 29. Turning Points and the Cross-national Diffusion of Popular Protest. Reprinted in J. Tucker, Cross-national diffusion of protest (blog entry), http://themonkeycage.org/blog/2012/02/29/cross-national-diffusion-of-protest/.

Pollock, J. 2011, August 23. Streetbook: How Egyptian and Tunisian youth hacked the Arab Spring. *MIT Technology Review* 114(5): 70–82.

Putnam, R. D. 2000. Bowling alone: The collapse and revival of American community. New York: Simon and Schuster.

Reporters Without Borders. 2004. Internet under surveillance 2004—Tunisia. Geneva: UNHCR.

Saidani, M. 2012. Revolution and counterrevolution in Tunisia: The forty days that shook the country. *boundary 2* 39: 43–54.

Schraeder, P. J., and H. Redissi. 2011. Ben Ali's fall. Journal of Democracy 22(3): 5–18.

Solimano, A. 2009. Stylized facts on the middle class and the development process. In Stuck in the middle: Is fiscal policy failing the middle class?, edited by Antonio Estache and Danny Leipziger, 24–53. Washington, DC: Brookings Institution.

Tilly, C. 2004. Social movements, 1768–2004. Boulder, CO: Paradigm.

Tullock, G. 1971. The paradox of revolution. Public Choice 11: 89–99.

Tunisian protests fueled by social media networks. 2011, January 12. CNN World. http://articles.cnn.com/2011-01-12/world/tunisia_1_protests-twitter-and-facebook-tunisian-government?_s=PM:WORLD.

Tunisie 2015. 2015. Country note. http://www.africaneconomicoutlook.org/en/country-notes/north-africa/tunisia/.

van Laer, J. 2011. Why people protest. Doctoral thesis. Universiteit Antwerpen.

Zuckermann, Ethan. 2011, September 22. Ben Ali and Bart: Understanding participatory media and protest. Video presentation at the international online conference "Facebook Revolutions? The Role of Social Media for Political Change in the Arab World," hosted by the Online Academy of the Friedrich Naumann Foundation. http://www.youtube.com/watch?v=Fzh1Trc-B7o.

NOTES

1. A good example is the Pacte Jeunesse, launched by the ruling party, Rassemblement Constitutionnel Démocratique (RCD), in 2008, which Ben Ali lauded as "a celebration of young people's independence" and an invitation for them to assume conscious responsibility in shaping the country's future job market by entering into a dialogue with the government and "expressing their concerns in freedom.

2. Yassine Ayari, interview conducted in Tunis, October 18, 2011.

3. *Takriz* is a Tunisian slang expression, roughly equivalent to "Bollocks" or "Don't break my balls."

4. See the website of Middle East Partnership Initiative, http://mepi.state.gov/.

5. Translation was essential, given that many Tunisian users post in Derya, the Tunisian dialect. In addition, young Tunisian Internet users, as elsewhere in the world, have developed their own particular argot and abbreviations. The resulting mixture is barely comprehendible to non-Tunisian Arabic speakers.

6. Yassine Ayari, blogger and cyberactivist, interview conducted in Tunis, October 18, 2011.

7. See for instance the "Tunisian Revolution Archive" on the YouTube channel of the blogger collective Nawaat: https://www.youtube.com/playlist?list=PLu9NNXunTgMOxAI52pb8PXI NCfRFRUc4n; and the synopsis of social media contributions on the Tunisian revolution the website of the international blogger collective Global Voices: https://globalvoices.org/specialcoverage/2011-special-coverage/tunisia-uprising-201011/.

8. Riots reported in Tunisian city, *Al Jazeera*, December 20, 2010, tp://www.aljazeera.com/news/africa/2010/12/2010122063745828931.html.

9. Yassine Ayari interview.

10. The video shows a scene from a Kasserine municipal hospital treating multiple victims during the time of deadly clashes between the protestors and local police between January 8 and 11. The video shows several grisly images of the carnage from the clashes, including multiple victims. Much of the video focuses on one young man who has suffered severe head injuries after being shot multiple times. "Warning Graphic Kasserine Tunisia Evidence of Civilian Massacre 10 01 2011," uploaded by YouTube user "cuervolegal" on January 11, 2011. https://www.youtube.com/watch?v=bwyHRC6nH8c.

11. Haythem El Mekki, blogger and political commentator on TV channel El Watanayah, interview conducted in Tunis, October 17, 2011.

12. Sara Ben Hamadi, blogger for Arte TV, interview conducted in Tunis, October 19, 2011.

13. Nadia Zouari, interview conducted in Tunis, October 17, 2011.

14. Yassine Ayari interview.

15. Nourredine al-Beheiri, An-Nahda organizer, interview conducted by the International Crisis Group in Tunis, January 24, 2011.

7   The Political Effects of Changing Public Opinion in Egypt
A STORY OF REVOLUTION
Ishac Diwan

SINCE THE EVENTS of the Arab Spring unfolded across North Africa, Syria, and Yemen, much debate and discussion has focused on the social drivers behind these uprisings. Further, as political dynamics in these countries had been defined by the status quo for decades, these events came as a shock to many observers—no other major event seems to have shifted so dramatically the nature of preexisting relations between governments and governed. Thus, one is left asking, what change has caused the uprisings? Toward answering this question, this chapter turns to the experience of Egypt. In the end, I assert that it was the political perspectives of the Egyptian people, not a dramatic event, that eventually broke the country's social contract and thus paved the way for revolution. Further, I argue that changes in these perspectives were manifested differently across various subgroups of the country's population, a development that facilitated two paths to democratic change. Egypt's middle class and youth embodied the convergence of these paths, thus becoming important influencers of their country's revolution.

While there has been a wealth of literature focusing on the "third wave" of democratization in other regions, little theoretical focus has been centered on political change in the Middle East. Instead, political dynamics in the region have been largely understood in the rentier state model (Beblawi and Luciani 1987), wherein citizens surrender political rights in exchange for economic security (Desai, Olofsgård, and Yousef 2009). Further, and at the expense of expanding understanding of how political dynamics may shift in this system, relevant academic research has focused more on the various ways regimes have maintained power than on how citizens influence the political process. Thus, the political upheavals of 2011 have highlighted an intellectual gap regarding political change in the region.

As no dramatic development seems to have changed the dynamics of the aforementioned autocratic (or social) contract—there was no major cut in subsidies, reduction in economic growth, or sudden increase in unemployment before the uprising—a push for change must have come from somewhere else. It seems likely that the social contract was broken slowly, with people's relative preferences between the status quo and an alternative political structure changing gradually over time, reaching a breaking point in 2011.

Perhaps the most logical drivers for changing Egypt's political system were those most disadvantaged by its application. From this perspective, theories of distributional motive, in which revolutions reflect structural conflicts between various parts of society over income distribution, are particularly relevant. In game theoretic models of distributional motives (see Acemoglu and Robinson 2006; Boix 2003; Przeworski 2009), poorer segments of a population are shown to favor taxation and redistribution, which the rich generally oppose. As a result, there is an incentive for the rich elite to govern in an autocratic way and for the poorer segment to attempt to take over and form a democracy, where the median voter determines policy.

While, admittedly, there is no direct evidence on the basis of distribution data that inequality has risen sharply in the recent past in Egypt (Bibi and Nabli 2010), there is reason to believe that many people had been disaffected by the country's governance.[1] Importantly, while the elite, and especially the military, worked to maintain the status quo, relying heavily on the country's growing middle class to provide a *legitimizing* coalition, the poor were largely denied economic advantages and were severely repressed (Richards et al. 2013). In addition, recent work by Belhaj (2012) and Chekir and Diwan (2015) suggests sharp increases in inequality of opportunity in education and in the labor market in Egypt, as well as rising cronyism. For their part, Egypt's middle class may have become increasingly disaffected with the governing contract[2]; there are indications that the economic liberalization of the 1990s, and especially its acceleration in the 2000s, took a toll on the economic well-being of this group.[3]

Adherents to political Islam, a group that has formed opposition to the country's military rule for decades, had also been greatly suppressed in Egypt and had much to gain from regime change (a fact evidenced by their rise to power with the election of Mohamed Morsi in 2012). Importantly, in the years before the revolution, several groups in the broad range of parties espousing political Islam moderated their messages and came to accept, at least nominally, the democratic system—in 2004, for example, the Muslim Brotherhood publicly committed to abide by a constitutional and democratic system (Shahin 2005).[4]

If it was not the strictly excluded who swayed public opinion toward political change, perhaps it was those new to the system, the country's youth, who in many ways had been unable to acquire the promises of the rentier state and had suffered its limitations. In "modernization" theories of revolution, where schooling (as well as wealth, urbanization, and industrialization) facilitates increased emancipation, which leads to an increasing interest in democracy among a population (Lipset 1959), youth are paramount. In such models, their increasing replacement of typically less educated older generations paves the way for further democratization (Tilley 2002). From this perspective, the current wave of political upheaval in the Arab world could be seen as an extension of the weakening of traditional authority, driven by education, urbanization, and economic growth, which made these societies *ready* for democracy; toward this end, youth are important agents of change.[5] Other modern values that are associated with emancipation typically include a greater preference for the private sector and competition, less support for redistributive policies, and more support for gender equality (Inglehart and Welzel 2010).

Indeed, indicators of human development show that "modernization" forces have made great strides over the past three decades in the Arab world as a whole. Egypt's Human Development Index rose from 0.39 in 1980 to 0.62 in 2012, faster than the average Arab country and double the average rate among Latin American countries during the same period. Average schooling rose from 7.5 years in 1980 to 11 years in 2012, faster than averages in the Arab world, Latin America, and Sub-Saharan Africa, and at the same average rate as that of East Asia (Kuhn 2012). Similarly, there has been significant improvement in Egypt on health indicators and urbanization, both of which are typically important variables in a modernization analysis.

Besides the hypotheses of modernization, distribution, and political Islam, an additional hypothesis that will be tested in this chapter is that political circumstances matter in shaping the political demands of various groups, that is, that there is a certain element of strategizing in their choices. In particular, three ideas will be investigated. First, there is reason to believe that as Islamist parties moderated their platforms, those in the middle class may have become more willing to turn any dissatisfaction into political action—in other words, it is possible that democratization was delayed in many countries of the Arab world because political Islam scared the largely secularist middle class into a "coalition of fear" with autocrats. Second, to the extent that richer and more educated individuals would fear that the ballot box would lead to governments that would implement policies that they dislike, such as income redistribution, this may neutralize their modern impulse to support democratic values. Third, one can expect circumstantial effects among the poor as well. Poor and uneducated individuals are affected by two opposite forces: by their economic interests toward redistribution and democracy and by their low levels of political emancipation toward a lack of interest in supporting political change. It may be that the political evolution of the Muslim Brotherhood has increased their interest in politics, encouraging them to participate more in the political life in order to further their economic interests.

Methods

If public opinion changed in ways that would suggest its strong influence on Egypt's 2011 revolution, one should be able to find such changes reflected in public opinion data. This is not to say that revolutions and uprisings are necessarily *caused* by changes in public opinion; such data, however, help measure the shifting political dynamics that do. To identity the drivers of Egypt's push for political change, this chapter studies the evolution of Egyptian public opinion as measured by the fourth and fifth waves of the World Values Survey (WVS). Further, to discern among which cross-sections of Egyptian society such changes were most pronounced, a set of variables are generated from the WVS data that relate to age, class, and level of education, as well as those that measure opinions regarding democracy (democracy versus order), redistributive economic policy (a rightist/leftist political economy dimension), and the role of religion in politics (secularist/Islamist orientation).[6]

As described on the WVS website, the WVS, using a common questionnaire, has organized "the largest non-commercial, cross-national, time series investigation of human beliefs and values" in the world. The survey covers nearly 100 countries, "almost 90 percent of the world's population," and just under 400,000 people.[7] The fourth and fifth waves of the survey, the ones used for this analysis, were collected in 2000, roughly a decade before the Arab Spring, and in 2008, only a few years before its advent and on the eve of the international financial crisis, respectively.[8] While the sixth wave of the WVS was collected closer to the outbreak of uprisings in Egypt (2012), its analytical import may be greatly affected by the political chaos that followed the uprisings and thus less instructive of the trends that led to them. As such, it is not included in this analysis.

As Beck and Dyer (chapter 1 here) show, the changing of the region's age structures has manifested significant policy challenges and opportunities throughout the region—a fact as true for Egypt as it has been for the wider region. In this context, youth have been important actors in the region's changing political dynamics. For this chapter, however, youth will be analyzed as one of many age groups, all of which importantly affect changing public opinion in some way. Organized by age, the respondents are divided into three broad categories. To start, those respondents aged 15–29 are labeled "youth," a designation shared throughout much of this book. In turn, those aged 30–59 are characterized as "adult," and those aged 60 years and above as "elderly." Between 2000 and 2008, the age shares of the sample population shifted, with the weight of the population aging. In 2000, the sample group consisted of 34 percent youth, 55 percent adult, and 11 percent elderly. By 2008, those shares had shifted to 25 percent, 62 percent, and 14 percent, respectively.[9]

To discern "class" among respondents, a WVS survey question asks respondents to indicate the class into which they self-identity (the choices being: poor, working class, middle class, upper middle class, and rich). Using these answers, the respondents are further organized into fewer groups, where those who identify as poor and working class are labeled "poor," those who identify as middle class and upper middle class as "middle class (MC)," and those who identify as rich as "rich." In the 2000 survey, 35 percent of the respondents self-identified as poor, while 65 percent and 1 percent identified as middle class and rich, respectively. In 2008, an increased 41 percent of respondents identified as poor, while 58 percent identified as middle class. The sample share of those who identified as rich remained at one percent.

The WVS divides its sample population into cohorts based on the level of education they have acquired, with groups ranging from "no schooling" to "university-level with degree." As with the class variable, WVS cohorts are reorganized into fewer groups, whereby those who have acquired some primary-level education or less are characterized as "primary," those who have attended or graduated from secondary school as "secondary," and those who have attended university as "tertiary."

Between 2000 and 2008, the educational composition of the sample groups notably shifted. (See Salehi-Isfahani, chapter 2 here, for an overview of expanding educational attainment across the region.) In 2000, for instance, the majority of the sample group (51 percent) had acquired no more than a primary education. The shares of those who had acquired secondary and tertiary levels were 38 percent and 11 percent, respectively. By 2008, however, the share of those characterized in the primary level had declined to 48 percent; in addition, that of secondary had declined to 34 percent, while that of tertiary had increased to 18 percent.

To measure opinions about democracy, a variable labeled "Preference for Democracy" (PfD) is constructed from responses to a question where respondents are asked to choose their first and second preferences from a list of four options that include "giving people more say in politics," "protecting freedom of speech," "maintaining order in the nation," and "fighting rising prices." A person is coded as preferring democracy when either of the two first choices is ranked higher than the third.[10] Having respondents chose from a restricted set is useful in that it controls for the fact that in unconstrained survey questions that simply ask whether or not one likes democracy, people tend to show overwhelming support for the former, a development that limits the analytical import of the data.

To better understand whether any increase in favorability for democracy is related to an interest in more economic equality, a variable to measure "Preference for Equality" (PfE) is created. This variable is important, because while one may see changes among the Egyptian population with regard to democracy, one is left with additional questions. For example, does a shift toward democracy signify an interest in the ability to influence income redistribution, does it change regardless of economic considerations, or is there some other relationship involved? "Preference for Equality" is constructed from a survey question that asks respondents to rank (on a scale of 1 to 10) whether "incomes should be made more equal" (high score) or whether "we need larger income differences as incentives for individual efforts" (low score).[11] Toward better understanding respondents' (possible) opinions regarding political Islam, this study relies on a question in which they are asked whether they believe that religious authorities provide answers to social problems.[12]

Results

With the analytical framework now explained, this chapter turns to the question of how public opinion in Egypt is manifested, and changed between 2000 and 2008, and how those changes may have affected the country's path to revolution. As all of the aforementioned theories of change rest on the assumption that there was, in fact, an increase in support for democracy from 2000 to 2008, the PfD variable is perhaps the most important for this analysis. As such, it is here where the analysis will begin. From 2000 to 2008, there was a remarkable increase in respondents' PfD, with the variable jumping from 24 percent to 52 percent over that time. Interestingly, this trend distinguishes Egypt significantly from other countries of the Middle East and North Africa measured by WVS. In Morocco and Iran, for example, 36 percent in both Iran and Morocco indicated support for democracy in 2000, notably higher than that shown in Egypt that year. At 26 percent, the share of those who supported democracy in Jordan that year was only slightly higher than that of Egypt. Interestingly, however, as support for democracy increased dramatically from 2000 to 2008 in Egypt, it increased only marginally in Iran, Morocco, and Jordan (to 40 percent, 37 percent, and 28 percent, respectively). These figures suggest that the uprising in Egypt does seem to represent a deep social wave that is specific to that country. While many other countries rate "order" ahead of "democracy" in ways similar to Egypt in 2000, such preferences generally remain consistent over time.[13] There may be many reasons for these changes in Egypt. Some could have been related to preferences for order, such as concerns about extremism that were more worrisome to the population in 2000. In addition, circumstances such as the presidential election that was to be held in 2011 (and fear of the constitution of a Mubarak/crony capitalist dynasty) may have played a role in the increased rejection of "order" by 2008 by a large share of the population. However, other reasons may run deeper, related to longer term social trends such as economic inequality, the rise of education among the youth, or the transformations in political Islam.

Examing figure 1, it is apparent that the rising support for democracy in Egypt is at least partially a class phenomenon. In particular, there is rising support for democracy among the poor and middle class but declining support among the rich. Interestingly, the middle class seems to have broadly switched from supporting autocracy in 2000 (with 75 percent of the middle class ranking "maintaining order" above "protecting freedom of speech" and "giving people more say") to supporting democracy in 2008 (with 55 percent ranking one of the other two alternatives above "maintaining order"). Among the poor, PfD increased from 22 percent in 2000 to 47 percent in 2008, while among the rich it decreased from 44 percent in 2000 to 31 percent in 2008.

With regard to age, youth were much more likely than their elders to support democracy in 2000. A third of young people indicated as much (34 percent) that year, while in contrast, only 18 percent of adults and 20 percent of the elderly indicated the same. Interestingly, by 2008, the PfD age disparity had largely evaporated, with youth and adults holding similarly favorable views toward democracy, both at 53 percent. Elderly support for democracy also increased during that time, reaching 48 percent in 2008.

Turning to PfE, it is clear that there was a large increase in support for equality between 2000 and 2008, with the variable increasing from 23 percent to 53 percent over that

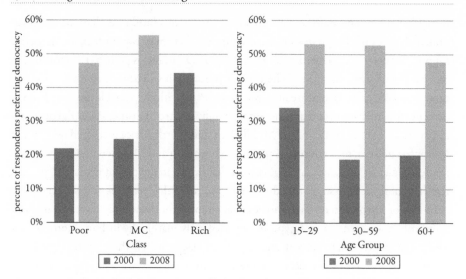

FIGURE 7.1 Preference for democracy by class (left) and age (right), Egypt, 2000 and 2008.
Source: World Values Survey, fourth and fifth rounds, author's calculations.

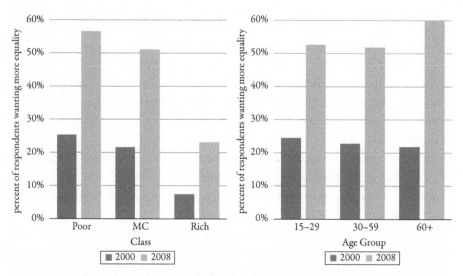

FIGURE 7.2 Preference for equality by class (left) and age (right), Egypt, 2000 and 2008.
Source: World Values Survey, fourth and fifth rounds, author's calculations.

period (see fig. 7.2). Similarly to changing PfD, this shift had a strong class correlation, with PfE strongest among the poor, followed by the middle class, and then, in turn, by the rich. This remained true in both 2000 and 2008. Despite these differences however, between 2000 and 2008, preference for equality increased among all three classes. In 2000, 26 percent of the poor, 22 percent of the middle class, and 7 percent of the rich preferred equality, while by 2008, those shares had changed to 57 percent among the poor, 51 percent among the middle class, and 23 percent among the rich.

In contrast to the effect of class, it is clear that age had little effect in influencing PfE (see fig. 7.2). Rather, preferences for equality increased among all age groups in a fairly consistent manner. In 2000, 25 percent of youth, 23 percent of adults, and 22 percent of the elderly preferred equality as opposed to inequality. By 2008, these shares had increased, reaching 53 percent, 52 percent, and a notably high 60 percent, respectively.

The popularity of political Islam seems to have declined from 2000 to 2008, although it retained majority favorability in both years. In 2000, 83 percent of respondents indicated a favorable opinion toward political Islam (in that they answered that religious leaders had solutions to social problems). By 2008, that share had decreased (albeit still a majority) to 60 percent.

Importantly, there was a strong class correlation to this shift, with the decrease in support for political Islam concentrated among the poor, where it fell from 81 percent in 2000 to 55 percent in 2008 (see fig. 7.3). Likewise, there was a fall in support for political Islam in the middle class. In contrast, support for political Islam remained relatively high among the rich in both 2000 and 2008, a surprising trend, given that education, which generally goes up with class, is usually correlated with a fall in religiosity. In 2000, 84 percent of the middle class and 85 percent of the rich supported political Islam. By 2008, those shares had declined to 62 percent and 78 percent, respectively. Thus, the decline in the middle class was 12 points, not that different than the 16-point decline for the poor. The only outlier was the rich, who saw only a four-point decline.

Similar to the changes in the preference for equality, there was not much of an age dimension to the decline in support for political Islam. In 2000, the youth were the least supportive of political Islam with 81 percent agreeing that religious authorities have

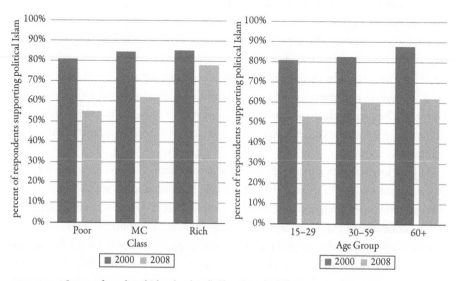

FIGURE 7.3 Support for political Islam by class (left) and age (right), Egypt, 2000 and 2008.
Source: World Values Survey, fourth and fifth rounds, author's calculations.

solutions to social problems, followed by adults and elderly with 83 percent and 88 percent, respectively. In 2008, all groups saw an approximate 25 percentage point decline in this variable. Youth support for political Islam fell to 53 percent, indicating a 28-point drop in support. However, this was not that dissimilar to what happened for adults (23-point decline to 60 percent) or for the elderly (26-point decline to 62 percent). Thus, while there appears to be some class component to the decline in support for political Islam, all age groups decreased their support (though it was still a majority of respondents) between the two waves of the survey.

Finding Meaning in the Data

As evidenced thus far, it is clear that public opinions greatly shifted in the decade preceding the 2011 Egyptian revolution. Moving forward, and framing the question in the theories of democratization introduced above, this chapter asks, what might these changes have meant for the eventual manifestation of that event?

To start, the rising support for democracy evidenced above is a necessary foundation for modernization theories of democratization. Importantly, though, it is not a sufficient one. One must also see intergenerational differences in opinions related to democracy, other modern values, and changing opinions about the role of the state in building opportunities for its citizens—generally, as modernization takes hold, individual agency, as opposed to reliance on the state, is increasingly viewed as the best path to opportunity.

In support of a modernization narrative, this chapter finds that higher levels of education are correlated with increased support for democracy. In 2000, among those Egyptians with a primary level of schooling or less, only 21 percent supported democracy. In contrast, 27 percent of those with a secondary level and 31 percent with a university level indicated the same. Further, the impact of education on PfD seems to have grown by 2008, a possible result, in part, of the Internet revolution, which increasingly allowed educated, or at least literate, individuals to more easily access large amounts of information. That year, 48 percent of those who had acquired some level of primary education, 55 percent of those who had reached a secondary level, and 57 percent of those with some university experience preferred democracy to autocracy—all notable increases from those recorded in 2000.

Higher levels of education tend to be closely correlated with age, reflecting the rapid rise in education attainments in the past decade. Education levels are also correlated in the data with other modern values, such as a preference for private over public ownership, more confidence in major private sector companies, more support for market competition and less support for income redistribution, and more support for gender equality (results not shown). As evidenced above, opinions regarding democracy also featured important age trends, with youth generally supporting democracy in higher shares than their elders. Further, the fact that the gap between youth and adult opinions was largely closed by 2008 does not necessarily challenge a modernization narrative; if anything, it might even support it—youth opinions may have influenced those of their parents. The common closeness of Arab families, as recognized by Alexander and Welzel (2011), further underscores this possibility.

Taken together, Egypt's rising support for democracy from 2000 to 2008, and its correlation with pertinent variables related to education and age, builds a plausible story of modernization-driven change.[14] Until one analyzes other contemporary trends, however, such as those related to equality and political Islam, one cannot say with more certainly how important these narratives are to understanding the causes of Egypt's 2011 revolution compared to competing narratives.

As noted earlier, the main implication of a distributional theory of democratization is that public opinion increasingly leans toward democracy as opinions shift in favor of redistributive policy—redistribution is the goal; democracy the tool. Further, shifting opinions would be formed along class lines. Importantly, from 2000 to 2008, this appears to be exactly what happened, with inclinations toward democracy strongest among the poor and weakest among the rich. As evidenced above, these trends differ from those related to age, with support for more equality increasing among all three age groups in a fairly consistent manner.

With the evidence considered, it seems clear that distributional motives played an important role in bringing Egypt closer to revolution. As such, a distributional narrative of political change must be added, or at least reconciled, to the story of modernization-driven democratization illustrated above. With that said, however, it is important to discern to which of these two paths of change carried the most weight in moving the Egyptian population closer to revolution. In short, from which sections of Egyptian society did the country's new supporters of a democratic order predominantly originate? Discerning these dynamics entails analyzing Egypt's changing public opinion between 2000 and 2008 against the changing composition of the country's population between those same years.[15]

Table 7.1 shows the distribution of all of those in the 2000 and 2008 survey who supported democracy over autocracy. Each cell in the table represents the proportion of the overall population who are "democrats" (were coded as preferring democracy over autocracy, as described in note 10) from that particular cell. For example, in the top panel, which shows the distribution of "democrats" by their level of PfE and class, the cell labeled "poor" on the column and "right" on the row shows that 5.6 percent of the people who preferred democracy did not prefer equality (thus "right") and were self-described as "poor." Notice the very small numbers in the "rich" category. Since the rich are 0.9 percent of the overall population, the highest value that any cell in the "rich" column can be is 0.9, even if everyone were a "democrat." Thus, more than in figures 7.1 and 7.2, table 7.1 allows to control for the size of these groups when analyzing the shift in attitudes.

The weight of changing opinion seems to have occurred on the redistribution rather than the modernization side; that is, a large share of the increased support for democracy

TABLE 7.1

Sources of the change in the number of "democrats" (share of total population), Egypt, 2000–2008.

Panel A: Preference for equality and class

	2000					2008					Change 2000–2008			
	Poor	MC	Rich	Total		Poor	MC	Rich	Total		Poor	MC	Rich	Total
Right	5.6	12.2	0.3	18.2	Right	8.9	15.8	0.2	24.9	Right	3.3	3.6	−0.2	6.7
Left	2.0	3.8	0.1	5.8	Left	10.5	16.7	0.1	27.3	Left	8.5	12.9	0.0	21.5
Total	7.6	16.0	0.4	24.0	Total	19.4	32.5	0.3	52.2	Total	11.8	16.5	−0.1	28.2

Panel B: Preference for equality and age

	2000					2008					Change 2000–2008			
	Youth	Adult	Elderly	Total		Youth	Adult	Elderly	Total		Youth	Adult	Elderly	Total
Right	8.4	7.8	1.9	18.1	Right	6.7	15.4	2.9	24.9	Right	−1.8	7.6	1.0	6.8
Left	3.2	2.5	0.4	6.1	Left	6.5	17.1	3.6	27.3	Left	3.4	14.6	3.2	21.2
Total	11.6	10.3	2.3	24.2	Total	13.2	32.5	6.4	52.2	Total	1.6	22.2	4.2	28.0

Source: World Values Survey, fourth and fifth rounds, author's calculations.

was due to a shift to the left. As shown in panel A of table 7.1, of the 28.2 point increase in support for democracy in the World Value Survey data (PfD moving from 24.0 percent of the population in 2000 to 52.2 percent in 2008), 21.5 points of it (or three-quarters of the total change) came from individuals moving toward the left. In 2000, only one-quarter of all the "democrats" came from the left (5.8 of 24.0). By 2008, a bit more than 50 percent of all those who supported democracy also supported equality (27.3 of 52.2).

But while the surge to the left seems to have provided a big push to the support for democracy, the forces of modernization were more persistent and gradual—in 2000, the modernizers that supported democracy on the right represented already 18.2 percent of the population, and their numbers continued to rise to become 24.9 percent of the population in 2008. Thus, both modernization and redistribution played an approximately equal role in making democracy the majority view, the first through a slow and steady process and the second in a surge that paralleled a surge in the perception of income inequality, between 2000 and 2008.

In this transformation of public opinion, the middle class played a central role. Of the 52.2 percent of the population who supported democracy in 2008, 32.5 percentage points come from the middle class and 19.4 percent from the poor. Moreover, of the 28.2-point increase in popular support for democracy, 16.5 points come from the middle class and 11.8 points from the poor. The reason for the leadership role of the middle class in the rise of the demand for democracy seems to be that it participates strongly in both modernist and distributional channels. The poor on the other hand participate less in the first modernization channel because they tend to be less educated. But they also participated less in the second distributional channel as well, even though their demand for redistribution was the highest among the population, for the various reasons the poor tend to be less involved in politics.

When the same exercise is conducted looking at the source of "new democrats" by right/left orientation and age group, one sees the relative importance of the shift of the population aged 30–59 (adults). In this panel, the change in the proportion of the total population who are adults who are prodemocracy makes up 80 percent of the total shift by age group. While nearly half of the "democrats" in 2000 were made up of the youth, by 2008 only a quarter of the total "democrats" were youth and 60 percent of the "democrats" were adults, as the adults shifted their views and began to adopt values that only youth championed earlier on, in 2000. This suggests that the revolution was not driven by the particular interests of the youth, a theme that is explored further by Desai, Olofsgård, and Yousef in chapter 8.

Importantly, when data regarding political Islam are incorporated into this analysis, it is clear that political Islam seems to have supported, rather than catalyzed, the Egypt's shift toward democratic change, with Islam serving primarily as a vehicle for change rather than as a cause for it.[16] This is consistent with Tessler et al (2012) findings that Egyptians who espoused the values of political Islam in the 2000s tended to favor democracy as much as the rest of Egyptians.

Indeed, this study finds that in 2008, both secularists and Islamists had similar propensities to support democracy. (Moreover, that preference for political Islam seems to vary little by class and by age.)

Nevertheless, it is useful to note that the composition of the Islamic group changed between the two periods. In 2000, 62.3 percent of the population supported both autocracy and political Islam, but this group shrank to 28.6 percent in 2008 (see table 7.2). It is as if the acceptance by the Muslim Brotherhood in 2004 of the democratic rules of the game forced citizens to choose new political orientations. Two major social transformations are apparent in the recomposition of the political field: a move toward secularism (an increase of 22.6 percent of the population) and a move towards democracy (an increase of 26.6 percent). As a result, the religious "autocrats" of 2000 were mainly replaced by Islamist and secular "democrats" in 2008—indeed, while new "democrats" come mostly from secular backgrounds (an increase of 15.4 points), a large proportion come from political Islam backgrounds (an increase of 11.2 points).

We are left with the hypotheses regarding strategic interactive effects. To test these hypotheses, it is necessary to look at the PfD among various subgroups in a more disaggregated manner (see table 7.3).

First, did the fear of redistribution affect the PfD of particular groups, especially given the large shift to the left that occurred between 2000 and 2008? The proportion of "democrats" among the right is as high as that among the population, at about 53 percent, suggesting that there was no major pushback on this account. Nevertheless, the collapse in the PfD among the rich suggests that the rich did change their levels of support in light of the looming threat of redistribution—but being a small group, this hardly affected the aggregate figures. More important, the support for democracy rose equally among the middle class on the left and on the right, suggesting that unlike the rich, they did not have a fear of redistribution that was strong enough to overcome their modernization ideals.

Second, how about the fear of political Islam—did it affect the political choices of some groups? Here, it is necessary to look at the support for democracy among secular groups. It might well be that their support for democracy was low in 2000 because of fear of political Islam (while it was low among Islamists because the Muslim Brotherhood did not support the electoral process then). The rise of the support for democracy in 2008 to around 53.percent, which is around the national average, suggests that this fear was largely gone by 2008.

Third, what can be said about the impact of the greater involvement of the Muslim Brotherhood in politics and the willingness of the poor to support democracy? Table 7.3 indicates that the negative effect of political Islam on the support for democracy was stronger in 2000 than in 2008, affecting both the poor and the middle class. Adherents of political Islam did not support democracy in 2000 as much as secularists, among all classes. By 2008, the share of "democrats" among Islamists of the middle class becomes as large as among middle-class secular individuals (at 55.5 for "rightists" and 56.7 for "leftists"), while it remains lowest among poor "Islamists," even when compared to the secular

TABLE 7.2

Changes in preferences along pro–political Islam/secular and "autocrat"/"democrat" dimensions (share of total population), Egypt, 2000–2008.

2000	Secularists	Supporters of PI	Total
Autocratic	11.8	62.3	74.1
Democratic	5.6	20.3	25.9
Total	17.4	82.6	100

2008	Secularists	Supporters of PI	Total
Autocratic	18.9	28.6	47.5
Democratic	21	31.5	52.5
Total	40	60	100

Change 2000–2008	Secularists	Supporters of PI	Total
Autocratic	7.1	–33.7	–26.6
Democratic	15.4	11.2	26.6
Total	22.6	–22.6	0

TABLE 7.3

Proportion of "democrats" in various groups, Egypt, 2000–2008.

	(2000)				(2008)			
	Poor	MC	Rich	Total	Poor	MC	Rich	Total
Right secular	26.1	28.8	66.7	28.1	52.0	55.1	0.0	53.3
Right political Islam	21.5	23.1	36.4	22.7	49.1	55.5	33.3	53.0
Left secular	28.6	28.8	100.0	29.4	47.8	56.8	0.0	52.5
Left political Islam	22.1	27.4	100.0	25.5	44.7	56.7	60.0	51.7
Total	22.6	24.7	44.4	24.2	48.0	56.1	30.8	52.5

Source: World Values Survey, fourth and fifth rounds, author's calculations.

poor. It seems then that the antidemocratic influences of political Islam had weakened by 2008 among the poor and disappeared among the middle class. It is probable that this is due to the fact that middle-class individuals were more influenced by moderate parties under the political Islam umbrella, such as the Muslim Brotherhood, while Salafi parties remained more popular among the poor (Masoud 2014).

Conclusion

Much of the analysis above has shown that the class-based versions of both modernization and distribution theories have strong support in the opinion data. Between 2000 and 2008 popular grievances increased, and the aspirations of a more educated population rose simultaneously. This concurrence explains why the middle class, which is at the intersection of both forces, turned out to be the main champion for democratization. In effect, if demand for democracy surged, it was because of the coincidence of large social change in the past decades, together with the rise of inequalities in the recent crony capitalism phase.

This chapter finds that the influence of political Islam operated mainly through its increased moderation over time. The political landscape in 2008 was reconfigured by the dissolution of the large "pro-autocracy" and pro–political Islam majority that prevailed in 2000. Moreover, the reduced adherence to political Islam by the poor and the reduction in the antidemocratic bias among them may have fostered the middle class's shift toward democracy by 2008. However, the distribution of Islamists along "democratic"/"autocratic" and "left"/"right" dimensions is similar to that in the overall population, supporting the argument that, in broad terms, political Islam has facilitated the emergence of grievances and aspirations rather than generating them. Indeed, the mix of aspirations and grievances was contained in several home-bred narratives along the religious/secular and left/right genres that have roots in Egyptian political history, and that were reflected in the programs of the four "democratic" presidential candidates in 2012, which represented the secular right (Mussa), the secular Nasserist left (Sabahi), the Islamist Muslim Brotherhood right (Morsi), and the Islamist left (Abdel-Fotouh).

It remains to be seen how these attitudes to democracy will evolve after the political chaos created by the uprisings. The more recent 2012 sixth wave of the WVS indicates that the support for political Islam has collapsed. At the same time, support for democracy has also taken a hit, while support for strong rule has risen. Interestingly, though, it appears that the intensity of the support for democracy among the middle class and of the poor may have switched. This suggests the possibility that the modernization motive that led to the uprisings was readily neutralized by the fear of insecurity and chaos that ensued. On the other hand the uprisings may have led to the political emancipation of the poor, lifting the veil of conservatism among them by demonstrating that street power works. If these new trends are maintained, the political field in Egypt may become over time more focused on distributional issues than in the past.

REFERENCES

Abdelhamid, D., and L. El Baradei. 2009, June. Reforming the pay system for government employees in Egypt. Egyptian Centre for Economic Studies working paper no. 151. Cairo: Egyptian Centre for Economic Studies.

Acemoglu, D., and J. A. Robinson. 2006. *Economic origins of dictatorship and democracy.* Cambridge: Cambridge University Press.

Alexander, A., and C. Welzel. 2011. Islam and patriarchy: How robust is Muslim support for patriarchal values? *World Values Research* 4(2): 40–70.

Alvaredo, F., and T. Piketty. 2014. Measuring top incomes and inequality in the Middle East: Data limitations and illustration with the case of Egypt. Economic Research Forum working paper No. 832. Cairo: Economic Research Forum.

Beblawi, H., and G. Luciani, eds. 1987. *The rentier state.* Vol. 2. New York: Routledge.

Belhaj Hassine, N. 2012. Inequality of opportunity in Egypt. *World Bank Economic Review* 26(2): 265–295.

Bibi, S., and M. Nabli. 2010. Equity and inequality in the Arab world. Economic Research Forum policy research report no. 33. Cairo: Economic Research Forum.

Boix, C. 2003. *Democracy and redistribution.* Cambridge: Cambridge University Press.

Chekir, H., and I. Diwan. 2015. Crony capitalism in Egypt. *Journal of Globalization and Development* 5(2): 177–211.

Cincotta, R., and J. Doces. 2011. The age-structural maturity thesis: The youth bulge's influence on the advent and stability of liberal democracy. In *Political demography: How population changes are reshaping national politics and international security,* ed. J. A. Goldstone, Eric Kaufmann, and Monica Duffy Toft, 98–116. Oxford: Oxford University Press.

Demiralp, D. 2009. The rise of Islamic capital and the decline of Islamic radicalism in Turkey. *Comparative Politics* 41: 315–335.

Desai, R. M., A. Olofsgård, and T. M. Yousef. 2009. The logic of authoritarian bargains. *Economics and Politics* 21(1): 93–125.

Gandhi, J., and A. Przeworski. 2006. Cooperation, cooptation, and rebellion under dictatorships. *Economics and Politics* 18(1): 1–26.

Inglehart, R., and C. Welzel. 2010. Changing mass priorities: The link between modernization and democracy. *Perspectives on Politics* 8(2): 551–567.

Kuhn, R. 2012. On the role of human development in the Arab spring. *Population and Development Review* 38(4): 649–683.

Lipset, S. M. 1959. Democracy and working-class authoritarianism. *American Sociological Review* 24 (4): 482–501.

Masoud, T. 2014. *Counting Islam: Religion, class, and elections in Egypt.* Cambridge: Cambridge University Press.

Osman, F. 1989. *The Muslim world: Issues and challenges.* Los Angeles: Islamic Center of Southern California.

Przeworski, A. 2009. Conquered or granted? A history of suffrage extensions. *British Journal of Political Science* 39(2): 291–321.

Richards, A. I., J. Waterbury, M. Cammett, and I. Diwan. 2013. *A political economy of the Middle East.* 3rd ed. Boulder, CO: Westview Press.

Roushdy, R., and M. Gadallah. 2011. Labor market adjustment to the world financial crisis: Evidence from Egypt. Economic Research Forum working paper 643. Cairo: Economic Research Forum.

Schwedler, J. 2006. *Faith in moderation: Islamist parties in Jordan and Yemen.* Cambridge: Cambridge University Press.

Shahin, E. E. 2005. Political Islam: Ready for engagement? Working paper no. 3. Madrid: La Fundaci on para las Relaciones Internacionales y el Dialogo Exterior.

Tessler, M., A. Jamal, and M. Robbins. 2012. New findings on Arabs and democracy. *Journal of Democracy* 23(4): 89–103.

Tilley, J. 2002, March 1. Is youth a better predictor of sociopolitical values than is nationality? *Annals of the American Academy of Political and Social Science* 580(1): 226–256.

Urdal, H. 2006. A clash of generations? Youth bulges and political violence. *International Studies Quarterly* 50(3): 607–629.

NOTES

1. To start, household surveys are notorious for undercounting the rich. There are many indications that the income share of the richest 10 percent in Egyptian society has increased. Further, it is the richest Egyptians who are perceived to have benefited most from a more market-oriented economy, and the top 1 percent are perceived to have benefited most from the rampant crony capitalism of the last decade (Alvaredo and Piketty 2014).

2. More research is needed to understand more clearly the changing welfare of the middle class in this context.

3. In Egypt, for example, real wages in the public sector declined over time. The minimum wage, which anchors all wages, declined from 60 percent of per capita GDP in the early 1980s to a mere 13 percent in 2007 (Abdelhamid and El Baradei 2009). This can also be seen at the macro level: by 2009, 25 percent of the Egyptian labor force worked for the state but earned a total wage of less than 9 percent of GDP, implying that average wages were below GDP per capita, which is extremely low by international standards.

4. Similar processes of moderation through participation (Schwedler 2006) took place in other neighboring countries, notably Egypt, Tunisia, and Turkey (Demiralp 2009, Osman, 1989)

5. Cincotta and Doces (2011) assert that as countries age, they become increasingly inclined toward democracy. Countries with younger populations, the argument would go, face higher risks of political violence and armed conflict (see Urdal [2006] for a summary of this literature), and as a result, citizens of these countries prefer the security of an authoritarian bargain (Gandhi and Prezeworski 2006).

6. In this way, the role of political Islam in Egypt's changing political dynamics will be analyzed as both a dependent and an independent variable.

7. From the WVS website, http://www.worldvaluessurvey.org/WVSContents.jsp.

8. This timing is important, as the global financial crisis was associated with a large fall in real wages, and this development might have affected public opinion in several ways (Roushdy and Gadallah 2011). However, the global financial crisis had yet to impact the Middle East at the time that the fifth wave of the WVS was collected.

9. The percentages do not always sum to 100 due to rounding.

10. PfD is generated by ordering of V71 and V72 (all question references are in regard to the fifth wave of the WVS). A respondent who chooses 1 in V71 is taken to prefer autocracy; one who chooses 2 or 4 is categorized as preferring democracy. Question V71 reads: "If you had to choose, which one of the things on this card would you say is most important? (1) Maintaining order in the nation; (2) Giving people more say in important government decisions; (3) Fighting rising prices; (4) Protecting freedom of speech."

11. Preference for Equality (PfE) uses V116: "Now I'd like you to tell me your views on various issues. How would you place your views on this scale? 10 means you agree completely with the statement on the left (*Incomes should be made more equal*); 1 means you agree completely with the statement on the right (*We need larger income differences as incentives for individual effort*); and if your views fall somewhere in between, you can choose any number in between." In the actual survey, the scale is the reverse, but it was inverted to ease the interpretation of the results. Note that the exact level of this indicator depends on how one codes the information. Because opinions are very much clustered around the levels 1–3 in 2000, any score above 3 is taken to indicate a preference for equality.

12. To measure support for political Islam V191 is used. "Generally speaking, do you think that the religious authorities in your country are giving adequate answers *the social problems facing our society?*" (Y/N). "Yes" is coded as a 1; "No" is coded as a zero.

13. For example, the Pew Research Center Global Indicators Database, which measures preferences of "democracy" over "a strong leader," shows that countries such as Russia, Ukraine, and Pakistan have remained at such levels for many years. The Pew Global Indicators Database shows many countries with ratings at similar levels, including Mali, Kenya, Indonesia, Senegal, Turkey, and Peru.

14. While the shift away from an activist state does support a modernization view of the recent transformations in Egyptian society, one needs to recognize that this shift is only partial, as other values, which are typically seen as central to modernity, such as those associated with gender, do not seem to have improved over the period under consideration. Popular views on gender-related issues actually deteriorated. This is possibly due to unemployment. To the question "Is university more important for a boy than for a girl," for example, about 30 percent answered yes in 2000, and

nearly 40 percent in 2008. Marginal progress can be observed among the rich, as expected, but not among the poor and the middle class.

15. This comparison assumes that there is no churning in the data, since the data are repeated cross-sections and not a panel.

16. It has been argued by many that Islam, through the forum of mosques, is able to facilitate mobilization by resolving coordination problems, typically a central constraint in social movements.

8 Days of Rage and Silence

EXPLAINING POLITICAL ACTION BY ARAB YOUTH

Raj M. Desai, Anders Olofsgård, and Tarik Yousef

DURING THE ARAB Spring demonstrations, youth protesters were commonly depicted as deeply frustrated by numerous societal failings: corruption, nepotism, repression, inequality, and a lack of economic opportunity. General economic and political discontent, combined with demographic shifts where job seekers faced long periods of unemployment, stagnating wages, and higher costs of living precipitated an enthusiasm for revolution that the region had not seen since the anticolonial independence movements.

This chapter examines the participation of Arab youth in political life. Outside the Arab Spring, young adults have been generally absent from most popular movements that have dominated the region in recent decades. While youth movements have played a role in pivotal political events in the region's contemporary history, either they have tended to be "top-down" efforts to mobilize young people, or groups have tended to fragment after defining events. One author refers to them as "nonmovements": not organized groups poised for collective action but the common "practices of large numbers of ordinary people [that] are rarely guided by an ideology or recognizable leaderships and organizations" (Bayat 2010, 14). By and large, these "nonmovements" distrusted party politics, remained mostly disorganized, and mobilized only sporadically.

Despite (or perhaps because of) this general apathy, youth activism in Egypt, Jordan, Libya, Morocco, Syria, Tunisia, and Yemen during the Arab Spring uprisings formed one of the central narratives for the biggest demonstrations that have engulfed the region in modern history. Thus, we are left with two contrasting images of political engagement among Arab youth. On the one hand there is a prevailing perception that protests during the Arab Spring were often heavily youth-driven; on the other there is abundant evidence that Arab youth have generally excluded themselves (and were excluded) from the political arena. In this chapter we attempt to reconcile these disparate views by arguing that politically motivated youth in Arab states—as youth elsewhere—are often forced to rely on a very different repertoire of political actions than their elders. In particular, their actions must be more dramatic, must be potentially more violent, and must come at a higher personal cost.

Political actions are "signals" of support or discontent, but the strength of these signals depends on the personal costs incurred by taking action. For younger, unemployed citizens, the personal cost of participating in (nonviolent) street protests is low. At first glance, it would seem that low personal costs of political action should *encourage* participation. But this also means that these actions send little information to authorities regarding the true level of support or discontent. In other words, low-cost actions are not effective signals because they lack credibility (Lohmann 1993; Spence 2002). On the other hand older (and more likely formally employed, wealthier) citizens face a higher opportunity cost of political action due to their time-cost of participation and the risk that political involvement incurs to their economic and social status. The same actions— which are a weak signal of discontent coming from younger groups—therefore constitute a stronger signal when sent by older groups.

Taken together, this suggests that the more economically established and relatively better off are also better able to change policies, leaders, and regimes through peaceful means. By contrast, marginalized groups, perceiving a lack of credible influence, will have to resort to more personally costly forms of action to send credible signals of discontent. The result is threefold: (1) the propensities to engage in different types of political actions differ across age groups; (2) marginalized groups—in particular, youth, the unemployed, and the poor—are more inclined to self-exclude themselves from civic life; and (3) radicalization is concentrated among discontented youth who perceive that they lack an effective, nonviolent political voice.

Political Violence and Protest

Political participation can take many different forms, ranging from voting and campaign activism to demonstrations and strikes and to riots and revolutions (Barnes et al. 1979; Verba, Nie, and Kim 1971). A street protest, for example, may aim at overthrowing the regime or just as well serve as a peaceful means to communicate an opinion (Norris, Walgrave, and Van Aelst 2005). What, then, determines how individuals and groups choose to express their political opinions? In particular, what drives certain groups to engage in actions such as boycotts, demonstrations, and petitions, and what makes others willing to engage in even more costly actions such as violent street protests, riots, and revolutions? At the micro level, scholars in psychology, political science, and sociology have linked individual activism to both attitudinal orientations and socioeconomic factors (Krueger and Maleckova 2003; Piazza 2006; Tadjoeddin and Murshed 2007).

Grievances

Evidence from studies of regime durability and transition shows the myriad ways groups that are more likely to act out of discontent can be selectively pacified (Bueno de Mesquita et al. 2005). In the Middle East and North Africa (MENA) region, rentier states have used natural resource revenues to fund welfare projects targeted to key constituencies (Aslaksen and Torvik 2006; Chaudhry 1997). The resulting generous social expenditures and public employment programs have created and reinforced allegiances to the state that have proven deeply resilient (Yousef 2004). But in the face of rising demographic pressures and constrained state budgets, youth have disproportionately borne the costs of economic adjustment over the past two decades, with their benefits dramatically curtailed and their vulnerability to economic downturns increased (Dhillon and Yousef 2009).

Public sector employment—the mainstay of economic opportunity for Arab youth in a previous era—has been typically cut by the reduction or freezing of new hiring. While there have been very few large-scale layoffs, the share of new entrants to the public sector—especially of young, educated professionals—has fallen dramatically (Assaad 2002). At the same time, labor market reforms have usually grandfathered current older workers with existing contracts while applying newer, flexible rules to new hires (Wahba 2009). The small size of the formal private sector, combined with slow job creation, has pushed young job seekers into low-skill jobs in the informal economy (see Barsoum, chapter 9 here). Partly as a result, the time between leaving school and getting a first job for Arab youth—during which young people typically remain unemployed or languish in the informal sector—is measured in years rather than months.[1]

Education does little to help; indeed, in Arab states, more education infamously *reduces* one's chances of finding a job. This is a consequence of the region's approach to postcolonial modernization, whereby the guarantee of public sector employment was used to increase demand for formal schooling. The result has been dramatic, with the MENA region experiencing the highest increase in educational attainment (average total years in schooling) since 1950 (Barro and Lee 2010). This inducement for mass education, however, has not produced concomitant increases in labor productivity. Between 1991 and 2010, Arab states have posted small productivity gains despite their increases in educational attainment, particularly when contrasted with the experience of Asia. The inefficiency of Arab educational systems is shown by Salehi-Isfahani (chapter 2 here): Arab states' spending on education covers similar ranges to that of advanced economies but student performance is consistently among the worst in the world.

Mobilization

In assessing political mobilization among Arab youth, the distinction between "preferences" and "opportunities" is crucial, since that which determines attitudes may not motivate action against regimes (Hirshleifer 1993). Perceived inequities or deprivation alone are unlikely to destabilize or threaten governments, unless groups take the necessary steps to mobilize. Here we make a distinction between two types of political activity—conventional, nonviolent forms of activism (voting, petition signing, and other forms of civic engagement) and radical, violent forms of direct action.

Rational actor perspectives suggest that the degree of political mobilization will depend on individuals' expectations of private benefit. This extends to multiple modalities of political behavior—from voting to violent political action. In voting models, voters' preferences do not translate into electoral outcomes where citizens do not see any private benefit to voting given the costs involved (Verba, Schlozman, and Brady 1995). Most conventional, nonviolent political acts, in this sense, are no different from voting (Inglehart 1997; Norris 2002). If the likelihood of affecting outcomes is small, discontent is not enough to motivate action.

Similarly, with respect to acts of collective political violence, this logic points to the role of individual incentives (to surmount coordination costs), opportunities for rebellion, and expectations of gains from violence (Collier and Hoeffler 2004; Deininger 2003; Fearon and Laitin 2003). Suicide terrorism, in addition, has been considered an especially lethal form of violent political action. Numerous analyses have indicated that poverty and unemployment are not directly related to the occurrence of suicide attacks (Krueger and Laitin 2008). There is greater evidence supporting the idea that terrorism and suicide terrorism constitutes a strong signal of political discontent, rather than economic deprivation (Atran 2004; Pape 2005; Sayre 2009). The recruitment of individuals into terrorist organizations, however, can be dramatically influenced by economic conditions. Bueno de Mesquita (2005), for example, argues that terrorism is more likely when individuals' utility from terror attacks is greater than that of employment. Data on Palestinian suicide terrorists during the Second Intifada shows that less educated individuals are generally more likely to participate in terrorism than better educated individuals, but that the better educated are more readily recruited when conditions deteriorate (Benmelech, Berrebi, and Klor 2012).

While long spells of unemployment among educated Arab youths caused frustration, the lack of economic opportunities did not translate into interest in politics or participation in conventional political action (Hoffman and Jamal 2012). A lack of trust in (mostly rigged) elections pushed youth further away from voting, while severe restrictions on universities across the region limited the normal route to politics among youth: campus activism. Some (mostly middle- or lower-middle-class) youth may have been mobilized into Islamic movements in countries such as Egypt in the 1980s, with varying degrees of success, but as one author describes it, this phenomenon "did not repeat itself in other political fields. In the late 1990s political activity on campuses was paltry, as state security intervened to prevent Islamist, leftist, and Nasserist candidates from running for student unions.... Even the youths of elite families, whose social and financial resources often make them the prime source of donations, remained indifferent" (Bayat 2010, 130). The Arab Spring revolutions, of course, were widely seen as youth-powered movements, with young activists and bloggers demanding regime change. However, following the collapse of the Ben Ali and Mubarak regimes in Tunisia and Egypt, youth involvement in politics did not grow. Prior to Tunisia's parliamentary elections in 2011, only 17 percent of eligible youth were registered to vote (POMED 2011, 17), and only 38 percent correctly identified the purpose of the election: to choose an assembly to write the constitution (IFES 2011). In Egypt, parliamentary and presidential elections in 2011–2012, as well as a constitutional referendum in 2014, have all seen low (and declining) young voter turnout (Hashem 2014).

On the other hand these same educated youth in Tunisia and Egypt had been (for years) carrying out small-scale and occasionally violent protests and strikes, calling attention to high unemployment, police harassment, and corruption (Goldstone 2011). The same pattern of limited and localized violent protests by youth groups in response to socioeconomic conditions has been observed in Egypt, Iraq, Iran, Libya, Morocco, and Yemen in the past decade (Costello, Jenkins, and Aly 2015). It has been suggested that the combination of expansion in schooling and weak prospects for employment among Arab youth has increased their support for more radical political activities (Campante and Chor 2012). In the next section we argue that, due to a combination of high discontent *and* the limited credibility of peaceful political signals, aggrieved young Arabs have become more likely to support or engage in violent forms of political action.

Political Behavior as Costly Signals: A Simple Framework

We begin with the assumption that citizens have private information about their own level of discontent with current policies. This information cannot be conveyed to regime authorities through communication alone, since all individuals have incentives to express strong discontent, for example, to induce transfers or other privileges such as subsidies or public sector jobs. Instead, *credible* signaling requires that individuals take actions that are costly to them; the more personally costly the action, the stronger the signal of discontent. We posit further that different categories of individuals (rich v. poor, employed v. unemployed, young v. old), depending on their level of economic exclusion or "marginalization," face very different personal costs of engaging in political action. This is due to the different opportunity or time costs for different groups. In particular, more marginalized groups face lower opportunity costs and lower risks to income, status, and employment from engaging in these activities.[2]

Desai, Olofsgård, and Yousef (2012) have formally developed a model to capture these assumptions. Intuitively one could expect that the marginalized groups would have stronger incentives to participate due to this lower opportunity cost. However, when political behavior is meant to signal discontent, this lower cost also means that participation is a less informative—and therefore weaker—signal to an incumbent. Consequently, marginalized groups are more likely to exclude themselves from conventional political activities, in contrast to dissatisfied groups with higher opportunity costs who can signal support for political change through the same activities. For the marginalized, peaceful political signals are too weak to matter; for the elite, the cost of foregone income and risk to status from political activity is simply too high. Conceptualized this way, unemployed Arab youth are likely to self-exclude not because they lack access to organizational resources, nor because they lack social capital. Rather, their withdrawal is chiefly because they are only able to use weak signals of discontent through normal political activity.

The alternative available to groups without a peaceful voice is political action that carries a uniformly high opportunity cost, namely, radical or violent action: sabotage, blockades, assaults on or clashes with police forces, and supporting or joining radical or insurgent groups. By contrast, nonmarginalized influential groups (business elites, bureaucrats, formal sector employees, etc.), who have a political voice, need not resort to violent actions, since for the same level of discontent they can take effective and peaceful action while others remain on the sidelines. Indeed, one result of the decades of Arab youth's self-exclusion is that economic policies, through two decades of reform, protected these groups at the expense of youth, resulting in a vicious cycle of marginalization, exclusion, and rising discontent. Eventually their level of discontent may have increased to the point where they resorted to radical or violent action, suggesting that the lack of peaceful voice eventually is likely to breed conflict.

Explaining Political Action in the Arab World

Our framework predicts that, due to the weakness of the signals sent via conventional political engagement, Arab youth—and other marginalized groups—are more likely to self-exclude than other groups, all else being equal. We hypothesize, further, that marginalized groups will respond to high levels of discontent by engaging in or supporting more violent or radical activity. In this section we examine the extent to which our approach is empirically justified.

Finding evidence for the full range of the varieties of political acts in the Arab world is difficult in a region where surveys regarding political behavior do not have a long lineage. The main source of information for the remainder of this chapter comes from four rounds of the Arab countries' section of the Gallup World Poll, undertaken annually between 2009 and 2012. The data cover over 20 countries in the MENA region. Sample sizes of 2,000 (in 2009, 2010, and 2011 in most countries) and 1,000 (in 2012) per country were designed to ensure national representation. The strength of the Gallup survey is that the identical questionnaire was implemented in all countries, providing a unique opportunity to examine cross-country comparisons as well as individual-level relationships.

Deprivation

The Gallup World Poll uses the Cantril "Self-Anchoring" Scale (Cantril 1965), derived from responses to the following:

> *Please imagine a ladder with steps numbered from zero at the bottom to 10 at the top. The top of the ladder represents the best possible life for you and the bottom of the ladder represents the worst possible life for you.*
> *On which step of the ladder would you say you personally feel you stand at this time? (ladder-present)*
> *On which step do you think you will stand about five years from now? (ladder-future)*

The Cantril Scale is used on the premise that measurement of well-being is multidimensional and that respondents evaluate their well-being according to multiple criteria (Diener et al. 2009). Cross-national evidence shows strong correlations between the Cantril Scale and income (Deaton 2008). Gallup further combines the ladder-present and ladder-future scales to form a "Life Evaluation Well-Being Index," grouped in three distinct (and independent) categories, for summary purposes: (1) thriving, or well-being that is "strong, consistent, and progressing"; (2) struggling, or well-being that is "moderate or inconsistent": and (3) suffering, well-being that is at high risk (Gallup 2015).

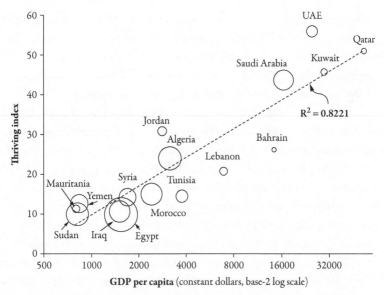

FIGURE 8.1 Life satisfaction and income across Arab states, 2009–2012 averages. Graph shows unweighted averages (2009–2012) of the percentage of the population "thriving" according to the Gallup World Poll and GDP per capita (constant 2005 US dollars) for Arab states listed (averages from 2009 to 2011 are used for Kuwait, 2009 to 2010 for Syria). Area of circles is scaled to average population for the relevant period. The trend line is given by 10.4 × Log_2(GDP/capita) - 62.1.

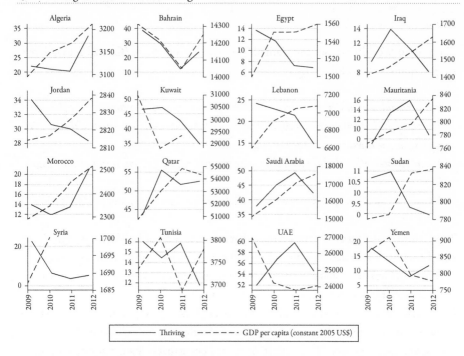

FIGURE 8.2 Satisfaction and income in the Arab world. Graphs plot percentage of the population "thriving" according to the Gallup World Poll (solid line, left axes) alongside GDP per capita (dashed line, right axes).

Figure 8.1 shows the percentages of respondents considered "thriving" against per capita income in constant US dollars, averaged over the period 2009–2012. The strong correlation between income and well-being ($R^2 = 0.82$) is shown. Figure 8.2 focuses on the percentages of the populations who are "thriving," as compared to changes in constant per capita income over the four-year survey period. In some states (Algeria, Bahrain, Morocco, Qatar, and Yemen) the two are related. In others (Egypt, Iraq, Jordan, Lebanon, Sudan, Syria, and Tunisia) the percentages of the populations thriving were declining even as income was rising. Algeria, Mauritania, Morocco, and the Gulf Cooperation Council countries all experienced increases in percentages thriving over time. In all other countries, the percentages of those at the top of the Cantril Scale declined.

Table 8.1 explores the determinants of life satisfaction among Arab populations by adult and youth groups. Our basic specification regresses the specific Gallup index on income and employment status (including both unemployed and self-employed dummies), as well as controls for age, education, gender, marital status, and urban-rural location. All specifications—here and throughout—take account of population weights, country and year fixed effects, and (country) clusters.

The problems of comparability when respondents are asked to use ordinal response categories are well known (Bertrand and Mullainathan 2001; King and Wand 2007). Different respondents may interpret subjective questions in different ways on the basis of

TABLE 8.1

Determinants of life satisfaction by age group in 21 MENA countries, 2009–2012.

	(1) Thriving > 30 years old	(2) Thriving 15–29	(3) Ladder of life (today) > 30 years old	(4) Ladder of life (today) 15–29	(5) Ladder of life (5 years from today) > 30 years old	(6) Ladder of life (5 years from today) 15–29
Income (Ln)	5.262***	6.102***	0.444***	0.422***	0.423***	0.421***
	(0.485)	(0.516)	(0.033)	(0.041)	(0.041)	(0.041)
Unemployed	1.188	−2.748**	−0.244**	0.408***	−0.285**	−0.285***
	(0.971)	(1.122)	(0.093)	(0.066)	(0.100)	(0.066)
Self-employed	1.950**	−2.137**	0.135**	−0.083	−0.029	−0.213**
	(0.763)	(0.970)	(0.055)	(0.065)	(0.057)	(0.076)
Age	−0.029	0.353***	−0.001	−0.021***	−0.010***	−0.023***
	(0.019)	(0.111)	(0.001)	(0.006)	(0.002)	(0.008)
Education	3.372***	1.728*	0.252***	0.189***	0.217***	0.218***
	(0.671)	(0.902)	(0.029)	(0.035)	(0.031)	(0.039)
Male	−1.945***	−2.440***	−0.187***	−0.190***	−0.231**	−0.203**
	(0.449)	(0.668)	(0.043)	(0.049)	(0.089)	(0.092)
Single	−1.863**	−0.705	−0.105**	−0.015	−0.135**	0.064
	(0.729)	(0.866)	(0.037)	(0.040)	(0.053)	(0.046)
Urban	1.423*	0.973	0.151**	0.118*	0.205***	0.205***
	(0.717)	(0.810)	(0.055)	(0.063)	(0.053)	(0.059)

(continued)

TABLE 8.1 (continued)

	(1) Thriving > 30 years old	(2) Thriving 15–29	(3) Ladder of life (today) > 30 years old	(4) Ladder of life (today) 15–29	(5) Ladder of life (5 years from today) > 30 years old	(6) Ladder of life (5 years from today) 15–29
Bias	0.309***	0.317***	0.019***	0.018***	0.021***	0.019***
	(0.031)	(0.032)	(0.001)	(0.001)	(0.002)	(0.002)
N	50,292	38,221	53,929	39,891	50,339	38,258
R^2	0.209	0.207	0.296	0.292	0.267	0.250
Countries	21	21	21	21	21	21

"Thriving" is the Gallup World Poll "thriving" index; "Ladder of life" asks respondents to place themselves on a 10-step scale. Estimations are ordinary least-squares with population weights. All regressions include intercepts with country and year fixed effects (not reported here). Standard errors clustered by country are in parentheses.

*p < 0.1;
**p < 0.05;
***p < 0.01.

unobservable characteristics. Ordinal scales, moreover, may mean different things to different respondents on the basis of idiosyncratic factors such as mood or overall optimism. Individual-level perceptions would similarly be affected by measurement error where identical individuals may have unequal probabilities of answering questions about their own well-being in the same way. In addition, the measurement error in subjective responses may be correlated with a wide variety of individual characteristics and behaviors.

"Anchoring vignettes" or other hypothetical questions to establish baselines that could normally correct survey responses for interpersonal incomparability are not included in the Gallup World Poll. Consequently, we attempt to correct our specifications in the following manner. In all estimations, we include a "bias" proxy. We derive that proxy by regressing a "financial well-being" response variable (coded from 0, "dissatisfied," to 100, "satisfied") against personal income, along with country and year effects, taking into account population-sampling weights, with errors clustered by country. The residuals from this equation reasonably approximate an individual's personal "bias": the level of perceived economic well-being that cannot be explained by one's actual level of wealth.

Across the different measurements of well-being in table 8.1, we see that income levels are strongly associated with greater life satisfaction—both today and in the future—across age groups. In addition, unemployment has a strong, consistently negative effect, while age is negatively related to satisfaction. Coefficients on other controls enter with expected signs: those with less education, men, single persons, and rural residents are less satisfied on the whole. We note two differences when splitting the sample between adult and young respondents. First, the magnitude of the (negative) effect of unemployment on well-being is much greater for young people than it is for adults, suggesting the heightened importance of employment in well-being among youth. Second, self-employment has the opposite effect on adults versus youth. For adult respondents, being self-employed increases the extent to which those are thriving, or are on the higher end of the present ladder (there is no effect on the future ladder). For young persons, by contrast, self-employment decreases well-being. This difference may be attributable to the possibility that adults have chosen self-employment, that is, to become small-scale entrepreneurs or single proprietors. For youth, the decision may be forced on them after years of fruitless job seeking. Alternatively, it may be that those who remain self-employed into older age are likely successful, or content.

Civic Engagement

We postulate that marginalized groups and those on the lower end of a socioeconomic or well-being scale are more likely to exclude themselves from civic life due to their lower opportunity cost of political participation. Table 8.2 replicates the specifications in table 8.1 but examines determinants of civic engagement instead. We also split the sample across within-country income quintiles. (We only report coefficients for income level, employment status, and age.) For the full sample, civic engagement is increasing in

TABLE 8.2

Civic Engagement, full sample and by quintiles, in 21 MENA countries, 2009–2012.

	(1) Full sample	(2) 1st quintile	(3) 2nd quintile	(4) 3rd quintile	(5) 4th quintile	(6) 5th quintile
Income (Ln)	0.262***	0.116***	0.438*	0.487***	0.132	0.133***
	(0.039)	(0.030)	(0.228)	(0.186)	(0.152)	(0.040)
Unemployed	0.069	0.056	0.144	0.010	0.081	0.055
	(0.080)	(0.150)	(0.100)	(0.081)	(0.101)	(0.120)
Self-employed	0.295***	0.259**	0.319***	0.226**	0.395***	0.238**
	(0.063)	(0.115)	(0.120)	(0.093)	(0.086)	(0.094)
Age	0.005***	0.002	0.004	0.007***	0.005**	0.007***
	(0.001)	(0.003)	(0.003)	(0.002)	(0.002)	(0.002)
Education	0.313***	0.290***	0.260***	0.274***	0.291***	0.335***
	(0.041)	(0.066)	(0.082)	(0.059)	(0.035)	(0.054)
N	89,783	17,203	18,680	18,367	18,192	17,341
Pseudo R^2	0.089	0.094	0.084	0.084	0.082	0.078
Countries	21	21	21	21	21	21

Dependent variable is a binary indicator based on the Gallup World Poll "civic engagement" index. Estimations are logit regressions with population weights. All regressions include additional controls for education, gender, marital status, location (urban-rural), correction for individual-specific systemic bias, and intercepts with country and year fixed effects (not reported here). Standard errors clustered by country are in parentheses.

*$p < 0.1$;
**$p < 0.05$;
***$p < 0.01$.

income, self-employment, age, and education. However, we note that the magnitude of the effects of income and self-employment are greatest for the middle quintiles, consistent with what the framework predicts, namely, that those facing intermediate opportunity costs are more likely to participate. This also suggests the possibility that the political behavior of the middle quintiles in Arab societies are more susceptible to changes in income and employment than richer or poorer groups—broadly in line with findings that consumption patterns among the middle classes in middle-income countries remain the most vulnerable to shocks (Ravallion 2009).

Radicalization and Extremism

Our framework also points to the potential of vicious cycles of marginalization—leading to self-exclusion, causing further political inaction, and eventually breeding a deep-rooted sense of discontent. In other words, we expect radicalization to characterize the attitudes of those who are the most marginalized economically and politically. Moreover, our framework predicts that members of different socioeconomic groups express discontent in different ways. The relatively well-off trust they can influence policies through nonviolent action and therefore find it worthwhile to engage in petition writing, perhaps the occasional demonstration, or general strike. By contrast, marginalized groups, perceiving a lack of voice to influence decisionmakers, resort to actions that carry a higher personal cost in order to signal their discontent credibly. Political violence, according to our framework, should be highly concentrated among those for whom nonviolent means represent low-cost actions.

In table 8.3 we examine three measures of radicalization and extremism. The Gallup World Poll, conducted in a handful of Arab states, includes questions on support for violent political action and on violence against civilians. The first variable codes respondents who answered "sometimes justified" to the question "Some people think that for an individual person or a small group of persons to target and kill civilians is sometimes justified, while others think [violence] is never justified: which is your opinion?" as 1, otherwise 0. The second variable does the same to the response "peaceful means alone will not work" to the question of how those "suffering from injustice" can improve their situation. Our third variable is coded 1 for those who say that attacks on civilians are "completely justified," 0 otherwise. Logit model estimations of these three binary outcomes are shown in table 8.3. As with previous specifications, we include separate country and year fixed effects, use population-sampling weights, and cluster errors by country.

Although richer respondents are less likely to support attacks on civilians, the income effects are relatively weak and inconsistent. Moreover, we do not see unemployed respondents more or less inclined to support violence. We do observe that youth, as expected, is associated with support for violence. There are reasons that the very poorest or the worse-off might not be more likely to engage in political violence than other groups. Recall that, in our model, the incentives to engage in violent actions depends on two factors: (1) the

TABLE 8.3

Violence and radicalization in 14 MENA countries, 2009–2012.

	(1) Violence justified	(2) Nonpeaceful means	(3) Attacks on civilians
Income (Ln)	−0.018	−0.020	−0.192[*]
	(0.024)	(0.025)	(0.114)
Unemployed	0.044	0.042	0.150
	(0.092)	(0.078)	(0.183)
Self-employed	−0.011	0.001	0.087
	(0.055)	(0.057)	(0.213)
Age	−0.005[***]	−0.007[***]	−0.007
	(0.002)	(0.001)	(0.012)
Education	0.054	0.020	−0.113
	(0.058)	(0.034)	(0.118)
N	19,910	24,557	11,556
Pseudo R^2	0.160	0.068	0.112
Countries	12	14	13

Dependent variable is a binary indicator based on the Gallup World Poll "civic engagement" index. Estimations are logit regressions with population weights. All regressions include controls for age, education, gender, marital status, location (urban-rural), correction for individual-specific systemic bias, and country and year fixed effects. Standard errors clustered by country are in parentheses.

[*]$p < 0.1$;

[**]$p < 0.05$;

[***]$p < 0.01$.

ability to send credible signals of discontent through peaceful means, and (2) the level of discontent with the current regime. The most vulnerable may have strong reasons for discontent, but their support is also relatively inexpensive to "buy" through redistributive policies or other "pro-poor" programs that target benefits to marginalized groups. Under these conditions, beneficiaries at the lowest end of the income scale may perceive less discontent with the sitting regime than those who, while still struggling, are slightly better off. Moreover, the credibility of peaceful actions in our model depends on the opportunity cost of time, which may not necessarily be decreasing with lower income at the lowest end of the distribution, as the poorest are more likely to require time and effort to secure necessities for their own survival.

To examine these possibilities, we explore the effect of two factors—income and life satisfaction—on support for violence using nonparametric means (for further details, see Desai, Olofsgård, and Yousef 2012). We first regress the outcome of interest on our main controls (employment status, age, marital status, location, and bias, along with country and year fixed effects). Residuals from these estimations represent the propensity to support violence, adjusting for these independent variables. We then estimate kernel (local-polynomial) regressions of these residuals on income decile and on steps on the present ladder, taking account of weights and country clusters. We also split the samples between adult and youth respondents. We do see small, nonmonotonic drops in support for violence for both youth and adults as income increases. When we turn to the multidimensional measure of deprivation—the Cantril Scale—we see less clear patterns. Support for violence shows a double-peaked pattern, rising rapidly as individuals transition from poor to "lower" middle class, falling between the fourth and sixth income deciles, and then rising again before falling sharply.

Conclusion

The political lives of Arab youth have been characterized by two distinct patterns of behavior. On the one hand there is ample evidence of the withdrawal of young Arabs from civic and political engagement relative to older cohorts for much of recent history. (See Breuer, chapter 6 here, on how this was experienced in Tunisia.) On the other hand youth played a prominent role in the popular uprisings that led either to the overthrow of dictators or to serious internal fracturing within regimes, most recently during the Arab Spring. We explain the discrepancy by arguing that youth—among other marginalized groups in the Arab world—perceive peaceful political organization to be a weak signal of discontent to governments and unlikely to instigate change. Therefore, youth apathy persists until the level of discontent is so high that they are willing to resort to forms of political action that carry high personal cost—actions that are more dramatic and place the participants at significant risk of reprisal.

Using Gallup World Poll data for Arab countries, we have demonstrated that youth are less civically involved, less likely to engage in volunteerism, and less likely to contact public officials directly. We also found that support for political violence is greater among youth; age was one of the consistent predictors of support for extremist violence. Exploring these relationships further with simple nonparametric methods, we showed that youth in the lower (but not lowest) income deciles were the most supportive of radical methods. This finding, if true, is in line with micro-level evidence of the connection between poverty and violence showing that rising incomes increase the support for and participation in violence and terrorism but that that support and participation fall once income levels cross certain thresholds.

After leading the political movements that dislodged incumbent dictators during the Arab Spring, youth are once again turning away from the traditional avenues of political influence. Youth voter turnout rates, which rose dramatically during the post–Arab Spring parliamentary elections in several countries, have plunged back down to historic lows, while youth complain that the democratic process has been "hijacked" by the old establishment (Kirkpatrick and El-Sheikh 2014). Growing economic challenges combined with the lack of political inclusion risk a repetition of a cycle of self-exclusion and resentment. The revival of youth apathy, if it persists, deprives the political discourse of a critical voice in support of policy reform. Resulting frustrations accumulate, eventually resulting in increasing radicalization and conflict. Finding a way to integrate youth into the political process is an important step toward avoiding such a scenario.

REFERENCES

Aslaksen, S., and R. Torvik. 2006. A theory of civil conflict and democracy in rentier states. *Scandinavian Journal of Economics* 108(4): 571–585.

Assaad, R. 2002. *The Egyptian labor market in an era of reform.* Cairo: American University in Cairo Press.

Atran, S. 2004. Mishandling suicide terrorism. *Washington Quarterly* 27(3): 65–90.

Barnes, S. H., et al. 1979. *Political action: Mass participation in five western democracies.* Beverly Hills, CA: Sage.

Barro, R. J., and J. W. Lee. 2010. A new data set of educational attainment in the world, 1950–2010. *Journal of Development Economics* 104C: 184–198.

Bayat, A. 2010. *Life as politics: How ordinary people change the Middle East.* Stanford, CA: Stanford University Press.

Benmelech, E., C. Berrebi, and E. F. Klor. 2012. Economic conditions and the quality of suicide terrorism. *Journal of Politics* 74(1): 113–128.

Bertrand, M., and S. Mullainathan. 2001. Do people mean what they say? Implications for subjective survey data. *American Economic Review* 91(2): 67–72.

Bueno de Mesquita, B., A. Smith, R. M. Siverson, and J. D. Morrow. 2005. *The logic of political survival.* Cambridge, MA: MIT Press.

Bueno de Mesquita, E. 2005. The quality of terror. *American Journal of Political Science* 49(3): 515–530.

Campante, F., and D. Chor. 2012. Why was the Arab world poised for revolution: Schooling, economic opportunities, and the Arab Spring. *Journal of Economic Perspectives* 26(2): 167–188.

Cantril, H. 1965. *The pattern of human concerns.* New Brunswick, NJ: Rutgers University Press.

Chaudhry, K. A. 1997. *The price of wealth: Economies and institutions in the Middle East.* Ithaca, NY: Cornell University Press.

Collier, P., and A. Hoeffler. 1998. On economic causes of civil war. *Oxford Economic Papers* 50(4): 563–573.

Collier, P., and A. Hoeffler. 2004. Greed and grievance in civil war. *Oxford Economic Papers* 56(4): 563–595.

Costello, M., C. Jenkins, and H. Aly. 2015. Bread, justice, or opportunity? The determinants of the Arab awakening protests. *World Development* 67: 90–100.

Deaton, A. 2008. Income, health, and well-being around the world: Evidence from the Gallup World Poll. *Journal of Economic Perspectives* 22(2): 53–72.

Deininger, K. 2003. Causes and consequences of civil strife: Micro-level evidence from Uganda. *Oxford Economic Papers* 55(4): 579–606.

Desai, R., A. Olofsgård, and T. Yousef. 2012. Inequality, exclusion, and dissent: Explaining political actions of Arab youth. Unpublished working paper. Available at http://www.youthpolicy.org/wp-content/uploads/library/2012_Inequality_Exclusion_Youth_Arab_World_Eng.pdf.

Dhillon, N., and T. Yousef, eds. 2009. *Generation in waiting: The unfulfilled promise of young people in the Middle East.* Washington, DC: Brookings Institution.

Diener, E., D. Kahneman, W. Tov, and R. Arora. 2009. Income's association with judgments of life versus feelings. In *International differences in well-being*, ed. E. Diener, J. Helliwell, and D. Kahneman, 3–15. New York: Oxford University Press.

Fearon, J. D., and D. D. Laitin. 2003. Ethnicity, insurgency, and civil war. *American Political Science Review* 97(1): 75–90.

Gallup. 2015. Understanding how Gallup uses the Cantril scale. http://www.gallup.com/poll/122453/understanding-gallup-uses-cantril-scale.aspx.

Goldstone, J. 2011. Understanding the revolutions of 2011: Weakness and resilience in Middle Eastern autocracies. *Foreign Affairs* 90(3): 8–16.

Hashem, M. 2014. The dangers of alienating Egypt's youth. *Sada*. http://carnegieendowment.org/sada/2014/03/06/dangers-of-alienating-egypt-s-youth/h2l2.

Hirshleifer, J. 1993. Cooperation, conflict, and all that. UCLA Economics Department Working paper 695. Department of Economics, University of California, Los Angeles.

Hoffman, M., and A. Jamal. 2012. The youth and the Arab spring: Cohort differences and similarities. *Middle East Law and Governance* 4(1):168–88.

International Foundation for Electoral Systems (IFES). 2011, February. Elections in Tunisia: Steps towards elections in 2011. IFES Tunisia briefing paper no. 2. http://www.ifes.org/~/media/Files/Publications/White%20PaperReport/2011/IFES_Tunisia_Briefing_Paper_feb2011.pdf.

Inglehart, R. 1997. *Modernization and postmodernization: Cultural, economic, and political change in forty-three societies*. Princeton, NJ: Princeton University Press.

King, G., and J. Wand. 2007. Comparing incomparable survey responses: Evaluating and selecting anchoring vignettes. *Political Analysis* 15(1): 46–66.

Kirkpatrick, D., and M. El-Sheikh. 2014, February 16. In Egypt, a chasm grows between young and old. *New York Times*, A1.

Krueger, A. B., and D. D. Laitin. 2008. Kto Kogo? A cross-country study of the origins and targets of terrorism. In *Terrorism, economic development, and political openness*, ed. P. Keefer and N. Loayza, 148–173. New York: Cambridge University Press.

Krueger, A. B., and J. Maleckova. 2003. Education, poverty and terrorism: Is there a causal connection? *Journal of Economic Perspectives* 17(4): 119–144.

Loayza, N., and T. Wada. 2010. Informal labor in the Middle East and North Africa: Basic measures and determinants. Mimeograph. Washington, DC: World Bank.

Lohmann, S. 1993. A signaling model of informative and manipulative political action. *American Political Science Review* 87(2): 319–333.

Norris, P. 2002. *Democratic phoenix: Reinventing political activism*. New York: Cambridge University Press.

Norris, P., S. Walgrave, and P. Van Aelst. 2005. Who demonstrates? Antistate rebels, conventional participants, or everyone? *Comparative Politics* 56(1): 189–205.

Pape, R. 2005. *Dying to win: The strategic logic of suicide terrorism*. New York: Random House.

Piazza, J. A. 2006. Rooted in poverty? Terrorism, poor economic development, and social cleavages. *Terrorism and Political Violence* 18(1): 159–77.

Project on Middle East Democracy (POMED). 2011. *A guide to the Tunisian elections*. http://pomed.org/wordpress/wp-content/uploads/2011/10/tunisian-election-guide-2011.pdf.

Ravallion, M. 2009. Why don't we see poverty convergence? *American Economic Review* 102(1): 504–523.

Sayre, E. A. 2009. Labor market conditions, political events, and Palestinian suicide bombings. *Peace Economics, Peace Science and Public Policy* 15(1): 1–12.

Spence, M. 2002. Signaling in retrospect and the informational structure of markets. *American Economic Review* 92(3): 434–459.

Tadjoeddin, M. Z., and S. M. Murshed. 2007. Socio-economic determinants of everyday violence in Indonesia: An empirical investigation of Javanese districts, 1994–2003. *Journal of Peace Research* 44(6): 689–709.

Verba, S., N. H. Nie, and J. Kim. 1971. The modes of democratic participation: A cross-national comparison. Sage Professional Papers in Comparative Politics 2. No. 01-13. Beverly Hills, CA: Sage.

Verba, S., K. L. Schlozman, and H. E. Brady. 1995. *Voice and equality: Civic voluntarism in American politics*. Vol. 4. Cambridge, MA: Harvard University Press.

Wahba, J. 2009. The impact of labor market reforms on informality in Egypt. Working paper no. 3. Cairo: Population Council.

Yousef, T. M. 2004. Development, growth and policy reform in the Middle East and North Africa since 1950. *Journal of Economic Perspectives* 18(3): 91–116.

NOTES

1. Arab economies are among the most informal in the world. The typical Arab country produces about 27 percent of its GDP and employs 67 percent of its labor force informally (see Loayza and Wada 2010).

2. This may not be true at the very lowest income levels, where individuals may need to allocate their time toward subsistence.

9 A Generation without Work Contracts
YOUTH IN THE INFORMAL ECONOMY IN EGYPT
Ghada Barsoum

UNEMPLOYMENT, SPECIFICALLY YOUTH unemployment, has long been a central issue of concern in the policy discourse in Egypt. The concern has stemmed from the political volatility of this group. The demonstrations in Egypt of January 25, 2011, and the subsequent political upheaval showed that the political fear about employment issues was rightfully placed. However, it was not the unemployed alone who were dissatisfied. Without downplaying the issues of freedom of expression, corruption, and police brutality, it is safe to argue that the anger on the street was fueled by compromised quality of jobs in the informal economy. It is important to remember that the Arab Spring, which showed its first bloom in Tunisia, followed by Egypt, was sparked by a frustrated street vendor who burned himself to death in protest of his government's violent exclusion of the working poor.

Work in the informal economy is central to the economic exclusion of young people in Egypt. Labor is the main asset of young workers at the beginning of their work careers. They are at a disadvantage when this employment does not provide them with social protection, in the form of pension benefits, at times of inability to work due to unemployment, illness, or reaching old age. They are also at a disadvantage when the compensation they receive for their labor does not cover basic needs or access to services such as health care. Lack of social protection is a direct outcome of informal work in Egypt.

It is safe to note that informal work is the norm among working youth, as data provided in this chapter show. The data show that the majority of new labor market entrants acquire jobs that provide them with no work contracts or access to social insurance contributory schemes. For these young people, work provides income but no protection. While it may cover the financial needs of the present, it leaves the future vulnerable.

Building on interviews with young people working in the informal economy, this chapter describes the lived experience of informal work and lack of social protection among youth in Egypt. The chapter focuses on young people who are wage workers in employment relations that are not documented by work contracts. The chapter's focus is on educated youth: specifically, young people with high school diplomas and above. This chapter provides an understanding of the process of informal work as experienced and described by working youth themselves. How do young people perceive their lack of social protection and social security? If the needs of the present are barely covered by the income that comes from work, how do these workers foresee their futures? What policies need to be put in place to address this situation of vulnerability? Qualitative interview data is embedded in quantitative data on the situation of informal work among wage-earning young people. By including the survey data, this chapter also shows, through qualitative data, the overarching structural constraints facing young people and the prevalence of the phenomena being described.

The concerns young people express about their lack of social protection highlight the seriousness of the issue of informal work in Egypt. As the qualitative data in this chapter show, while some youth are denied access to social security by their employers, others are making the conscious decision to compromise their social protection. Some of the youth interviewed note that they could not afford to pay social security contributions, as these amounts get deducted from their already meager income. From a generational perspective, young workers' limited access to social protection means that Egypt is witnessing a new generation of workers, specifically educated workers, who will have no access to old age pensions. This is a relatively new phenomenon for educated workers in Egypt, where older generations had access the government's guaranteed employment scheme, which came with social security and health insurance. More serious social repercussions of this problem will start to appear as this cohort of workers ages and becomes unable to work. Lack of social protection is adding a further cause for young people's dissatisfaction with the government's performance, as they continue to believe that the government should sustain its earlier role as the main employer of the educated, as they note in interviews. The continued valorization of government jobs is a direct result of the lack of social protection in Egypt's predominantly informal private sector. Another aspect of the importance of this problem relates to the fact that the contributions of these new entrants to the labor market are needed to sustain the social security system, which is currently skewed toward supporting an aging population of earlier contributors.

Research Methodology

This study is based on the ethnographic field methods of in-depth interviews, taking a life history approach. Qualitative research typically seeks in-depth and intimate information about a relatively small group of people, with the objective of learning about how and why they behave, think, and attach meaning as they do. Qualitative research spans the micro-macro spectrum and touches on issues of both structure and process (Ambert et al. 1995). Such research primarily seeks to show the voice of those affected by the issues studied and follows an inductive epistemology, where the researcher is learning from the data collection process (Marshall and Rossman 2011).

The interviews conducted as part of this study took the approach of following the career path of the informant, taking the life history approach. This approach does not just involve the individual being interviewed but explores the overarching social and economic structures that define the life trajectory of the informant (Bertaux 1982). Life histories also allow the researcher to understand evolutionary processes instead of depending on a snapshot of the present. In life histories, the analysis focuses not on isolated lives of individuals but on the individual as embedded in social relationships and structures. In this way, the analysis eschews a view of culture as a monolithic phenomenon and treats it as process of continuity, change, and conflict that is played out in the lives of individuals.

The interviews informing this study were conducted in two stages. The first stage took place in January 2009 and included female wage workers in the informal economy. In-depth interviews were conducted with eight female workers, in addition to one focus group discussion in the city of Minia in Upper Egypt that was carried out with the help of a NGO. The second stage extended the study's focus to both male and female wage workers in the informal economy and took place in October and November 2012 in Cairo. Overall, 20 young people were interviewed as part of this stage. The young people included in the analysis in this chapter are those with a minimum of a secondary education who have had work experience in the nonagricultural private sector. This was the case for the young men and women interviewed in Cairo and the majority of the young women included in the focus group discussion in Minia.

I will introduce the qualitative data after a discussion, in the next section, of the issue of the prevalence of informal work based on data from the Survey of Young People in Egypt (SYPE). The survey, fielded in 2009, covered a nationally representative sample of 10,000 young people aged 10–29. The analysis presented in this chapter only focuses on young people 15–29, as the working age begins at 15 in Egypt (Population Council 2010). The purpose of this statistical descriptive section is to provide the overarching social and economic structures in which these interviewees make choices.

Understanding Informal Work and Social Protection

Chen (2005) notes that the notion of the informal sector was "discovered" in Kenya, when an International Labour Organization (ILO) interdisciplinary mission wanted to describe persisting traditional forms of economic activities that had even expanded to include enterprises with unregistered and undocumented economic activities (ILO

1972). Building on fieldwork, the Kenya mission opted to describe these activities as falling in the "informal sector." The term itself had been coined a year earlier by British social anthropologist Keith Hart, as part of a study on the Ghanaian economy (Chen 2005; Hart 1973).

The state of thinking at the time was that informal work was an ephemeral phase that is bound to end as an economy moves away from its precapitalist mode of operation and becomes modernized. The structuralist school, pioneered by Alejandro Portes, was a major exception to this widespread view, arguing that the informal sector was a feature of capitalist economy that is exploited by the formal sector (Portes 1989). As Chen (2005) notes, the enthusiasm about studying the informal sector and the debates surrounding it had subsided by the late 1980s and early 1990s, as the concept went out of favor in academic circles.

Renewed interest in the informal work economy came after the ILO's 2002 International Labor Conference, as part of the larger agenda of "decent work" (ILO 2002). The ILO provided an operational definition of informal work and emphasized the focus on an informal "economy" as opposed to an informal "sector," shifting the focus from enterprise characteristics to work relations. The informal economy was defined as economic activities not "covered by formal arrangements" (ILO 2002). This includes all forms of employment without secure work contracts, worker benefits, or social protection in the form of social insurance or health insurance. This definition of the informal economy refers to two distinct groups. The first group consists of own-account workers in unregistered enterprises that are engaged in the production of goods and services for sale or barter. The second group consists of paid workers in undocumented employment relations, either in documented (formal) or undocumented (informal) enterprises. Educated youth among this group are the focus of this study.

Limitations of the Policy Discourse on Youth Unemployment

In comparison to the issue of youth unemployment, informal work and the decent work deficit in the informal economy are hardly discussed in relation to the plight of Egypt's youth. Only recently did Egypt's central statistical bureau, the Central Agency for Public Mobilization and Statistics (CAPMAS), start to include data on job quality and access to social security and work contracts in its regular labor statistics. These statistics, however, are rarely mentioned in policy circles or even in the press coverage when the results are released. The focus on unemployment remains paramount.

Unemployment statistics do give a bird's-eye view of problems of employment in Egypt's labor market, particularly among the youth. By definition, the unemployed are those who are not working for at least one hour in the week and are actively searching for a job. Two large groups are not included in unemployment figures. The first group consists of the young people who have given up searching for a job. This group of "discouraged" youth is significant and is particularly high in rural areas. Jobless, these young people have given up searching on realizing that the search does not lead to finding jobs. The joblessness rate is defined the number of youth who are neither in education nor in employment as a proportion of the relevant age group. Analysis of recent survey data in Egypt shows that the joblessness rate among youth aged 15–29 reaches 60 percent (Assaad 2010).

The second group that is not included in the unemployment figures, and is the focus of this chapter, is those employed in the informal economy. This omission pertains to the quality of jobs of those who are employed. Jobs that provide low income and no social protection or potentials for growth. A recent ILO report (2012) shows that 51.2 percent of nonagricultural employment in Egypt is informal employment. This statistic includes those who are own-account workers in unregistered businesses, employers in unregistered businesses, and workers without contract in both registered and unregistered businesses. These figures do not include the large segment of workers in the agricultural sector, which constitutes one-third of the workforce (30.7 percent, according to CAPMAS estimates in 2011).

Informal Work Is a Serious Youth Employment Issue in Egypt

In all the interviews with employed youth, informal work, identified here as working without a work contract and social security, was the norm in the private sector. In this section, I use data from the 2009 Survey of Young People in Egypt (SYPE) to show that the qualitative sample included in this study reflects clear patterns that are confirmed by quantitative data.[1] There are many methodological hurdles in measuring aspects of informal work that go beyond the scope of this chapter. I follow Gatti and colleagues (2011) in defining informal work as performing wage work without work contracts and social security coverage. The following analysis will look at the prevalence of work contracts among wage workers in nonagricultural activities, along with access to social insurance.

According to the SYPE data on those aged 15–29, wage work is the most common employment status among youth in Egypt. More than 86 percent of working youth are wage workers. The remaining working youth are mainly unpaid family workers (10 percent), and a small minority are employers or self-employed. Among young workers, the private sector is the main employer, providing employment to more than 78 percent of nonagricultural wage workers.

For the overwhelming majority of youth who are wage workers, informal work is the norm. As shown in table 9.1, among those wage workers aged 15–29, only 18.9 percent have access to work contracts. When looking at all wage workers, including those in agriculture, this figure is lowered to 15 percent, as contracts are virtually nonexistent among this group (not shown in table 9.1). While the private sector is the main employer of young people, only 7.5 percent of youth working in the private sector had access to social insurance, and only 7.1 percent had access to medical insurance. These benefits are closely related to access to a work contract, with only 7.7 percent of workers in the private sector having access to work contracts.

Table 9.1 shows a glaring disparity between young people working in the government and those working in the private sector in terms of access to work contracts, social insurance, medical insurance, and permanent employment. The government provides employment to only 14 percent of wage working youth. However, 65.5 percent of them have access to social insurance, 54.1 percent have access to medical insurance, and 68.1 percent have access to work contracts.

It is worth noting that informal work is a youth-specific problem in Egypt. Comparing youth-specific data to data on the general population, taken from recent official statistics from CAPMAS, shows that informal work is far more prevalent among youth than in the general population (see table 9.2). Table 9.2 includes agricultural and nonagricultural workers. While only 20.1 percent of nonagricultural wage workers from the youth have access to work contracts, the prevalence rate is 58.0 percent for wage workers from all age categories. While 18.9 percent of youth nonagricultural wage workers have access to social insurance, the prevalence rate is 55.0 percent for wage workers from all age categories. Likewise, while 18.7 percent of youth nonagricultural wage workers have access to medical insurance, the prevalence rate is 50.0 percent for all wage workers.

Informal work is also an enduring state. Based on the analysis of panel data from Egypt, Gatti and colleagues (2011, 203) note that between 2008 and 2009, an informal worker in Egypt had a 4 percent chance of moving to a formal private sector job and a 5 percent chance of moving to a public sector job. This pattern shows little possibility for the large

TABLE 9.1

Access to work contracts, social insurance, and health insurance among nonagricultural wage workers aged 15–29, Egypt, 2009.

Employment sector	Government	Public sector	Private sector	Investment sector	Other	Total
Nonagricultural wage workers with social insurance	64.48	75.30	7.50	46.64	25.12	18.92
Nonagricultural wage workers with medical insurance	54.13	75.30	7.10	37.98	25.12	18.67
Nonagricultural wage with legal work contract	68.18	66.77	7.77	66.56	60.02	20.12

Source: Survey of Young People in Egypt, 2009.

TABLE 9.2

Access to work contracts, social insurance, and health insurance among wage workers (all working-age population, all sectors), Egypt, 2009.

Indicator	Gender	Employment sector					Total
		Governmental	Public sector	Private sector	Investment	Others	
Employed	Male	98	96	29	88	69	55
with social	Female	97	91	25	81	54	84
insurance	Total	98	96	30	88	64	60
Employed	Male	97	94	13	72	64	44
with health	Female	95	90	15	74	54	78
insurance	Total	96	93	14	72	61	50
Employed who	Male	99	98	23	91	66	51
have work	Female	100	99	30	90	66	88
contract	Total	99	98	24	91	66	58
Employed in	Male	96	93	47	87	94	64
permanent	Female	93	93	43	80	68	85
work	Total	95	93	47	86	87	68

Source: Survey of Young People in Egypt, 2009.

pool of young workers who start their work life in informal work to move away from it and carries little hope for them to move into formal work with the possibility of access to social protection in the form of social insurance and health insurance. Gatti and colleagues compare the implied average job duration of informal wage work between countries. The implied duration of an informal job is about three years in Egypt; that in Mexico, for example, is about two years.

The foregoing descriptive statistics speak to three facts about the employment opportunities available to new entrants to the labor market. First, most of the jobs they obtain as wage workers are informal in nature. Second, the fortunes of these new entrants to the labor market are more skewed toward informal work than were those of earlier cohorts. Third, young people mostly start in informal employment relations; young people are more likely than those in other age categories to continue in informal work; and their fortunes are much worse than those of workers in other wage categories. Gatti and colleagues (2011) even demonstrate that between 2006 and 2009, the probability of transitioning from the informal sector to the formal sector decreased, though this was partially due to the impact of the financial crisis (see Said, chapter 3 here).

For many young people, good jobs that offer financial stability, employment security, and social protection are concentrated in the government. For this reason, as the interviews in this chapter and the SYPE data show, the government remains the preferred employer of many youth, particularly women. With the exception of the limited number of formal jobs in the private sector, the government remains the sector of employment predominantly offering job security in Egypt. Analysis of the SYPE data shows that about 72 percent of young people noted that working in the government was better than working for the private sector. The preference for a government job was inversely correlated with socioeconomic background. Young people in poorer households, those who are more likely to be disadvantaged in the labor market, show greater propensity to prefer a government job. Because a government job becomes a highly valued job, young people speak of favoritism as the key obstacle to finding a job in the government.

The legal framework governing social security provision contributes to the increased amount of informal work among new entrants to the labor market in Egypt. The contributory social insurance system in Egypt is governed by Law 79 of 1975, which allows access to the contributory pension system only to employees in the government public service and publicly owned enterprises, commonly known as the public sector, and the formal private sector. This law excludes those who do not have work contracts with a registered enterprise from access to social protection. This exclusion also applies to wage workers in unregistered informal enterprises. The Egyptian Labor Law (2003) states that social security is a public program designed to protect individuals and their families from income losses due to unemployment, old age, sickness, or death and to improve their welfare through public services. Contributions by the private sector under social security regulations are provided for those who are employed full-time. According to the law, on a basic monthly salary of up to 650 EGP (about $100), social security contributions are at the following rates: 26 percent paid by the employer and 14 percent paid by the employee. The fundamental benefits granted by the law include a pension, disability payments, sickness payments, maternity and death allowances, and unemployment insurance. Without a work contract, these benefits are not tenable.

While workers in the informal economy are unable to contribute to social security schemes, they also fail to qualify for the noncontributory safety net schemes. There are two main regulations governing the noncontributory pensions system in Egypt. Law 112 of 1980 (the Comprehensive Social Insurance Service) provides a fixed amount to those not covered by contributory schemes in old age and allows for survivor and disability benefits ($10–15/month). Law 30 of 1977 (*daman* pension) provides pensions to orphans, widow(er)s, divorcees, women remaining unmarried at age 50, and families of the imprisoned. These schemes leave out workers in the informal economy who may lose their jobs at times of economic shocks and thus are left with no income, even if they are heads of households including children and other vulnerable groups.

Informal Work among Working Youth

Discussions with young people show different patterns of living with informal work and lack of social insurance. Concerns about lack of access to social security schemes are clearly voiced in the qualitative data. However, despite the eagerness to have social security, some young people are not willing to contribute to it. The following section discusses these reasons and young workers' views on issues of access to social security, based on data collected through interviews and focus group discussions.

Social Insurance as an Unattainable Goal

Many interviews showed young people's eagerness of to have access to social insurance and their concerns about their lack of work contracts. One young man, Mustafa, connected access to social insurance to job security, noting that not having a contract is a sign of lack of stability. His description of his relationship with his private sector employer is one of limited trust and a sense of being deceived. He notes:

> There is no sense of security in a job [aman wazifi] in the private sector. No company would insure you or renew an annual contract for you. It is all by word, [they say] 'come start to work and give us a copy of your identification card [el bitaka]. They take it [the ID copy] and throw it in a drawer. They give you an illusion that you will have a contract, but nothing is signed. (Mustafa, November 2012)

Mustafa was a graduate of the Workers University, which is an open university, and had studied the software package for engineering drawings. His job as a drafter had been changed recently by the construction company that had hired him to work on a construction site, which added to his dissatisfaction. To him, the limited access to social insurance was another way he was being cheated and exploited by his employer, and so he referred to the "illusion" of social security that they gave him.

Laila, a young woman working as a shop assistant, did not stop at silently wanting social security. She discussed the issue with her employer, but with no positive results. She noted:

> When I tell the shop owner to provide me with insurance, he says the shop is not bringing in enough money to pay your salary; now you want insurance. (Laila, January 2009)

As noted earlier, employers are required by law to pay a monthly contribution of 26 percent of the salary as their contribution to the employee's social insurance cost. However, to save on their labor costs, employers resort to not contributing to insurance. As the following section shows, some young workers might accept their employers' decisions in order to save on their own contributions. This also allows young employees to negotiate higher take-home pay. Because there is no effective monitoring and inspection system, this strategy is allowed to persist.

Employers resort to a number of strategies, which were explained in different interviews, to evade the requirement to contribute to social insurance for their employees. For instance, they physically hide the employee in various ways. In one interview, a shop assistant noted that she was asked to pretend that she was a customer. Tricks used to evade social insurance monitoring by the government vary and can be quite innovative. In one interview, another shop assistant noted that the employer had insurance files in the names of relatives (his wife, for example). When the government inspectors visited the shop, the employee pretended to be the person in whose name the insurance file was created.

Not All Youth Want to Contribute to Social Insurance

Despite valorization of social security among interviewed youth, not every young person is willing to contribute to social security. This section describes the main reasons interviewees offer for not contributing to social insurance when allowed, despite the value they see in having it.

The high cost of contributions remains the most commonly identified reason. To many of those interviewed, any deducted contribution takes away from an already limited income. Abeer, a factory worker, noted:

> I don't have any benefits, no social insurance or medical insurance. But I don't want them anyway, because it gets deducted from my salary. (Abeer, January 2009)

The same notion was repeated by Mariam, a shop assistant who took part in the focus group discussion in Minia. She questioned the cost of any deductions from her salary because it was so low, noting:

> The salary is already not enough, what else will they deduct from it? (Mariam, January 2009)

Mustafa, who was quoted earlier lamenting not having access to social security, explained the calculation behind his decision to withdraw from the social insurance system after it was arranged for him to get enrolled through his current employer:

> I went to the company owner and told him, "I don't want insurance." They were deducting LE [EGP] 150 for two months...Yes, this amount makes a difference. My salary is LE 1000, I work in Dokki and I live in Helwan. After (the cost of) my food and transportation, I am left with LE 700. After he takes the LE 150, I am left with 550. My savings group [gameiati: an informal rotating saving group] takes about LE 200. When you look at it, you will find that it is not working. Even if I am insured, it is difficult that he takes LE 150 from me. (Mustafa, November 2012)

Many young workers fear that the money being deducted is not being paid into the government insurance scheme. Because the system does not allow workers to know about their monthly contributions payment submission or accumulated funds, there is a sense that the money will be lost. If the money that is deducted as contributions is very much needed, contributors need to know where exactly these funds are going. Because of the lack of system transparency, young people feel that if they stop working, the accumulated funds will be considered as lost. This notion was clearly exemplified in the case of Mustafa, who noted:

> If I saw them sending the money to the Ministry of Insurance, I would have accepted to continue. I found them deducting the money for two months and no one was going to the Ministry office to submit the contributions. (Mustafa, November 2012)

Information on accumulated funds is only available at the offices of the Social Insurance Authority and is only be provided on submitting a written request. The hurdle of having to go to a government office to learn about one's accumulated savings adds to the complexity of the system.

Young women offer more reasons for not contributing to the social security scheme. Hoda, who worked in a textile factory in Cairo, believed that not contributing was the safest option because that way she would not lose her contributions when she stopped working. Not married during the time of the interview, Hoda believed that she was bound to leave her job at the factory once she got married because of its long hours and nonexistent maternity benefits. Hoda believed that not contributing to social insurance was a marker of her freedom to leave her current job at any point. She noted:

> I know nothing about this insurance thing. In the factory they tell me have social insurance, I tell them I am not sure I'll stay [in the factory], that's why I don't like to have insurance. It gives me freedom. What do I know? They will take money from my salary, and if I stay at home, who will continue to pay? (Hoda, January 2009)

Hoda's statement not only describes the lack of system transparency but also relates to the system's perceived lack of flexibility. Most young female workers expect maternity to interrupt their work life. However, the system does not have the flexibility to deal with employment volatility, particularly that of female workers, who tend to drop out of the labor force in association with childbearing. In a focus group discussion, young working women expressed concerns about the possibility of losing the prospect of being hired by the government if one has social insurance through a private sector firm. There are no laws stipulating the exclusion of private sector employees from attaining positions in the government. However, the government's efforts to hire "the unemployed" support this misconception. A young woman noted:

> If social insurance will eliminate the options of working in the government, we don't want social insurance. My friend's brother worked in a restaurant for four

months, and they covered him with social insurance. All graduates in his cohort got jobs in the government. He didn't because he had social insurance. For the insurance of four months, he lost the government job. (Hind, January 2009).

It is very difficult to verify the reason for the friend of the informant's brother not getting a government job. What really matters is that these beliefs play into the decision not to contribute to social security.

The fact that most young people are working in the informal economy and not contributing to pension schemes has a number of serious repercussions. These youth, lacking social security contributions, constitute a new generation of workers who will have no access to social security payouts when they need them. The impact of this problem will be ubiquitous as this generation of workers ages and becomes unable to work. Contributions from new entrants to the labor market are also needed now to sustain the social security system, which is currently skewed toward supporting an aging population of earlier contributors. The system is heavily lopsided, with a lower proportion of young subscribers than of old ones, who are approaching the demographic stage of retirement and receiving pensions. El-Gibally (2006) argues that the low contributions from young workers are affecting the sustainability of the social security system in Egypt.

The Preference for Government Jobs among Youth

Young people prefer government jobs. This was clearly shown in survey results, as noted earlier. This preference is a result of the disparity between the predominantly informal employment in the private sector and the "good" government jobs, leading to a dual labor market system. Such a dual, or segmented, configuration is a key feature of labor markets throughout the Arab world (Assaad 2013).

In Barsoum (2004) I discussed the benefits young women list of a government job. These include job security, pension schemes, job stability, a relatively light workload with shorter hours than the private sector, and a limited power differential between the supervisor and the supervisee. In a government job, according to the young women I had interviewed at that time (Barsoum 2004), no one "owns" you, unlike the private sector, where relations of power are very strong.

Among youth I interviewed in Egypt after January 25, 2011, the preference for a government job was very strong, and there was little gender difference in the data. Mustafa, asked about the solution he saw to having no social security, noted:

I am thinking that I should find a job in public sector company. I am convinced of this. They will give me insurance. They will deduct the insurance money from my salary, and I know where the money goes. I don't believe the private sector...My father worked in a public sector company and he has early retirement. I talked to him to see anyone he knows in the company to get me a job. (Mustafa, November 2012)

The only solution—a public sector job, according to Mustafa—could only be reached through favoritism and the family network. If this was not going to work, he believed that the government had to offer yet another solution:

> I think the government should start factories. There are actually many factories that have been closed. If they open these factories that were privatized, this will solve the solution. (Mustafa, November 2012)

The same notion was repeated by Ahmed, who noted:

> They [the government] has to hire the youth. That's the only solution. The country will be better than before. People will be able to live better than ever [a ḥan min el awal], and people will be able to live [tikdar te'ish]. (Ahmed, November 2012)

The era when the government could be the main employer of educated youth is gone. That social pact was broken with the slowing of government hiring from the early 1990s, upon the implementation of economic reforms and structural adjustment policies. However, many young people, dissatisfied with working conditions in the private sector, continue to cling to this hope. This is particularly the case in Egypt since January 25, 2011; many of the young interviewees talked about change in the direction of the government offering more jobs.

The preference for government jobs was played by the Mubarak regime during the protests of January 25, 2011. In a desperate attempt to clear Tahrir Square, the government announced vacancies in the government for youth. Journalistic accounts portrayed thousands of young people, both male and female, flocking into government organizations with job applications. The foregoing quotes show that this governmental strategy perpetuates the illusion of a solution in the minds of many young people.

The Direct Cost of Informal Work: Lack of Access to Medical Insurance

Informal work is very costly to workers, particularly the working poor. The lack of work contracts leaves conditions of work, such as work hours and pay, and benefits, such as paid leave and health insurance, subject to negotiations with employers. The ILO (2009) refers to "glaring decent work deficits" in the informal economy, where working conditions can be unsafe and incomes uncertain and lower than in the formal economy, even when employees work longer hours. Collective bargaining and representation rights are nonexistent.

Informal work eliminates access to health care insurance in Egypt. The Health Insurance Organization, the main health insurance service provider in Egypt, is mandated to provide service to three main groups: public sector/government employees and their families; enrolled students; and school-aged children (Shawky 2010). Workers in the informal economy are often engaged in hazardous jobs with particularly high exposure to risk. Because the majority of these workers are poor, they are more subject to poor-quality nutrition and reduced access to safe drinking water and sanitary facilities. Such high exposure to risk, combined with low social protection coverage, places most informal economy workers in a very vulnerable situation (ILO 2009).

Rashad (2012) notes that access to quality health services is very expensive in Egypt even in comparison to many other lower middle income countries. Research has repeatedly documented the impoverishing effect of catastrophic health spending in Egypt and the limitations of its current health insurance system (e.g., Shawky 2010). Targeted schemes to reach vulnerable uninsured households need to be developed to address the need to expand access to health insurance beyond employment-based schemes (Shawky 2010), which only cater to workers in the formal economy.

The Egyptian labor law (2003) states that all private sector companies in Egypt are required to provide health care for employees either privately or through the Medical Insurance Plan of the Ministry of Social Insurance. Without a work contract, these workers have no access to medical insurance. Besides, the near universality of small-scale enterprises in the private sector makes it difficult for employers to provide employees with group insurance plans.

When asked about access to medical insurance in a focus group discussion of female young workers, a young woman who works as a shop assistant noted:

Medical insurance is a big illusion. It doesn't exist. (Minia, focus group discussion, January 2009)

If a respondent in the focus group discussion mentioned medical insurance, it was with cynicism and describing it as nonexistent. Interviewed youth often mentioned access to medical insurance in connection with access to social insurance. This is not surprising, since both are provided to government employees. Ashraf, a teacher in a private school, noted:

I want job security, insurance, and a pension [plan]. I want that when I need [medical] treatment, I get it for free, and not for a lot of money in private hospitals. (Ashraf, Cairo, March 2013)

Also related to health insurance, the Egyptian labor law stipulates that if the sickness or injury is work-related, the employee is entitled to as much as six months of annual sick leave with pay between 75 percent and 100 percent of the employee's usual wage. Asmaa, who worked in a textile factory, recounted her recurrent encounters with workplace injuries. Her case illustrates glaring violations of these regulations.

I cut my finger when I was working on the machine. I accidently put my hand inside, and it cut half my finger. This has happened to me three times. I went to the central hospital and stayed at home because I couldn't work. My boss sent me 100 LE, and I managed to stitch my finger back on. I didn't go to work for a week afterward, and my boss split my weekly wage with me—he gave me three days' worth of my salary and deducted the other three days. (Asmaa, January 2009)

This account reveals glaring violations of workers' rights in this factory. Of particular concern is the recurrence of injury, the lack of medical support in the workplace, and the limited support the employee received. Not paying her wages for the week was a clear violation of the law. It is important to note that Asmaa, who was 19 at the time of the interview, had never been to school.[2]

Policy Options for Extending Social Protection to Workers in the Informal Economy

While this chapter voices the views of young people on the value of getting a government job, the policy solution cannot be to create more government jobs. Decades of guaranteed employment have resulted in a bloated, inefficient government sector, despite the implementation of structural reforms since the early 1990s. The demand for jobs in the government is an outcome of the failure of the private sector to provide social protection to its workers. This requires shifting the focus to extending social protection measures to workers in the informal economy. As noted, social protection refers to workers' access to social security schemes in the informal economy along with access to health care insurance. In the first area, the international experience in extending social security to workers in the informal economy highlights a number of approaches. For instance, the ILO (2009) highlights the need for flexible, simplified, and diversified contributory social security schemes. Such flexibility would accommodate the inconsistent income of workers in the informal economy. Contributory schemes would allow these workers to accumulate insurance funds to be used at times of unemployment or illness or in old age. The ILO (2009) also highlights the importance of subsidizing social insurance systems, particularly for the self-employed. There is also a renewed focus on the need for measures for the enforcement of contributory schemes for wage workers.

My earlier discussion of young people's reluctance to contribute to the social insurance system because of its lack of transparency and its high cost relative to the limited income of young people working in the informal economy shows the need to address these concerns. System transparency and efficient communication with contributors would alleviate concerns about the loss of one's contributions or the possibility of fraud by one's employer. More urgently, intervention is needed to subsidize social insurance schemes for young workers to encourage them to contribute.

The ILO has also been at the forefront of advocating for the provision of micro-insurance schemes as a tool to extend social protection to the working poor (Churchill and Matul 2012). These programs are provided by a diverse set of players, including cooperatives, unions, nongovernmental organizations, and the private sector. The rationale of micro-insurance programs is to combine savings with insurance and help the working poor build assets. These schemes seek to protect policyholders against the financial consequences of various risks, including illness and death. According to Churchill and Matul, more than 500 million micro-insurance policies are active in Asia, Africa, and Latin America. A similar approach, *takaful*, which has grown in a number of Arab and countries, is seen as an Islamic alternative to conventional insurance, based on the concept of mutuality (Vizcaino 2012). The program has grown significantly in recent years in Saudi Arabia, Bahrain, and Malaysia. Adaptations in program implementation to lower-income clientele are needed to encourage contributors.

Because labor is the main asset of the poor, health shocks have an especially detrimental impact on their income. There is a global movement toward the extension of health care coverage to excluded groups, particularly those working in the informal economy. "Social health protection" refers to guaranteed effective access to affordable quality health care and financial protection at times of illness (ILO 2009). Models in this direction include:

1. India's government launched in 2008 a social insurance scheme that provides smart-card-based, cashless health insurance coverage of 30,000 rupees per annum (about US$640), covering hospitalization, including maternity, for families below the poverty line in the informal economy. In August 2011, the program had more than 24 million smart cards, each covering five persons. The program extends health insurance to regularly excluded groups, such as construction workers, street vendors, and domestic workers, with plans to extend it to mine workers, rag pickers, railway porters, and cab drivers (ILO 2011).

2. In Thailand, a universal health care coverage scheme has been fully implemented providing basic health care and maternal care. The Thailand Constitution recognizes health and social security as citizens' rights (ILO 2011).

3. Micro-insurance has been used as a mechanism for pooling funds to purchase health service. In some African countries, civil society organizations take part in initiating micro-insurance programs that are delivered in different forms (ILO 2009).

The political will to put these programs into action is central. Indonesia, as part of its democratic transition, amended its 1945 Constitution in 2002 to commit the government to the extension of social security to the entire population, stating: "Every person shall have the right to social security in order to develop him or herself as a dignified human being" and "The state shall develop a social security system for all the people and shall empower the vulnerable and poor people in accordance with human dignity" (ILO n.d.). Following the constitutional amendment, a new labor law (Law 40 of 2004) was issued to create a "National Social Security System." The system covers the entire population and has five programs: (1) health insurance, (2) occupational injury insurance, (3) an old age benefit, (4) a pension benefit, and (5) a survivor's benefit. Similarly, as noted, Thailand recognizes health and social security as citizens' rights in its Constitution.

Finally, to once again mention an often-repeated recommendation, young workers need to be aware of their rights and need to be offered effective channels for grievances at times of violation. When young people choose not to have social security, this is a choice made out of necessity. There is need to support young people so that they do not compromise their social security and future needs because of the needs of the present.

Conclusion

The impact of informal employment on young people's lives is not sufficiently addressed in policy circles in Egypt. Youth unemployment dominates the policy discourse on employment issues. This focus ignores the concerns of a significant majority of working youth in Egypt: those who are employed in the informal economy with little access to social protection.

Informal work has become the norm among educated youth in Egypt working in the nonagricultural sector. This is a development witnessed at a new scale for this generation of youth in Egypt. The pact that was started by the Nasser regime in 1964 to provide guaranteed employment to youth was first broken by a process of slowed hiring and then stalled hiring, with the implementation of structural adjustment policies. A bloated government structure that suffered from overstaffing and inefficiency provided impetus for these policies. For educated youth, who have witnessed their parents getting jobs in the government, there is a heavy realization that the stalling of government hiring represents a breakdown of the social pact. This is particularly the case in that the private sector has failed to absorb the large population of graduates seeking jobs and offers jobs with compromised benefits and limited access to social protection. The private sector's failure to provide good jobs, combined with an image of the past where the government provided better jobs for the earlier generation, continues to feed into the valorization of government jobs among youth. When these jobs are not obtainable, young people speak bitterly of favoritism as a mechanism for their exclusion.

The qualitative data in this chapter show different patterns of living with informal work and lack of social insurance among youth working in the private sector. While young people strongly voice concerns about lack of access to social security, many are not eager to contribute to the social security system. A main reason is cost: the impact of one's contribution on one's meager monthly income. Other problems relating to the lack of transparency of the system and its lack of flexibility to support the volatile conditions of informal work have also been highlighted.

Extending social protection to young people working in the informal economy is a major policy challenge in Egypt. To do so requires a strong political will to move social protection higher up on national policy agendas. This issue is even more urgent today, given the fact that the problems of informal work have reached one of Egypt's most politically volatile groups: educated youth.

REFERENCES

Ambert, A., P. A. Adler, P. Adler, and D. Detzner. 1995. Understanding and evaluating qualitative research. *Journal of Marriage and the Family* 57(4): 879–893.

Assaad, R. 2010. Human development and labor markets. In *Egypt human development report. 2010,* 147–158. Cairo: United Nations Development Programme and Institute of National Planning.

Assaad, R. 2013, August. Making sense of Arab labor markets: The enduring legacy of dualism. Institute for the Study of Labor (IZA) discussion paper 7573. Bonn: Institut zur Zukunft der Arbeit.

Barsoum, G. 2004. *The employment crisis of female graduates in Egypt: An ethnographic account.* Cairo Papers in Social Science, vol. 25, monograph 3. Cairo: American University in Cairo Press.

Bertaux, D. 1982. The life-cycle approach as a challenge to the social sciences. In *Aging and life course transitions: An interdisciplinary perspective,* ed. T. Hareven and K. Adams, 127–150. New York: Guilford Press.

Chen, M. 2005. Rethinking the informal economy: From enterprise characteristics to employment relations. In *Rethinking informalization, poverty, precarious jobs, and social protection,* ed. N. Kudva and L. Beneria. Cornell University Open Access Repository

Churchill, C., and M. Matul, eds. 2012. Protecting the poor: A micro-insurance compendium. Vol. 2. Geneva: International Labour Organization.

Gatti, R., D. F. Angel-Urdinola, J. Silva, and A. Bodor. 2011, December. Striving for better jobs: The challenge of informality in the Middle East and North Africa region. MENA knowledge and learning quick notes series no. 49. Washington, DC World Bank.

Gibally, A. F. 2006. The future of the social insurance system in Egypt. Strategic papers of Al Ahram's Center for Political and Strategic Studies. Cairo: Al Ahram's Center for Political and Strategic Studies.

Hart, K. 1973. Informal income opportunities and urban employment in Ghana. *Journal of Modern African Studies* 11: 61–89.

International Labour Organization (ILO). 1972. Employment, incomes, and equality: A strategy for increasing productive employment in Kenya. Geneva: International Labour Organization.

International Labour Organization (ILO). 2002. Resolution concerning decent work and the informal economy. International Labour Organization 90th Session, 2002. Geneva: International Labour Organization.

International Labour Organization (ILO). 2009. The informal economy in Africa: Promoting transition to formality: Challenges and strategies. Geneva: International Labour Organization.

International Labour Organization (ILO). 2011. Social protection floor for a fair and inclusive globalization. Report of the Social Protection Floor Advisory Group. Geneva: International Labour Organization.

International Labour Organization (ILO). 2012, June. Statistical update on employment in the informal economy. ILO—Department of Statistics. 2012. Geneva: International Labour Organization.

International Labour Organization (ILO). n.d. Overview of major social security legislation (in Indonesia). http://www.ilo.org/jakarta/whatwedo/publications/WCMS_170622/lang—en/index.htm.

Marshall, C., and G. Rossman. 2011. Designing qualitative research. 5th ed. Los Angeles: Sage.

Population Council. 2010, February. Survey of Young People in Egypt: Preliminary report. Cairo: Population Council.

Portes, A. 1989. La mondialisation par le bas [L'émergence des communautés transnationales]. *Actes de la Recherche en Sciences Sociales* 129(1): 15–25.

Rashad, A. 2012. Catastrophic health expenditure and poverty in Egypt: An analysis of household survey data. Master's thesis, American University in Cairo.

Shawky, S. 2010. Could the employment-based targeting approach serve Egypt in moving towards a social health insurance model? *Eastern Mediterranean Health Journal* [La Revue de Santé de la Méditerranée orientale] 6(16): 663–670.

Vizcaino, B. 2012, April 19. Analysis: Slower Takaful growth prompts strategy rethink. thedailynewsegypt.com. http://www.dailynewsegypt.com/2012/04/18/analysis-slower-takaful-growth-prompts-trategy-rethink/.

NOTES

1. I am grateful to Ali Rashed for research assistance in analyzing the SYPE data, which are available at populationcouncil.org.

2. While her education background would not include her in this study, I include her account to show the danger of lack of medical insurance and the glaring violations of workers' rights in some private sector firms.

10 Does Labor Law Reform Offer an Opportunity for Reducing Arab Youth Unemployment?
Jeffrey B. Nugent

THE ISSUE OF creating enough meaningful jobs is at the center of the socioeconomic challenges facing the Middle East. However, before making policy prescriptions, one must first fully understand the underlying labor market issues. If the private sector is going to hold the key to creating new opportunities for young people, then one must understand how private sector firms operate in the economic environment of the Middle East in order to make meaningful policy recommendations.

First, consider the hiring decision by a private sector firm. This hiring decision is extremely risky. Only after a firm makes this decision does it become possible to assess the diligence, conscientiousness, and honesty of a worker, and an employer's needs, in terms of both the number and type of workers, which may change in unpredictable ways over time. Second, from the worker's perspective, there are also risks involved when deciding to take a job. The integrity of the employer in protecting workers from danger and following through on employment commitments, contributions to pensions, social security, vacations, and rest time may be equally hard to assess.

If labor regulations are quite rigid, they may cause firms to become unwilling to take on the uncertainty of hiring new workers. Labor market rigidity arises when firms cannot use short-term contracts and when regulations provide considerable job protection to workers on long-term contracts. These long-term contracts require firms to be able to predict today their employment needs into a very far-off future, regardless of the likelihood of changing technology and market conditions. With so much uncertainty in the employment relationship, if firms can only hire for long-term contracts, fewer workers are likely to be hired when facing these strict employment regulations: managers and owners attempt to avoid taking on all of the risk of the employment relationship. The purpose of this chapter is to examine the possibility that removing labor regulations could be a means to increasing employment and productivity in those countries in the Middle East and North Africa (MENA) that have both high youth unemployment and rigid labor regulations.

By making it easier for firms to hire (and lay off) workers, deregulation can lower the costs of labor, thus stimulating employment. Nevertheless, since some of the labor market regulations are those designed to make it harder for firms to dismiss redundant workers, deregulation can, alternatively, decrease employment (by increasing firing). Moreover, since labor regulations serve to protect workers from various kinds of exploitation, labor market deregulation may also discourage employment via reduced labor supply. Given strong reasons for seeing both positive and negative effects on employment, it is not surprising that labor market deregulation is so controversial. Proposals to remove existing labor regulations are likely to receive a great deal of political heat, explaining why substantial labor market reforms are relatively rare in MENA countries.

While deregulation may have many effects on current labor market conditions in the MENA countries, assessing the effect on employment is the most important. To date, most assessments of the effects of changes in labor regulations have been limited to highly developed OECD countries and to a lesser extent Latin American countries where some significant reforms have taken place in the last couple of decades. Nevertheless, an increasing a number of studies in the MENA region (e.g., Agenor and El-Aynaoui 2003; Devlin 2010) have claimed that the labor market institutions of the countries of the MENA region constitute a severe constraint on the region's economic development and are a contributor to their generally high level of unemployment and the high rates of informal work (see Barsoum, chapter 9 here). The validity of such claims, however, is very difficult to prove, and hence they remain controversial.

The seriousness of this issue is primarily due to the current demographic youth bulge in the MENA countries (see Beck and Dyer, chapter 1 here). In the MENA countries the share of youth in the population is 30 percent whereas it is 20 percent or less in Europe, North America, Australia/New Zealand, and Japan and generally 25 percent or less in Sub-Saharan Africa and Asia. An important implication of this youth bulge is the record number of new labor market entrants each year. With this surge in new entrants, any obstacles to labor absorption are of much greater significance to youth unemployment problems in the MENA countries than in other regions (see Said, chapter 3 here).

Unemployment rates in the MENA region have been averaging 15 percent and are often at least twice that for young men and higher yet for young women. These high unemployment rates cause an absorption challenge and a host of related problems for those in the youth bulge including delayed marriage, inability to afford housing, and inability to live independently from parents (Assaad and Tunali 2001; Dhillon and Yousef 2009).

Indeed, these factors are credited with contributing very substantially to the unprecedented political unrest and uprisings that erupted throughout much of the MENA region in the Arab Spring of 2011 and 2012. Even the rapid growth in the MENA countries, triggered in large part by high and rising oil prices over much of the past decade prior to the financial crisis and the Arab Spring, were unable to make a dent in these unemployment rates.

While the overall level of labor law rigidity (LLR) for the region is not that high, there are three reasons for taking this issue seriously in the MENA countries: (1) these rigidity indexes are higher in the countries, such as Morocco, Syria, Tunisia, and perhaps also Egypt, that are facing more serious youth unemployment than are other countries of the region; (2) these are the very countries that, because of somewhat lower wage rates and greater experience in labor intensive manufactures exports, have the best potential for increasing job growth through exports; and (3) research from around the world (e.g., Heckman and Pages 2000) suggests that stiffer regulations on both hiring and firing workers disproportionately disadvantage new entrants to the labor force and young people in general.

On the other hand several important reasons for doubting that LLR could really be a serious obstacle to job creation in the MENA countries (or even elsewhere) can also be identified. First, to the extent that these laws are rigid, they are only de jure and may not operate in practice because of lack of enforcement. Second, even if they are in principle enforced, corruption payments to the relevant officials—which are known to be relatively high in the MENA region—could provide a way around measures taken to enforce the rules. Third, even if the rules were enforced without corruption, the informal sector, which operates outside these rules, would still thrive. To support this claim, Elbadawi and Loayza (2008) have demonstrated that in the MENA countries more rigid regulations are associated with more informal employment.

The remainder of this chapter is organized as follows. The next section presents some information relevant to the rigidity of labor laws for the MENA and other regions. I also briefly review existing literature, making use of various methods for linking labor laws to employment outcomes. The following section then summarizes the results obtained from the two different studies that I draw on, which make use of the World Bank Enterprise Surveys, and compares the results with other studies that make use of the same surveys. The results show the potential importance of not only job creation but also job destruction in MENA countries. In the final section I pay considerable attention to policy implications and suggestions for further research.

Rigidity of Labor Regulations in the MENA Region

While numerous scholars have suggested that labor markets in the MENA countries are problematic, few studies examine LLRs, and to my knowledge, none examines such effects at the firm level. The most comprehensive attempts to measure LLRs in the MENA countries are those of Botero and colleagues (2004), Angel-Urdinola and Kuddo (2010), and to a lesser extent Aleksynska and Schindler (2011).[1] Botero and colleagues (2004) included six MENA countries (Egypt, Jordan, Lebanon, Morocco, Tunisia, and Turkey) among the 85 countries for which LLR indexes were constructed for a single year in the late 1990s. Botero and colleagues (2004) examined only the determinants of labor market rigidity, including income per capita, the political orientation of government, trade openness, and the origins of the country's legal system.

Angel-Urdinola and Kuddo (2010) constructed similar indexes, based on the World Bank's Doing Business Surveys, for more MENA countries. The Doing Business database provides consistent measures of components of LLR indexes for the period 2005–2011. These indexes are built up from large numbers of yes/no answers to questions about various aspects of the labor laws, thereby making the coding of the LLRs relatively objective and replicable. Unfortunately, these indicators do not capture everything of relevance in these laws to the functioning of labor markets; the weighting of the various subindicators into the various indicators and indexes is arbitrary; and alternative independent attempts to develop such indicators for the MENA countries are lacking.

Most studies on the effects of changes in labor laws have been limited to OECD countries and, to a lesser extent, Latin American and "transition economies." While the countries of the MENA region have received less attention in the literature on labor market regulation and their effects, they have not been altogether neglected. Kpodar (2007) attempts to analyze the effects of labor regulations in 15 MENA countries and 14 transition economy countries. Explanatory factors included not only an LLR index, taxes on wage rates, social security payments by the employer, and firing costs but also macroeconomic factors such as labor productivity, real interest rates, inflation rates, terms-of-trade shocks, and lagged unemployment rates. The results obtained from his 24-country panel data set showed that differences between Algeria (the study's focus) and any particular country were better explained by the differences in macroeconomic shocks than by those in the labor and tax wedge variables.

Elbadawi and Loayza (2008) studied the relationship between informal work, and regulations. This study, like this chapter, was motivated by the employment crisis that Arab countries have had and will be facing through 2030. The study analyzed the effects of regulations on informal work and in turn on firm performance; their proxies for such institutions and regulations were a law-and-order index and a business regulatory freedom index, but no attempt was made to make use of labor market rigidity indexes.

Some researchers have also attempted to make more direct connections between labor laws and employment problems in two MENA countries (Egypt and Morocco, the two countries analyzed in this chapter). Agenor and El-Aynaoui (2003) have shown that in Morocco extremely high transaction costs in labor markets have had the effect of impeding firms from both laying off redundant workers and hiring new workers. There have been even more frequent attempts in the literature to relate relatively rigid labor regulations to the dominance of the informal sector in Egypt than in Morocco (Assaad 2002, 2009; Assaad and Tunali 2001; Wahba 2009).

Pierre and Scarpetta (2006) used firm-level perceptions of labor regulations as an obstacle to doing business, taken from the Investment Climate Surveys (forerunners to the Enterprise Surveys of the World Bank), to show that country-specific scores on LLRs were positively and significantly related to firm-level perceptions of the seriousness of labor regulations as an obstacle. Also relevant to the present study is that they showed that the effect of the LLR was stronger in firms that were either expanding or contracting employment and in those that were innovators. Nugent and Wu (2012) demonstrated the existence of this relation based on a much larger number of countries and Enterprise Surveys and showed that it holds for various alternative indexes of the rigidity of the regulations.

The three studies making use of these Enterprise Surveys that come closest to the present study are Kaplan (2009), Bhaumik et al. (2012), and Seker (2012). Kaplan (2009) made use of country averages of firm-specific responses to a hypothetical question in these surveys about the extent that the firm would change its employment level if all labor regulations were eliminated. Based on the average scores for this variable from the Enterprise Surveys of 14 Latin American countries, Kaplan's results showed that on average removal of all labor regulations would result in a significant but relatively modest (2 percent) increase in employment. Bhaumik and colleagues (2012), on the other hand, examined the effect of Botero and colleagues (2004) measure of LLR as well as of other institutional indicators on firm-level productivity both across and within countries on firm performance from the Enterprise Surveys for a single industry, textiles and clothing. They hypothesized that the effects of labor market rigidity (or in their case flexibility) on productivity would vary across different types of firms, and they found results supporting this hypothesis. Finally, Seker (2012) made use of responses to the same question in the Enterprise Surveys of 26 countries to compute firm-specific values of net job creation at the industry level to help explain variation at the firm level in firms' ability to export.

Labor Law Rigidity Indexes and Employment Outcomes

In an attempt to establish the links between LLR and firms' views about the severity of labor regulations as an obstacle to doing business, this chapter uses the same World Bank Enterprise Surveys but attempts to mitigate the rather severe problems of selection and simultaneity in such analyses. In particular, I follow Li and Nugent (2012) and Nugent and Wu (2012) in making use of a two-step estimation procedure. In the first step, firm-specific estimates of the severity of labor regulations as an obstacle to its business (Labor Obstacle) are obtained based on factors exogenous to the firm. Then, in the second step, these estimates of Labor Obstacle are used, along with other relevant controls and certain firm, industry, and country characteristics, to explain variations across firms in their responses to that hypothetical question concerning the employment change that would result from complete removal of all existing labor regulations.

Below I report results obtained by Li and Nugent (2012) for separate country studies for Egypt and Morocco, two MENA countries that have relatively rigid labor regulations and high youth unemployment and are facing the challenge of generating jobs in a time of political and economic turmoil. In the case of the single country studies for Egypt and Morocco, we cannot take advantage of differences in the LLRs, which vary across countries. Instead, we tried to detect such a link by identifying those firm and industry characteristics that seem to lead firms to view the given labor regulations as "serious." Since both Egypt and Morocco used somewhat different versions of the Enterprise Surveys, Egypt and Morocco could not be included in the larger sample of countries treated in Nugent and Wu (2012).

The perceived severity of Labor Obstacle in the survey was defined as a categorical variable ranging from "No Obstacle," to "Minor Obstacle," "Moderate Obstacle," "Major Obstacle," and "Very Serious Obstacle." These are coded from 0 for "No Obstacle" to 4 for "Very Serious Obstacle." Similar responses were obtained in the survey to questions about a number of other obstacles to the firm's business. I make use of three of these other obstacles: (1) an inadequately educated workforce; (2) practices of competitors in the informal sector, who presumably do not abide by the various regulations, including of course labor regulations; and (3) the difficulty of business licensing and permits. Each of these is defined and coded in the same way as Labor Obstacle, and all three are then averaged to form Average Other Obstacle.

Egyptian and Moroccan Country Studies

In the first stage, the dependent variable (Labor Obstacle) is specified to be related to two instruments: the first is a dummy variable for the textiles sector, and the second is Average Other Obstacle.

In the second stage, estimates are obtained of the effects of Labor Obstacle and controls for firm size, firm age, firm ownership, and other factors on the magnitude and direction of changes in employment that the firm would undertake if all existing labor regulations were removed. These measures can be constructed in various ways. For simplicity, here I present the results of only the most important controls on only two measures of employment changes, namely, Job Creation and Job Destruction. Job Creation is measured by the percentage increase in employees that the firm manager thinks would result from the elimination of all existing labor regulations. Job Destruction is similarly measured by the percentage by which the existing number of employees would decline after the hypothetical elimination of the existing labor regulations.

The Enterprise Surveys for Egypt and Morocco used in the analysis are those for 2007, with data collected in 2006 and mostly pertaining to 2005. To obtain a flavor of the key relationship investigated in this chapter, that between Labor Obstacle and the Job

TABLE 10.1

Mean percentages of job creation and job destruction, by Labor Obstacle group, numbers of firms, and tests for intergroup differences, Egypt (2004) and Morocco (2006).

	Egypt		Morocco	
	Job Creation (Obs)	Job Destruction (Obs)	Job Creation (Obs)	Job Destruction (Obs)
Labor Obstacle = 0 or 1	4.428 (542)	4.192 (542)	9.643 (674)	5.530 (674)
Labor Obstacle = 2–4	13.061 (98)	6.755 (98)	12.316 (311)	12.791 (311)
Difference (2.0 - 1.0)	8.633	2.563	2.673	7.261

Numbers in parentheses represent numbers of sample firms in these categories.
Source: World Bank Enterprise Surveys. Calculations based on original data.

Creation and Job Destruction variables, table 10.1 (replicated from Li and Nugent [2012]) shows separately for Egypt and Morocco the means of the percentages of jobs that would be created or destroyed in each firm in the event of complete deregulation of labor, for firms in two different categories of the Labor Obstacle categories: those for which the obstacle was coded 1 or less, and those for which it was coded 2–4. In both countries, the differences are rather striking. First, the likelihood of hiring, firing, or both after the complete elimination of the labor regulations is generally higher in Morocco, the country with the more rigid labor laws (as revealed in the World Bank's Doing Business Surveys). Second, in both countries the averages of the changes attributable to deregulation of labor are considerably larger for firms that rate the Labor Obstacle as more serious (2–4) rather than less serious (0–1). The size distributions of firms in the two surveys are extremely different; the Moroccan sample consists almost exclusively of small firms (those with fewer than 20 workers), but firms in the Egyptian sample are much more equally divided among small, medium, and large size groups.

A simplified version of the estimates from the second step in the empirical analysis, those for both Job Creation and Job Destruction from Li and Nugent (2012), is presented in table 10.2, for both Egypt and Morocco. The parameters of greatest importance to the present study are those for Labor Obstacle. For both countries the effects are positive, though the magnitudes as well as significance levels of these effects are considerably larger in Egypt than in Morocco. As also indicated in table 10.2, (1) the effects of firm size (number of workers) on both Job Creation and Job Destruction are positive in both countries, (2) the effects of age of the firm are negative on Job Creation and positive on Job Destruction in both countries, and (3) the effects of government ownership are positive on Job Destruction and are negative and not significant on Job Creation. The latter results could well arise from the likelihood that public sector firms would have been much more inclined to have been respecting the labor laws more carefully than private firms.

TABLE 10.2

Estimates of the effects of Labor Obstacle and other firm characteristics on the percentages of job creation and destruction attributable to labor deregulation in Egypt (2004) and Morocco (2006).

Explanatory Variables	Egypt Dependent Variables		Morocco Dependent Variables	
	Job Creation	Job Destruction	Job Creation	Job Destruction
Labor Obstacle	15.81**	40.585*	7.051	10.136
Size	0.0088	0.0074	2.47	4.389
Age of Firm	−0.722	1.241*	−0.076	0.219
Percent Government Ownership	−0.15	1.261**	−0.142	0.79
Percent Foreign Ownership			0.023	0.099
Number of Observations	987	987	637	637

All regression coefficients obtained by Tobit procedure; the appearance of *, **, and *** next to the reported coefficient indicate that the coefficient is statistically significant at the 10, 5, and 1 percent levels, respectively.

Source: World Bank Enterprise Surveys. Calculations based on original data for 2007.

Even though these results could be subject to estimation biases, for at least these MENA countries, the regression results offer at least suggestive evidence that, for firms that view labor regulations to be a relatively serious obstacle to their business, job destruction could be a consequence of labor deregulation that is just as important as, or an even more important than, job creation.

The Larger Sample of Countries

Next I turn to results obtained by Nugent and Wu (2012) from the larger sample of Enterprise Surveys. After omitting all surveys with entirely missing information on any of the most relevant measures, this left me with a sample of 73 countries and 107 Enterprise Surveys. While the sample included a few highly developed countries like Germany and South Korea, some southern European countries, several very poor countries from Africa, and Asia, middle income countries are well represented in the sample. These poorer countries share some of the same characteristics (per capita income, country size, and industrial structure) as the MENA countries that are not in the Gulf Cooperation Council (GCC). Unfortunately coverage of MENA countries in this sample was limited to Lebanon, Oman, and Turkey.

The estimation using more countries offers a distinct improvement over the approach shown in table 10.2. With more countries, ordered probit estimates for the first stage equation for Labor Obstacle, shown in table 10.3, now include one or another of three country-specific measures of LRR (overall rigidity of employment or its separate components difficulty in hiring and difficulty in firing) that are taken from the Doing Business Surveys database, as in the case of the 2005 and 2011 data. Other explanatory variables include the average of three other subjective obstacles to doing business (Average Other Obstacle) identified above and controls for firm size (dummy variables for Medium and Large firm size). Since small firms are more likely to be informal themselves, and therefore not likely to view labor regulations as a serious obstacle to their business, dummy variables for medium and large sizes were also included.

The ordered probit estimates for Labor Obstacle (first stage) in table 10.3 show the effects of LLRs on the perception of labor regulations as being an obstacle to the firm's business (Labor Obstacle), using alternatively the overall LLR index, the hiring subindex, and the firing subindex. The other instruments are Average Other Obstacle, and then medium size and large size are added as controls. As can be seen in table 10.3, as expected, firms facing higher LLR indexes are estimated to reflect larger positive and more significant effect on Labor Obstacle. Note also that in each of the three columns, the effects of the medium and large size dummy variables on Labor Obstacle are positive and significant. This is as expected, because the excluded small sized firms could be expected in many cases to be "informal" firms, not abiding by the regulations. Notice from the reported values of the Pseudo R2 that these few measures alone explain almost 18 percent of the total variation in Labor Obstacle.

TABLE 10.3

Ordered probit estimates of the determinants of Labor Obstacle (based on three different indexes of labor law rigidity and other firm characteristics) across the full sample of firms in MENA countries in different years ranging from 2003 to 2008.

Obstacle Labor	Overall Index	Hiring Index	Firing Index
Index	0.00571***	0.00166***	0.00147***
	(0.000468)	(0.000284)	(0.000292)
Obstacle avg	0.522***	0.528***	0.531***
	(0.0108)	(0.0107)	(0.0107)
Medium Size	0.130***	0.131***	0.134***
	(0.0141)	(0.0141)	(0.0141)
Large Size	0.228***	0.221***	0.229***
	(0.0154)	(0.0154)	(0.0154)
Observations	38,764	38,764	38,764
Pseudo R2	0.1771	0.176	0.1759
Log likelihood	−41992.06	−42049.224	−42053.638

Standard errors in parentheses. *** p < .01, ** p < .05, * p < .1.

Source: World Bank Enterprise Surveys. Calculations based on original data.

For still another means of relating the severity of the labor obstacle to the firm's business, I divided the sample countries into three groups based on another question, namely, one asking each firm to identify which of the 15 obstacles to success in their business constituted the most serious one. Countries included in the preferred group (Group 1) were those where a minimum of 1.5 percent of the firms in the survey mentioned labor regulations as the most important obstacle. Group 2 was the group of countries for which less than 1.5 percent identified labor regulations as the most important obstacle. The remaining countries, put into Group 3, were those for which this information was not available. Hence, ex ante, the Group 1 sample would be expected to be the most promising one for measuring the possible effects of removing the labor regulations, the Group 2 sample the least promising, and Group 3 somewhere in between.

In this large sample case, the second stage analyses for Job Creation (table 10.4) and Job Destruction (table 10.5) were modified to include Age^2 to allow for nonlinearity in the effect of firm age, location in the capital city (where labor and other regulations may be better enforced), export orientation (dummy variables for Large direct exporter or Large indirect exporter), medium and large size, dummy variables for the different values of Labor Obstacle an index for Labor Intensity of the industry to which the firm belongs, and a dummy variable for Textiles and garments in which flexibility in labor regulations are often deemed to be very important.

Table 10.4 presents the Tobit estimates for Job Creation, separately for each of the three groups and for the full sample. Table 10.5 does the same for Job Destruction. Of crucial importance to the basic objective of this chapter are the effects of Labor Obstacle. The results in table 10.4 show that for Group 1 at least, the effects of the dummies for all four of the nonzero values of the levels of Labor Obstacle are all positive and highly significant and that the magnitudes of the coefficient rise quite sharply with higher values of Labor Obstacle. Each of these coefficients represents the estimated percentages of Job Creation over the existing workforce that would occur if all existing labor regulations were eliminated. For Group 1 firms for which Labor Obstacle = 1, this is estimated to be a 12.7 percent increase. For those with Labor Obstacle = 2, 3, and 4, the corresponding estimated increases in Job Creation would be 27 percent, 41 percent, and 72 percent, respectively. In groups 2 and 3 these estimates are generally negative and less significant, indicating that labor deregulation would not have job creation benefits in all countries. In the full sample, however, the overall effects of the variables are positive and significant though smaller in magnitude than for firms in Group 1.[2]

With respect to the effects of the other controls on Job Creation, it can be seen that effects of age are nonlinear, declining by age up to a certain point and then flattening out. They are also larger in the capital city, where the regulations may be better enforced, and larger in either large direct or large indirect exporters, but smaller in medium and large size firms (relative to the excluded small size firms), and slightly larger in more labor intensive industries and especially in firms in the textiles and garments industries.

Table 10.5 presents the corresponding Tobit estimates for Job Destruction. In this case notice that the effects of the various levels of Labor Obstacle are small, negative, and generally not statistically significant. Of the other determinants of Job Destruction, many have opposite effects to those identified for Job Creation. Indeed, the signs of the age and age-squared terms are reversed, as they are for medium and large size firms, large indirect exporters, and firms in the textiles and garments industries, from what they are in table 10.4. On the other hand the effect of labor intensity remains positive, as in table 10.4.,

TABLE 10.4

Tobit estimates of the effects of Labor Obstacle and other firm characteristics on gross job creation, based on one or more individual country-year surveys between 2002 and 2009.

Gross Job Creation	Group 1	Group 2	Group 3	All
Age	−0.546***	−0.780***	−0.435***	−0.646***
	(0.0944)	(0.151)	(0.0839)	(0.0624)
Age²	0.00226**	0.00647***	0.00235***	0.00353***
	(0.00103)	(0.00179)	−(.000743)	(0.000654)
Capital City	6.274***	7.719***	0.636	5.828***
	(1.572)	(2.106)	(1.411)	(1.022)
Large Direct Export	−0.632	7.474**	0.549	1.138
	(2.572)	(3.642)	(2.323)	(1.715)
Large Indirect Export	9.654**	8.672	2.375	8.141***
	(3.826)	(5.376)	(3.945)	(2.625)
Medium Size	−0.223	−9.877***	−7.263***	−3.929**
	(2.593)	(3.098)	(2.165)	(1.614)
Large Size	−17.42***	−16.89***	−15.22***	−15.70***
	(3.388)	(4.054)	(2.637)	(2.056)
Obstacle Labor = 1	12.74***	−9.281*	−4.724	1.908
	(4.118)	(5.375)	(3.566)	(2.641)
Obstacle Labor = 2	27.12***	−14.75**	−8.187**	8.165***
	(4.354)	(7.092)	(4.108)	(2.986)
Obstacle Labor = 3	41.30***	−25.40**	−7.574	17.20***
	(5.207)	(10.07)	(5.382)	(3.731)
Obstacle Labor = 4	72.36***	−79.76***	−116.7***	40.73***
	(8.472)	(21.88)	(37.06)	(6.918)
Labor Intensity	1.307***	−1.154**	−0.362	0.663***
	(0.387)	(0.47)	(0.286)	(0.233)
Textile and Garment	7.788***	10.29***	3.05	7.121***
	(2.574)	(3.707)	(2.786)	(1.754)

Standard errors in parentheses. *** p < .01, ** p < .05, * p < .1.
Source: World Bank Enterprise Surveys. Calculations based on original data.

TABLE 10.5

Tobit estimates of the effects of labor obstacle and other firm characteristics on job destruction, based on one or more individual country-year surveys between 2002 and 2009.

Job Destruction	Group 1	Group 2	Group 3	All
Age	0.163***	0.379***	0.278***	0.202***
	(0.0496)	(0.0898)	(0.0563)	(0.0337)
Age^2	0.000003	−0.00301***	−0.00155***	−0.000690**
	(0.000476)	(0.00107)	(0.000493)	(0.000327)
Capital City	−0.88	6.928***	−0.342	1.933***
	(0.967)	(1.315)	(1.037)	(0.619)
Large Direct Export	−2.667*	−3.585	−1.777	−2.172**
	(1.543)	(2.256)	(1.643)	(1.015)
Large Indirect Export	−1.799	−7.032*	−0.765	−2.896*
	(2.428)	(3.629)	(2.859)	(1.650)
Medium Size	9.558***	9.955***	5.380***	9.125***
	(1.571)	(2.046)	(1.640)	(0.998)
Large Size	14.98***	16.18***	9.411***	14.67***
	(1.838)	(2.488)	(1.874)	(1.169)
Obstacle Labor=1	−5.592**	4.582	0.514	−0.891
	(2.612)	(3.497)	(2.778)	(1.673)
Obstacle Labor=2	−1.713	3.286	1.637	−0.0781
	(2.783)	(4.672)	(3.105)	(1.891)
Obstacle Labor=3	2.731	6.585	4.216	3.044
	(3.354)	(6.530)	(3.898)	(2.353)
Obstacle Labor=4	−1.117	1.902	15.64	−2.782
	(6.093)	(11.31)	(21.08)	(4.809)
Labor Intensity	1.572***	−0.229	0.379*	0.768***
	(0.205)	(0.291)	(0.205)	(0.131)
Textile and Garment	−6.394***	−8.375***	1.858	−4.870***
	(1.563)	(2.432)	(2.000)	−1.073

Standard errors in parentheses. *** p < .01, ** p < .05, *p < .1.

Source: World Bank Enterprise Surveys. Calculations based on original data.

In contrast to the results from the country studies for Egypt and Morocco, the results obtained from the larger multicountry sample show that the effects of removing labor regulations are strong and positive for Job Creation but not for Job Destruction. The magnitudes of the effects of the various Labor Obstacle terms on Job Creation are also quite high. Since these estimates also reflect the link to LLR indexes from the first step ordered probit estimates of table 10.3, the results of the cross-country samples clearly suggest the relevance of labor law deregulation as a vehicle for job creation.

Conclusion

The results of this study extend the work of earlier studies about the extent to which firms would want to change their employment if all existing regulations on labor were removed. Yet the heavy reliance on international cross-sections of data on firms means that the results reported here could be subject to some biases. Thus, further research should be undertaken with panel data from countries with comparable Enterprise Surveys taken at years before and after the labor regulations were changed. The enormous gap between the results for the two countries (Egypt and Morocco in table 10.2) and the large sample of countries (tables 10.4 and 10.5) suggest further research is warranted.

In view of the rather ample evidence presented here concerning the differences in the effects of labor deregulation from one sector to another, it is beneficial to identify those specific industries and firm types where deregulation has the greatest positive employment effects. For example, the results presented here suggest targeting sectors or locations with large exporters and firms in labor-intensive activities like textiles and garments. This suggests the idea already built into export processing zones around the world that the less restrictive labor laws could be confined to those operating in these specific sectors and zones. This could also make labor deregulation more politically feasible than it would otherwise seem to be in much of the region.

This is not to say, however, that reduction in existing high levels of LLR is justifiable only in those sectors or countries where one can be assured that job creation would outweigh job destruction. Indeed, examples in which deregulation would lead to substantial job destruction are precisely those where the existing inefficiencies in labor markets are likely to be most damaging. As noted, this would seem especially likely in older and government-owned firms. Forcing these firms to hold onto redundant workers creates huge allocative inefficiencies.

Given the possibility that labor deregulation in the MENA countries could give rise to substantial job destruction, the deleterious effects of labor law deregulation on (1) worker well-being, (2) the incentives of firms to provide training, (3) the commitment by workers to their employers, and (4) management-worker cooperation, it is important to take these negative effects into consideration and to identify policies to mitigate these adverse effects. To this end, we deem it important to encourage the development of social safety nets so as to get the benefits of such reforms without some of the costs, as demonstrated by Acemoglu and Shimer (2000). As suggested by Barsoum (chapter 9 here), worker and young people opinion surveys indicate that the vast majority of wage workers in Egypt are employed in the informal sector, without labor contracts. These results may well explain why even employed youth are extremely dissatisfied with their jobs and why worker-management relations may be far from optimal.

But this is not to say that as long as one builds these safety nets with unemployment insurance, and active labor market policies, all will be well. Algan and Cahuc (2006) have pointed out that even in Europe cultural values may vary to the extent that a combination of unemployment insurance and active labor market policies that works well in one country might not work in another country. A key issue is whether or not the incentives for job search and participation in training are weakened by the generosity and other features of these in different cultures. But reasonable balance in the design of these schemes as has occurred in several European countries, limiting the generosity of such schemes, would seem to have been successful in this regard (Laporsek and Primoz, 2012). For example, this would involve sharply lowering the wage replacement rates in unemployment insurance schemes over time and increasing the need for participation in well-designed training programs. Furthermore, there are interrelationships between other obstacles to doing business and labor regulations. Thus, there may exist strong complementarities between deregulation of labor markets and encouraging international trade along the lines of comparative advantage. Evidence in support of this from Fiori and colleagues (2007) and Seker (2012) supports the important role of trade in job creation, and the effect of the lack of trade openness on employment generation and firm productivity can be seen in the effects of the blockade of Gaza (Zimring 2012).

It is clear that what needs to be fixed in the labor markets of the MENA countries goes well beyond reform of labor laws themselves. The employment protection systems, the rigidity in working hours, and the benefits of civil service employment are often set at such a high level that even without labor laws, the private sector would find it hard to compete for employees, especially for female employees, without offering much higher benefits that are likely to make the firms noncompetitive. (This is seen extensively in GCC countries.) The effect of labor deregulation on the private sector's ability to absorb labor is therefore very much undermined by large and excessively generous government wage and benefits systems. While this problem is most serious in the Gulf countries where incumbent regimes find it convenient to fend off even the slightest hints of discontent by raising the wages and benefits of government workers, this also happens in non-GCC countries, where the effects on the private sector employment can be even more constraining.

REFERENCES

Abruhart, A., I. Kaur, and Z. Tzannatos. 2002. Government employment and active labor market policies in MENA in a comparative context. In *Employment creation and social protection in the Middle East and North Africa*, ed. H. Handoussa and Z. Tzannatos, 21–48. Cairo: American University in Cairo Press.

Acemoglu, D., and R. Shimer. 2000. Productivity gains from unemployment insurance. *European Economic Review* 44: 1195–1224.

Agenor, P. R., and K. El-Aynaoui. 2003. Labor market policies and unemployment in Morocco: A quantitative analysis. World Bank Policy Research working paper 3091.Washington, DC: World Bank.

Aleksynska, M., and M. Schindler. 2011. Labor market regulations in low, middle and high-income countries: A new panel database. International Monetary Fund working paper 11/154. Washington, DC: International Monetary Fund.

Algan, Y., and P. Cahuc. 2006. Civic attitudes and the design of labor market institutions: Which countries can implement the Danish flexicurity model? (IZA) discussion paper no. 1928. Bonn: Institut zur Zukunft der Arbeit.

Angel-Urdinola, D. F., and A. Kuddo, with support from K. Tanabe and M. Wazzan. 2010. Key characteristics of employment regulation in Middle East and North Africa. Washington, DC: World Bank.

Assaad, R., 2002. The transformation of the Egyptian labor market: 1988–98. In *The Egyptian labor market in an era of reform*, ed. R. Assaad, 3–64. Cairo: American University in Cairo Press.

Assaad, R. 2009. Labor supply, employment, and unemployment in the Egyptian economy, 1988–2006. In *The Egyptian labor market revisited*, ed. R. Assaad, 1–52. Cairo: American University in Cairo Press.

Assaad, R., and I. Tunali. 2001. Wage formation in the construction sector in Egypt. In *Labor and human capital in the Middle East: Studies of Markets and Household Behavior,* ed. D. Salehi-Isfahani, 293–335. Reading, England: Ithaca Press.

Bhaumik, S. K., R. Dimova, S. C. Kumbhakar, and K. Sun. 2012, February. Does institutional quality help firm performance? Insights from a semiparametric approach. Institute for the Study of Labor (IZA) discussion paper 6351. Bonn: Institut zur Zukunft der Arbeit.

Botero, J. C., S. Djankov, R. La Porta, F. Lopez-de-Silanes, and A. Shleifer. 2004. The regulation of labor. *Quarterly Journal of Economics* 119(4): 1339–1382.

Dennis, A. 2006. Trade liberalization, factor market flexibility and growth: The case of Morocco and Tunisia. World Bank policy research working paper 3857. Washington, DC: World Bank.

Devlin, J. C. 2010. *Challenges of economic development in the Middle East and North Africa region.* Hackensack, NJ: World Scientific.

Dhillon, N. and T. Yousef, eds. 2009. *Generation in Waiting: The Unfulfilled Promise of Young People in the Middle East.* Washington, DC: Brookings Institution Press.

Elbadawi, I., and N. Loayza. 2008, March 17–18. Informality, employment and economic development in the Arab world. Paper presented at "The Unemployment Crisis in the Arab Countries," International Conference of the Arab Planning Institute, Cairo.

Fiori, G. N., G.Nicoletti, S. Scarpetta, and F. Schiantarelli. 2007, May. Employment outcomes and the interaction between product and labor market deregulation: Are they substitutes or complements? Institute for the Study of Labor (IZA) discussion paper no. 2770. Bonn: Institut zur Zukunft der Arbeit.

Heckman, J., and C. Pages. 2000. The cost of job security regulation: Evidence from Latin American labor markets. NBER working paper 7773. Cambridge, MA: National Bureau of Economic Research.

Kaplan, D. S. 2009. Job creation and labor reform in Latin America. *Journal of Comparative Economics* 37(1): 91–105.

Kpodar, K. 2007. Why has unemployment in Algeria been higher than in MENA and transition countries? International Monetary Fund working paper 07/210. Washington, DC: International Monetary Fund.

Laporsek, S., and P. Dolenc. 2012. Do flexicurity policies affect labor market outcomes? An analysis of EU countries. *Croatian Journal of Social Policy* 19(2): 107–130.

Li, Y., and J. B. Nugent. 2012, June 30. What can be learned about the employment effects of labor market deregulation from the answers to hypothetical questions about it to firms? Evidence from Egypt and Morocco. Paper presented at the annual conference of the Western Economic Association, International, San Francisco.

Nugent, J. B. 2012. Detecting corruption and evaluating programs to control it: Some lessons for MENA. Economic Research Forum (ERF) working paper 738. Giza, Egypt: Economic Research Forum.

Nugent, J. B., and Y.Wu. 2012, June 30. How would firms adjust employment if labor market regulations were eliminated? Evidence from the enterprise surveys. Paper presented at the annual conference of the Western Economic Association, International, San Francisco.

Pierre, G., and S. Scarpetta. 2006. Employment protection: Do firms' perceptions match with legislation? *Economic Letters* 90: 328–334.

Seker, M. 2012. Rigidities in employment protection and exporting. *World Development* 40(2): 238–250.

Wahba, J. 2009, August. The impact of labor market reforms on informality in Egypt. In *Gender and work in the MENA region working paper series: Poverty, job quality, and labor dynamics.* Population Council paper no. 3. New York: Population Council.

Zimring, A. 2012. Gains from trade: Lessons from the Gaza blockade, 2007–2010. Stanford Institute of Economic Policy Research discussion paper 12024 Stanford, CA: Stanford Institute of Economic Policy Research.

NOTES

1. For some other more general overviews of labor markets, labor regulations, education, and migration issues in one or more MENA countries see Abruhart et al. (2002), Agenor and El-Aynaoui (2003), and Dennis (2006). Dennis (2006) is especially interesting since it shows via simulations that in both Morocco and Tunisia, tariff reductions of 50 percent relative to their most favored nation (MFN) base rates would cause GDP to grow significantly faster if factor markets were more flexible (captured in the model by making labor more substitutable for capital). This is modeled as the effect of comparing the GDP increases with a low elasticity of substitution between capital and labor (0.1) and low responsiveness of investment to the rate of return on investment with those arising with a high elasticity of substitution (2.0) and high responsiveness of investment. Particularly telling was the fact that labor allocation increases in the labor-intensive and export-oriented clothing sector would more than quadruple in each case relative to the low-flexibility case in both countries (from a 4.6 percent increase to a 23.2 percent increase in Morocco and from a 5 percent increase to a 31.6 percent increase in Tunisia).

2. The overall effects are more complicated since they need to take into account the interaction effects between size and Labor Obstacle (not reported here).

11 Exploring the Impact of Reforms in the Moroccan Vocational Education System

A POLICY ANALYSIS

Brahim Boudarbat and Daniel Egel

HIGH UNEMPLOYMENT AMONG youth, and recent graduates in particular, is endemic to the countries of the Middle East and North Africa (MENA). The average rate of youth unemployment in this region is 26 percent, nearly half again as large as the next highest region, Sub-Saharan Africa, where youth unemployment is "only" 18 percent. In several MENA countries the unemployment rate is staggeringly high. Indeed, in the mid-2000s, both Algeria and Palestine had youth unemployment rates close to 40 percent, and Tunisia had a rate just over 30 percent (Assaad and Roudi-Fahimi 2007). These rates increased as a result of the financial crisis (see Said, chapter 3 here) and in several countries rose further as a result of the economic turmoil that followed the Arab Spring.

While the short-term economic, emotional, and psychological impacts of this unemployment can be quite devastating, it also has important long-term effects for the future economic and political stability of the region. This youth unemployment is heavily concentrated among recent graduates of secondary schools and higher education programs and may stunt the skill development of these youth by denying them opportunities to apply their education. As a result, this unemployment may result in both the political and social exclusion of this generation of educated youth. Without access to employment these youth remain dependent on their families and remain at home, unmarried, until they can find employment (Dhillon and Yousef 2009).

Amid a variety of other policies designed to either improve educational efficacy or labor market flexibility, a number of countries in the MENA region have implemented reforms to their vocational training (VT) programs as a way to address these employment challenges. Examples include Iran, where various reforms of the vocational education system have been attempted since the late 1990s (Salehi-Isfahani and Egel 2007); Lebanon, which benefited from several European Union–funded reforms to its vocational and technical programs in the early 2000s (World Bank 2005); and Tunisia, which established a ministry and a national vocational training system in the early 1990s (World Bank 2005).

In Morocco a variety of reforms to the educational system and labor markets were attempted throughout the 1980s and 1990s. One effort to improve the efficacy of technical and vocational training was the expansion and improvement of VT programs in 1984. Those efforts were designed to assist youth in gaining access to the private labor market by providing them with skills that were practical and appropriate. Later extensions of this program included a co-operative training program beginning in 1996 that sought to involve students in the private sector labor market during their vocational schooling and a postgraduation internship program. In addition, policies designed to encourage recent graduates of these programs to form small businesses were implemented in the 1990s. (See Boudarbat and Lahlou 2009 for a more detailed review.)

The existing literature for the developing world suggests that VT can be an effective policy tool. In Latin America, a voucher program to support private education in Colombia found significant benefits for youth attending private VT centers (Bettinger, Kremer, and Saavedra 2010); a Dominican Republic VT program significantly increased wages (Card et al. 2011); and a randomized intervention in Colombia estimated returns to vocational education of 10 percent or more, with a particularly large effect for young women (Attanasio et al. 2011). And in South Asia, Maitra and Mani (2013) found significant benefits from a program targeted for women living in Delhi slums. However, the experimental evidence from Africa is more mixed, with evidence from Malawi (Cho et al. 2013) and Kenya (Hicks et al. 2013) indicating that VT programs are not effective, while evidence from Uganda (Blattman et al. 2014) suggests that VT programs can increase earnings. However, despite the range of VT policies implemented across the MENA region, there is limited policy analysis from the MENA countries to help guide the development of these programs.

This chapter addresses to this gap in the literature by assessing the efficacy of technical and vocational training reform in Morocco. We find that postgraduation internship programs have a dramatic positive effect on employment outcomes. Using a recall questionnaire on employment activity from the 2004 Follow-up of Vocational Training Graduates survey (FVTG; conducted by the Moroccan Department of Vocational Training) data, we use quasi-experimental methods (e.g., Imbens 2004) to demonstrate that unemployment rates among VT graduates participating in an internship program following graduation are roughly one-half the rates among VT graduates from a classroom-only program. Furthermore, the length of the internship before entering the labor market is positively correlated with employment prospects at the completion of the internship—thus, youth who have a longer internship are less likely to be unemployed at the completion of their programs.

However, several recent policy initiatives seem to have been broadly ineffective. First, using the same recall questionnaire, we find that graduates of private VT institutes, which are often seen as more "market focused" and potentially more effective, do worse than their colleagues in public institutes. Second, we find that a program designed to support VT graduate entrepreneurs (Law 16/87) was largely ineffective, as evidenced by the extraordinary low take-up rates of this program.[1] Third, using a World Bank and Silatech-funded survey focused on challenges facing youth, we find that the project of the National Agency for the Employment and Skills Promotion (Agence nationale de promotion de l'emploi et des compétences; ANAPEC), a European Union–funded program designed to increase linkages between the private sector and job candidates, was also largely ineffective.

Vocational Training in Morocco

In 1984, the VT system in Morocco underwent significant reform. The goal of this reform was to make VT a genuine tool for socioeconomic development in a context marked by high dropout rates and rising unemployment among graduates. The reforms would both improve the employment prospects of new graduates and support the development of the Moroccan private sector by enhancing the quality of new labor market entrants.

The first year of the reform saw a dramatic increase in the number of VT students, and a rapid, sustained growth rate was maintained thereafter in both the public and private sectors (see fig. 11.1). The number of graduates from public vocational centers increased, on average, by more than 7 percent per year between 1984 and 2007, though the growth was particularly rapid from 2003 to 2007. The growth in the number of private sector graduates was equally impressive, averaging more than 6 percent per annum between 1988 and 2007. The growth in the number of private training institutions was similarly rapid, growing from 584 facilities in 1992 to 1,650 in 2003, amounting to a creation of about 100 institutions on average per year.

Despite the variety of efforts to improve the VT system and make it more responsive to the labor market, job prospects for graduates of these programs are quite poor. The unemployment rate among recent graduates of these programs is extraordinarily high. Though the unemployment rate for all youth is itself very high, with rates among comparably aged youth nearly 40 percent, the unemployment rate among vocational graduates is close to 60 percent one year after graduation and nearly 50 percent even two years after. The high unemployment rate among recent graduates of VT programs is particularly perplexing in light of the fact that these programs were specifically designed to provide employable skills and were very selective in choosing applicants, accepting only around 43 percent of total applicants.

Boudarbat (2007) examines the factors favoring or hindering the employment of this population. He relies on duration analysis to study the length of unemployment before the first job; this approach allows him to explore which observable characteristics of new

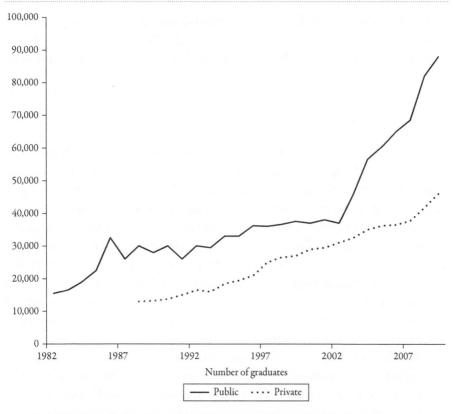

FIGURE 11.1 Number of public and private sector vocational training graduates, Morocco, 1982–2007.
Source: Statistics from Département de la formation professionnelle, http://www.dfp.gov.ma/.

job entrants reduce the length of unemployment. He finds that training geared toward work in the informal economy offers a greater potential for employment. There are, however, factors not related to training that significantly affect the duration of unemployment. For example, social networks (personal connections) substantially increase access to employment, particularly for girls. In the same vein, the father's profession is instrumental, with children of managers and skilled tradesmen more likely to find employment.[2] Furthermore, while these vocational programs do provide specific skills that are useful in particular vocations, they are not very effective in preparing individuals for the realities of the private sector labor market. Graduates are unwilling to take low-paying jobs that offer valuable experience and instead delay employment in the hope of obtaining the high wages they feel their education entitles them to.

Vocational Training Policy Reforms

Morocco has experimented with a variety of different initiatives to support its VT programs over the past two decades. This section reviews four general classes of VT reforms that have been implemented in Morocco: traineeship programs; direct support of VT entrepreneurs; creation of a job matching agency (ANAPEC); and reform of VT classroom teaching methods. The effectiveness of the first three reforms is evaluated in the following sections.

Traineeship Programs

Morocco's traineeship programs have the explicit objective of facilitating the transition between training and employment. Each program requires training in the workplace as a component. The belief was that direct integration into a workplace would ease the entry of graduates of these programs into the labor market. These programs were implemented as a direct result of the poor labor market outcomes of graduates of VT and other educational programs.

The first type of traineeship program, cooperative training, was the first initiative designed to augment the existing VT system. Participants in this program must spend at least one-half of the training period in a workplace and at least one-third in a VT center. Students receive a large part of their training in the workplace, which puts them in touch with the reality of the world of work and allows them to develop a profile that corresponds to the needs and specificities of businesses.

While the first cooperative education pilot projects started in 1993, cooperative training only become available throughout the country in 1996–1997 and started with a modest 1,000 trainees.[3] However, the number of trainees increased rapidly over time, reaching nearly 80,000 participants in 2014–2015 (Département de la formation professionnelle—Maroc, 2015).

The second type of traineeship program, the apprenticeship program, was first made available in 2000. Participants in this program must spend at least 80 percent of the training period in a workplace, while only a minimum of 10 percent of the training period is spent on general and technological training in a VT center. Thus, the share of the training period that takes place in a workplace is higher than that in cooperative training, in which a maximum of 67 percent of this time can be spent in the workplace. The training period varies from one to two years depending on the trades and qualifications of the apprenticeship training. The training can lead to a diploma (specialization and qualification levels) or can be qualifying only (a certificate that recognizes the skills acquired).

The implementation of the apprenticeship program in Morocco had two goals. The primary goal was to support youth employment, particularly among rural youth and youth who either left the education system too early or who did not meet the conditions (e.g., age, education) required for other forms of VT. The secondary goal was to support small and medium-sized enterprises (SMEs) in Morocco, with a particular focus on saving some traditional arts and crafts trades that were dying. Thus, these SMEs were given direct support from the apprenticeship program by being the recipients of many of the apprentices.[4]

After completing their traineeship program, many VT graduates participate in internships, with the aim of gaining work-based experience and improving their job prospects.

Our analysis of the cooperative and apprenticeship programs focuses only on these post-graduation internships, as our data do not allow us to distinguish between traineeship programs. Since the former programs focus on workplace training, we assume that their effectiveness can be inferred from the performance of graduates who participated in internships.

Direct Support for Vocational Training Entrepreneurs

Since the late 1980s, a variety of programs have provided loans at preferential interest rates to graduates who wish to start their own businesses. Among these programs are the Crédit Jeunes Promoteurs program, which provides loans to young entrepreneurs; the Programme Auto-Emploi, which provides a mixture of state grant support and loan financing; and a newer integrated program called Moukawalati, which provides technical assistance and loans for a selected group of educated youth starting small businesses. These programs tend to favor highly educated workers (i.e., those with postsecondary education) and largely exclude VT graduates.

Recognizing this gap in financing programs for VT graduates, the Moroccan government enacted Law 16/87, which was designed to provide direct financial support to the entrepreneurs among the graduates of VT programs. This program, implemented in 1989, provides tax exemptions (exclusively) for young entrepreneurs holding VT diplomas. Specifically, any necessary equipment can be purchased tax free by VT graduates (the VAT is currently 20 percent) and all businesses established by VT graduates do not pay taxes for five years and then pay 50 percent of the normal tax rate during the following five years. In addition, Law 16/87 listed 20 trades that could be carried out only by graduates holding VT diplomas or by experienced workers who succeeded at professional aptitude tests. This component was designed to protect graduates from being forced to compete against potential competitors who were both uneducated and unskilled (i.e., individuals who could undercut them by providing a substandard product).[5]

Job Matching

A third effort to support employment of VT graduates is ANAPEC (established in 2001), which differs from other VT programs in that it functions as an intermediary in the labor market rather than subsidizing entrepreneurship or training activities. The goal is to support effective matching in the labor market—that is, to help firms find employees and to help the unemployed find jobs that match their skills and interests. The agency is also unusual in that it functions as a liaison between European entrepreneurs and Moroccan candidates and thus supports legal migration to Europe, encourages returnees to Morocco, and targets primarily high-skilled workers.

The agency has been robustly supported with a budget of $100 million (Belghazi 2013). This funding supports a network of 547 staff in 74 branches across the country. The organization has even established liaison relationships with NGOs to reach remote areas.

By 2009 a total of more than 500,000 job seekers had been registered by ANAPEC. However, only a relatively small share of these job seekers—around 18 percent—were under 24 years of age.

The overall effectiveness of ANAPEC is not well established. Official reporting by ANAPEC during the first five years of operation suggested dramatic success—17,000 jobs were created during 2001–2003, and an additional 44,000 during 2004–2005. However, Belghazi (2013) indicates that ANAPEC succeeded in finding employment for only 4,355 job seekers in 2009, suggesting that the effectiveness of ANAPEC might be waning, despite continued robust financial support.

Skills-Based Approach

A fourth type of VT reform has been the modernization of the educational practices in VT institutions. This modernization, which would replace existing teaching methods with the skills-based approach (SBA), was first implemented in 2003 with a four-year experimental phase. This experimental phase included the establishment of five new institutions, one for each of the five training sectors: (1) textile/clothing industries, (2) the tourism/hotel and catering industry, (3) tertiary (in particular information and communication technology), (4) mechanical, metallurgical, and electrical industries, and (5) agriculture.[6] The perceived effectiveness of the experimental phase led to a subsequent round of donor funding that will continue to fund SBA-type approaches, with a particular focus on agriculture, marine fisheries, and tourism.[7]

Data

We assess aspects of each of the first three policy reforms discussed above using different types of data. Our first assessment draws on the FVTG longitudinal survey data that were collected by the Moroccan Department of Vocational Training in order to explore the effectiveness of postgraduation internships for VT graduates. The data we use include data on VT graduates from the 2000 cohort, surveyed four years after graduation in 2004. The FVTG collects relevant information on the evolution of the situation of graduates in the labor market during the four years following their graduation. The questions about the evolution of the labor force status are retrospective, covering the period July 1, 2000, to July 31, 2004. The 2004 FVTG included a total of 6,381 respondents, which was approximately a 10 percent sample of the 2000 cohort. The sample was approximately 50 percent female, and 90 percent of the respondents were between 20 and 30 years old at the time of the interview. These data are also used to assess the potential effectiveness of the privatization of VT.

Our second assessment, the evaluation of the Law 16/87, which provides support to VT entrepreneurs, relies on a nonlongitudinal component of the 2004 FVTG. This component collects graduates' opinions on the quality of their training compared to the reality of the workplace, the support that they have received postgraduation, and their knowledge about the myriad programs they could potentially benefit from.

Our third assessment, that of ANAPEC, relies on 2009 data collected by Silatech and the World Bank. These data contain information on nearly 2,900 Moroccan youth; these surveys ask basic questions on education and labor force participation, as well as on the types of job placement service these youth received, with a specific focus on ANAPEC.

Estimating the Effectiveness of Vocational Training Policy Reforms

In this section's evaluations, we show that participation in an internship after graduation from a traineeship program has a lasting and strongly positive impact on subsequent labor market outcomes. However, we find little evidence that privatization of VT, policies designed to encourage small business formation, or job placement services have been effective.

Traineeships

We assess one aspect of the traineeship program—postgraduation internships—by comparing the unemployment rates of traineeship graduates with internships to those of such graduates without internships.[8] We find that the internships lead to both short-term and long-term increases in the likelihood of being employed. Importantly, we offer evidence that this result does not seem to be driven by selection or other forms of endogeneity.

The short- and long-term difference in the employment trajectories of the participants in the internship program is demonstrated in figure 11.2. In particular, participating in an internship program seems to lead to a permanent reduction in the probability of unemployment—trainees have an approximately 20 percent lower unemployment rate for each month following the completion of their VT program.

Longer internships seem to be associated with enhanced employment outcomes. This is demonstrated in figure 11.3, which reports the employment trajectories of individuals with different lengths of internships. Longer internships are associated with lower unemployment rates at all points after completion of the VT program.

A significant empirical concern in assessing the effectiveness of the internship programs is that individuals who choose to participate in them are different in some important ways from nonparticipants. Thus, rather than just comparing participants to nonparticipants, it is important to estimate the average impact of the internship program on the participants in the program, referred to in the statistical literature as the "average treatment effect among the treated" (ATT). In this case, the ATT is the difference in the unemployment rate among those in an internship program and the estimated unemployment rate among those same individuals if they had not participated in an internship program. This ATT can be written as follows:

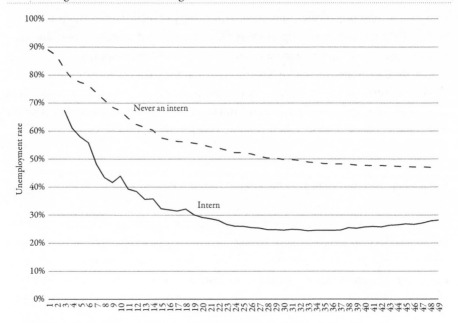

FIGURE 11.2 Unemployment rates of trainees with internships and those without internships. The "Intern" line includes all individuals who have completed their internship programs by the corresponding month.

Source: FVTG survey, author's calculations.

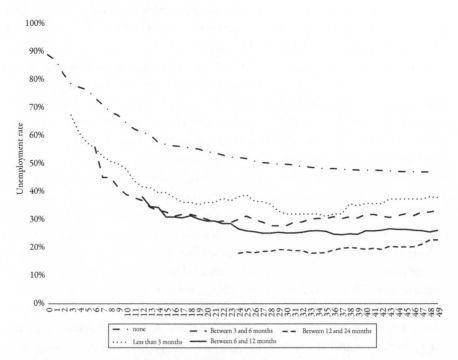

FIGURE 11.3 Unemployment rates and length of internship, Morocco, July 2000–July 2004. The plot for each group of interns begins at the end of the range for that group.

Source: FVTG survey, author's calculations.

$$ATT = E[U_T - U_N \mid T = 1],$$

where U_T is the unemployment rate among the treated, U_N is the unemployment rate among the nontreated, and T is a binary indicating whether the individual participated in an internship program.

The challenge in this approach, therefore, is finding data on individuals who are not in internship programs but are sufficiently similar to those in internship programs to serve as a counterfactual. We can observe $E[U_T \mid T = 1]$, the expected unemployment rate among those in internship programs, directly in the data. However, we do not observe the counterfactual unemployment rate, $E[U_N \mid T = 1]$, directly as we do not know what would have been the outcome of those in internships if they had not participated in an internship program. If the decision to participate in an internship was random, so that $E[U_N \mid T = 1] = E[U_N \mid T = 0] = E[U_N]$, then we could estimate the ATT using the prevailing unemployment rate among all vocational graduates. However, this is unlikely to be the case.

We estimate this counterfactual unemployment rate, $E[U_N \mid T = 1]$, in two stages. In the first stage we calculate the probability of being a participant. Following Friedlander, Greenberg, and Robins (1997), who model a similar voluntary training program, we estimate the probability of participating in the program as a function of specialization, region, field of study, father's vocation, gender, age, and age-squared.

In the second stage, we estimate $E[U_N \mid T = 1]$, following the approach suggested by Imbens (2004). Specifically, we calculate

$$E[U_N \mid T = 1] = \left(\sum_{i \in \{T=0\}} U_i \frac{\hat{e}_i}{1 - \hat{e}_i} \right) \Big/ \left(\sum_{i \in \{T=0\}} \frac{\hat{e}_i}{1 - \hat{e}_i} \right),$$

where $\hat{e}$ is the probability of an individual choosing to participate in the program. This approach assumes that the decision to participate in the internship is independent of one's unemployment outcome conditional on observables.

Figure 11.4 demonstrates the estimated causal impact of the internship program. Specifically, the dashed grey line reports what the unemployment rate would have been among the trainees if they had selected not to participate in the internship program. Thus the causal impact of the program is simply the difference between the dashed grey and the dashed black lines. That there is not a significant difference between $E[U_N \mid T = 0]$, the *observed* unemployment rate among individuals not in internship programs, and $E[U_N \mid T = 1]$, the *estimated* unemployment rate if these same individuals had been in internships, indicates that individuals participating in internships and those not participating are similar in their observable characteristics.

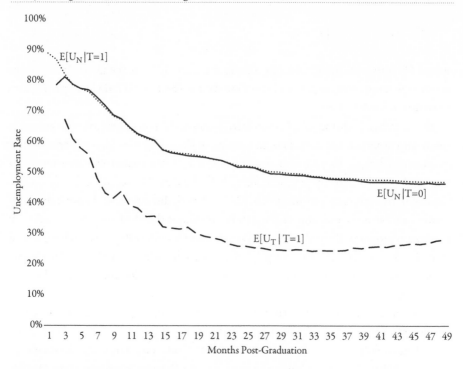

FIGURE 11.4 Causal impact of internships, Morocco, July 2000–July 2004.
Source: FVTG survey, author's calculations.

Privatization of VT Programs

The relative effectiveness of the private VT programs is examined in figure 11.5. Despite the fact that graduates of these centers have to pay the full cost of tuition, the employment prospects are appreciably worse. Indeed, even four years postgraduation, the unemployment rate among graduates of the public programs is nearly five percentage points lower than those of private programs.

Male graduates of these private vocational training centers do particularly poorly. Figure 11.6 compares outcomes for the private and public centers separately for men and women. The "employment" gap between the two types of center (private and public) seems to be driven by male graduates only. Indeed, this "employment gap" is as large as 10 percentage points one year after graduation.

Entrepreneurship Programs

There is little evidence that Law 16/87, which was designed to provide direct support to entrepreneurs among the vocational training graduates, was an effective program. Table 11.1 provides key summary statistics comparing Law 16/87 to the two other Moroccan programs

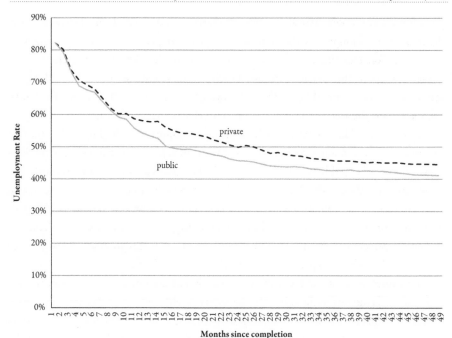

FIGURE 11.5 Comparative outcomes of private and public vocational training graduates, Morocco, July 2000–July 2004.

Source: FVTG survey, author's calculations.

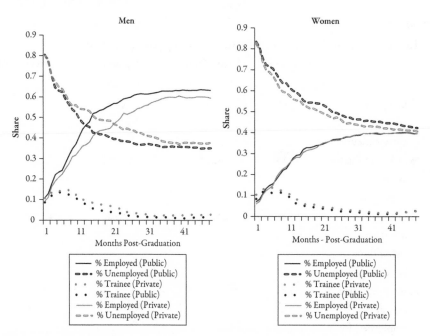

FIGURE 11.6 Gender differences in the public and private vocational training outcomes, Morocco, July 2000–July 2004.

Source: FVTG survey, author's calculations.

providing direct support to vocational training entrepreneurs, Crédit Jeunes Promoteurs and Programme Auto-Emploi; neither of these other programs provides preferential opportunities for vocational training graduates. The first row reports the take-up rate of each program; the second reports the overall awareness of each program; and the third and fourth report the average investment and size of firms benefiting from the specified program. The fourth column reports the average size and investment level for all surveyed firms.

The inefficacy of Law 16/87 in reaching the target population is highlighted by the fact that nearly twice as many recent graduates of vocational programs claim to have received some type of other public assistance, despite the fact that Law 16/87 was specifically designed to target these individuals. This can be seen in table 11.1 by comparing the first to the second and third columns: More than 6 percent of entrepreneurs (who are VT graduates) benefited from entrepreneurship programs targeted toward university graduates, and only 4 percent benefited from Law 16/87. Indeed, while this program was targeted to have approximately 1,000 participants annually, it only had an average of 100 annual participants, reaching a total of fewer than 600 youth during its first six years of operation.

The low take-up rate of the Law 16/87 benefits is likely driven by two factors. The first is ineffective publicity. As demonstrated in table 11.1, less than 20 percent of entrepreneurs were even aware of this program. However, among the 20 percent who were aware of the program, the vast majority of respondents said that they just were not interested in it.

TABLE 11.1

Key statistics from different types of entrepreneurship programs, Morocco, 2004

	Law 16/87	Crédit Jeunes Promoteurs	Programme Auto-Emploi	All entrepreneurs
Take-up rate among entrepreneurs	3.6%	1.1%	5.1%	—
% of VT graduates aware of program	19.8%	61.2%	30.9%	—
Average investment (MAD) for benefiting firms	77,800	202,500	127,800	37,300
Average firm size (no. of employees) for benefiting firms	2.5	3.7	3.1	1.9

Source: FVTG survey, July 2004, author's calculations.

The second factor is the additional cost to the firms associated with participating in the program. Specifically, while there are some short-term benefits from Law 16/87, a medium-term cost is that a recipient's firm must enter the formal sector eventually and begin to pay taxes, even if at a reduced rate (50 percent of regular taxes). It is thus unsurprising that those firms that were aware of the program and chose not to participate were significantly smaller than participating firms; the average participating firm had a total investment of approximately 75,000 MAD (Moroccan dirhams) and 2.5 employees, while a firm choosing not to participate had a total investment of 30,000 MAD and 2.0 employees.

The National Agency for the Promotion of Employment and Skills

For Moroccan youth, ANAPEC seems to have had very a limited total impact. In a 2009 data set of Moroccan youth collected by Silatech and the World Bank, only 4 percent had received job information through ANAPEC, and just over 1 percent had received any kind of services or training from this program. Thus, even though these data indicate that youth unemployment rates among ANAPEC beneficiaries were one-half those of similar Moroccan youth, the low take-up of the program indicates that it has not been not effective. The lack of effectiveness of the program seems to be primarily driven by limited awareness of it: only 14 percent of youth interviewed had heard of it.

Conclusion

Designing policies to reduce youth unemployment in the MENA region remains a key challenge facing both those countries' governments and international and regional donors. Our findings offer three lessons about the potential role of VT programs in supporting those efforts.

First, entrepreneurship is still not a panacea. Various types of entrepreneurship programs (e.g., microfinance) have been attempted in Morocco and throughout the region. In almost every case, after much fanfare and hype, there have been some successes and many failures. Similarly, we find no evidence that these efforts effectively support smaller entrepreneurs, though they may help larger enterprises.

Second, ANAPEC-like approaches might be attractive, particularly given the active role Europeans have demonstrated to be willing to play in the process; however, there is very limited knowledge of these programs despite 10 years of existence. More research is necessary to (1) establish impact, and (2) understand why penetration has been so limited.

Third, as we have demonstrated in this chapter, there is significant evidence that internship programs following graduation can be effective for supporting graduates of VT programs. We have shown that these postgraduation programs in Morocco brought significant job stability, which can support positive long-term career trajectories for youth. However, as these programs require the participation of cooperative and interested members of the private sector, to expand the benefit of these programs a significant advocacy effort needs to be made by both interested donors and the private sector. Further research exploring the benefit of these interns to firms could help support such an effort.

REFERENCES

Assaad, R., and F. Roudi-Fahimi. 2007. Youth in the Middle East and North Africa: Demographic opportunity or challenge? Population Reference Bureau policy brief. http://www.prb.org/pdf07/youthinMENA.pdf.

Attanasio, O., A. Kugler, and C. Meghir. 2011. Subsidizing vocational training for disadvantaged youth in Colombia: Evidence from a randomized trial. *American Economic Journal: Applied Economics* 3(3): 188–220.

Belghazi, S. 2013. Public employment programs in Morocco. In *Building effective employment programs for unemployed youth in the Middle East and North Africa*, ed. D. F. Angel-Urdinola, A. Kuddo, and A. Semlali, 101–114. Washington, DC: World Bank.

Bettinger, Eric, Michael Kremer, and Juan Saavedra. 2010. How do vouchers work? Evidence from Colombia. *Economic Journal* 546(8): F204–F228.

Blattman, Christopher, Nathan Fiala, and Sebastian Martinez. 2014. Generating skilled self-employment in developing countries: Experimental evidence from Uganda. *Quarterly Journal of Economics* 129(2): 697–752.

Boudarbat, B. 2007. La situation des diplômés de la formation professionnelle sur le marché du travail au maroc: Une analyse sexo-spécifique à l'aide des modèles de durée. *Revue Canadienne d'études du Développement* 28(2): 293–314.

Boudarbat, B., and M. Lahlou. 2009. Vocational training in Morocco: Social and economic issues for the labour market. In *Vocational training in the 21st Century: A comparative perspective on systems and innovations in ten countries*, ed. G. Bosch and J. Charest, 214–241. New York: Routledge.

Card, D., P. Ibarraran, F. Regalia, D. Rosas-Shady, and Y. Soares. 2011. The labor market impacts of youth training in the Dominican Republic. *Journal of Labor Economics* 29(2): 267–300.

Cho, Y., D. Kalomba, A. M. Mobarak, and V. Orozco. 2013. Gender differences in the effects of vocational training: Constraints on women and drop-out behavior. Policy research working paper 6545. Washington, DC: World Bank.

Département de la formation professionnelle—Maroc. 2015. Carte de la formation professionnelle alternée 2014/2015. Rabat. http://www.dfp.gov.ma/images/pdfdocs/2015/Carte_de_la_FP_Alternee_rece2014-2015_-_Nationale.pdf

Dhillon, N., and T. Yousef, eds. 2009. *Generation in waiting: The unfulfilled promise of young people in the Middle East*. Washington, DC: Brookings Institution.

Ernst and Young. 1989. Morocco: Constraints and opportunities in the SME Sector. Prepared for USAID/Morocco. http://pdf.usaid.gov/pdf_docs/PNABF822.pdf.

Friedlander, D., D. Greenberg, and P. Robins. 1997. Evaluating government training programmes for the economically disadvantaged. *Journal of Economic Literature* 35: 1809–1855.

Hicks, J., M. Kremer, I. Mbiti, and E. Miguel. 2013. Vocational education in Kenya: Evidence from a randomized evaluation among youth. Report for Spanish Impact Evaluation Fund (SIEF) Phase II. Washington, DC: World Bank. http://siteresources.worldbank.org/INTHDOFFICE/Resources/VocEd_SIEF_Report_2011-04-07_final.pdf.

Imbens, G. W. 2004. Nonparametric estimation of average treatment effects under exogeneity. *Review of Economics and Statistics* 86(1): 4–29.

Maitra, P., and S. Mani. 2013. Learning and earning: Evidence from a randomized evaluation in India. Fordham economics discussion paper series, Fordham University, Department of Economics, dp2013-02. New York: Fordham University, Department of Economics.

Montmarquette, C., F. Mourji, and A. Garni. 1996. L'insertion des diplômés de la formation professionnelles dans le marché du travail marocain: Une application des modèles de durée. *Revue Région et Développement* 3: 37–57.

Salehi-Isfahani, D., and D. Egel. 2007. Youth exclusion in Iran: The state of education, employment and family formation. Washington, DC: Wolfensohn Center for Development, Brookings Institution.

World Bank. 2005. *Reforming technical vocational education and training in the Middle East and North Africa*: Experiences and challenges. Washington, DC: World Bank.

NOTES

1. Other programs that provide technical and financial assistance to young entrepreneurs are also far from achieving their objectives. For instance, the program Moukawalati (My Enterprise), aimed at attracting university graduates toward self-employment, has participated in the creation of 600 small businesses so far, whereas the initial objective was creating 30,000 by 2008. Hence the realizations are only 2 percent of the expectations.

2. An early study by Montmarquette et al. (1996) of the graduates of the Office de la formation professionnelle et de la promotion du travail led to very similar findings.

3. The passing of Law 36.96 in 1996 instituted cooperative training (formation professionnelle alternée) as a formal component of the vocational training system.

4. The Charte Nationale d'Éducation et de Formation had recommended an apprenticeship program as a means both to support both youth employment and to improve the pool of skilled labor available for SMEs.

5. The law is published online at the website of the Ministry of Justice, http://adala.justice.gov .ma/production/html/Fr/liens/..%5C69343.htm. A summary of this work is provided in annex 6.C in Ernst and Young (1989).

6. The first round of this third approach was funded by the Government of Canada through the Canadian International Development Agency, which granted CAD $10.5 million worth of financial assistance. See the website of the Département de la formation professionnelle—Maroc, http://www.dfp.gov.ma/images/CooperationMaroco-Canada.pdf.

7. This was funded under Canadian International Development Agency project number Z020745-001 covering the period 2012–2019. For a short description, see http://www.acdi-cida .gc.ca/cidaweb/cpo.nsf/vLUWebProjEn/33795E0A17AAB4CC8525774B00373B54.

8. This analysis pools together graduates from either the cooperative training, the apprentice program, or the classroom-based training programs.

12 After the Arab Spring
REFORM, INNOVATION, AND THE FUTURE OF YOUTH
EMPLOYMENT
Tarik M. Yousef and Edward A. Sayre

AT THE WRITING of this final chapter, the Arab world is again in turmoil. While the bloodiest of the civil conflicts that erupted during Arab Spring, in Syria against the regime of Bashar Al-Asad, has run unabated since 2011, other conflicts are back in full force after an intermittent period of relative calm and initial steps toward peaceful political transition. The renewed threat of extremist militants in Iraq has led the United States and its allies to reengage militarily in Iraq and Syria against the so-called Islamic State. The political uncertainty and then promise in Libya after Moammar Gadhafi and in Yemen after Ali Abdullah Saleh has now dissolved into civil war fueled by regional intervention. While Egypt is stable by comparison, the regime of President Al-Sissi has begun to resemble if not exceed the authoritarian tendencies of ousted dictator Hosni Mubarak. The only qualified success at the current writing is the nascent democracy of Tunisia, which continues to show promise.

When the region exploded in the political protests of 2010–2011, the connection was not obvious at first between the Arab Spring and the socioeconomic and development conditions that had defined the region in the previous two decades: the youth bulge and rising youth unemployment; failed economic and political reform projects; rising inequality and institutionalized corruption; the spread of information technology; and, most recently, the effects of the global financial crisis (Gause 2011; Lynch 2014). Despite the lack of clear unidirectional causality from these suspected drivers of revolt to the events in question, what is not in dispute is the pivotal role played by youth in initiating and sustaining the Arab Spring revolutions and their messy aftermath. And while the precise role that youth grievances played in triggering the protests will remain an object of scholarly debate (as seen in the differences in perspective between chapters 7 and 8 here), the chapters in this book have, in our view, confirmed a long-standing belief that institutional rigidities in the economies of the Arab world, especially labor markets, lay at the heart of the youth exclusion and ultimately discontent that drove the demands for economic and political change (Dhillon and Yousef 2009; Malik and Awadallah 2013).

This chapter deals with the questions of reform in the post–Arab Spring period. Specifically, we assess the political space for addressing those rigidities in the economies of the region that account for the persistent weak outcomes affecting youth employment. We suggest an alternative approach based on social innovation that can overcome the obstacles and resistance to change in the short term and establish a foundation of knowledge for the emergence of a broader agenda for reform in the long term.

Demography, Exclusion, and Reform

Even with the registered fertility declines across the region, the projected profile of the demographic transition in the Arab world suggests that youth will continue to be a dominant force in the region's population structure for the foreseeable future. While the apex of the youth bulge has passed in many countries, and notwithstanding the oil boom period of the past decade, we have seen the ratio of youth to adult unemployment continuing to steadily grow in Tunisia, Jordan, Algeria, Morocco, and Syria into 2010. The inability of labor markets to deal with a large and more educated group of youth will continue to put strains on the region's economies and societies in the same way that the backlog of inactive, underemployed, and unemployed young people has forced them to wait until their thirties to make the transition to full employment and full adulthood.

In the context of this "youth bulge," young people, seeking to achieve the transition to adulthood, are competing with a large cohort of peers to secure places in preferred educational fields and gain employment in scarce positions in the formal sectors of the economy. At the same time, youth are struggling to successfully reach other important milestones in the transition to adulthood, such as marriage and household formation.[1] Over the past two decades, efforts to achieve these normative milestones have been increasingly met with growing frustration and failure, as evidenced most clearly by the poor outcomes in the region's labor markets. In the future, such efforts will take place in the context of greater domestic political uncertainty, regional economic dislocation, and a sluggish global economy. On the eve of the Arab Spring in 2009, regional youth unemployment stood at nearly 24 percent; today it has approached 30 percent.

The problems associated with labor markets often begin with the region's education systems. Despite significant public investments in education and a long history of reform efforts, the region's education systems have continued to fail in providing the region's youth with the skills demanded by the region's private sector employers (see chapter 2 here). Facing exclusion in the employment markets, the region's youth are, in turn, facing a host of additional challenges as they struggle to complete the transition to adulthood. This is perhaps most notable in regard to marriage and family formation. In a relatively short period, the average age of marriage in the region has risen to the point that 25- to 29-year-old men now have the lowest rates of marriage in the developing world, a trend driven largely by the high cost of marriage, poor labor market outcomes, and the difficulty of securing housing due to poor access to mortgage lending and restrictive rental markets.

The Legacy of Institutional Rigidities

Despite the widely acknowledged importance of the youth agenda to Arab governments, little progress has been made over the past two decades in confronting the challenge in an effective and sustained manner. A growing body of research, including chapters in this book, suggests that the determinants of the region's inability to deal effectively with the youth agenda are not due to demographic pressures, lack of investment, or even economic growth per se, as is best seen in the stubbornly high youth unemployment rates since the 1990s (Salehi-Isfahani and Dhillon 2008). Rather, the roots of youth's economic exclusion are found in the formal and informal institutions that govern the education, employment, marriage, and housing markets and the incentives that such institutions impose on the choices and behaviors of youth, their parents, their educators, and their potential employers (Nabli 2007; Dhillon and Yousef 2009).

Thus, despite the reduction in opportunities in the region's public sector, the legacy of government employment—in the form of relatively high wages and job security—means that many youth continue to queue for such jobs. Moreover, the lure of government employment shapes educational choices, with students pursuing degrees that will land them those jobs rather than investing in degrees or work experience that prepare them for private sector employment or entrepreneurship. In the past, public sector employment guarantees and pervasive job protections in the private sector provided important social benefits. But in the context of the region's changing demographics, these institutions have worked to the advantage of older and established workers at the expense of the region's youth. Moreover, they have provided the wrong market signals and incentives for helping young people make the right investments in education and secure gainful employment.

The Arab world's poor track record in creating economic opportunity for its youth does not arise from a lack of information about what needs to be done. Indeed, the core policy solutions to youth unemployment have been known and widely discussed for some time (Amin et al. 2012). Yet despite this knowledge of what needs to be done and the urgency of doing it, the reforms have stalled. While some countries have made limited progress on select aspects of reform, none has ambitiously restructured the framework in which these reforms have been embedded (Mazarei and Mirzoev 2015). As a result, proposed solutions have found little traction and have often been captured by vested interests that support the status quo. This has confirmed the belief that reform lacks credibility, has increased poverty, and has exacerbated social polarization (Benhassine 2009; Yousef 2011).

The Policy Reform Agenda Post-Arab Spring

But in the context of growing insecurity and uncertain political transitions across the region, the question arises as to how governments could effectively address the economic aspirations of youth. Specifically, can the region embark on reform of the institutional rigidities to revitalize markets and generate sufficient growth and job creation to respond to the economic demands of youth?[2] Such a broad objective requires societies to embark on sustained long-term reform projects to address the core drivers of youth exclusion, an effort that would require difficult choices in a complex environment of political instability, societal polarization, constrained fiscal space, and an uncertain global economic outlook (Amin et al. 2012). Moreover, and as Barsoum (chapter 9 here) has argued, many of the choices for reform might not, in the short term at least, align with youth's heightened expectations and demands for immediate results.

No less challenging is the task of absorbing short-term pressures without undermining sustained long-term policy reforms. To date, government response to the vulnerability and change brought forward by the Arab Spring has been largely reactionary (Beschel and Yousef 2015). While in some cases announcements of public sector hiring and wage increases have relieved immediate political tensions, such changes do little to address the long-term economic challenges facing youth. In fact, by reinforcing institutions that disincentivize job creation and skills development, such efforts could accentuate the challenges facing long-term institutional reform efforts. At the same time, none of the newly formed governments in the Arab Spring countries has put forward an economic vision that departs markedly from the status quo. As pressures build to alleviate postrevolution economic dislocation, transition governments will likely lean toward similar strategies of public-sector-led employment and investment, particularly as continued instability deters private investment (IMF 2014).

Social Innovation and Youth Employment

Increased public investments in the short term can help address the starkest employment outcomes and cushion the most vulnerable against the effects of economic downturns. However, serious efforts aimed at putting the next generation of youth on the pathways of healthy transitions to adulthood will require sustained efforts to address key institutional and regulatory rigidities. What is needed are well-designed programs that are implemented in ways that create incentives for young people to develop marketable skills; for educators to emphasize skills development; for private sector firms to hire first-time job seekers; and for parents to aid youth in taking risks in building their careers and aspirations. But in view of the political constraints and an outlook that suggests that instability and insecurity are likely to persist, if not deteriorate, for some time, youth employment in the Arab world can best be served in the short term by the targeted innovations in programs and policies that are championed by emerging actors in the post–Arab Spring public space.

In fact, there are many examples of social innovation aimed at tackling youth unemployment, from interventions in skill acquisition and career development to youth-focused microfinance and entrepreneurship programs (Bell 2011).[3] Actors from the public sector, civil society, and the private sector—often working in tandem and blurring the distinctions among them—are increasingly engaged in efforts to implement innovative solutions, even in the absence of knowledge about the efficacy of such programs in fundamentally shifting outcomes.[4] In the absence of proven "off-the-shelf" models of social innovation in the region, these efforts are responding to the growing need for new thinking and experimentation, in regard to both the creation of innovative programs and the introduction of innovative applications of more traditional programs (Murray, Caulier-Grice, and Mulgan 2010). These efforts mainly aim to bridge deficits created, or left unaddressed, by traditional education and labor market institutions. They tend to focus on skills development, job readiness, career guidance, job placement, entrepreneurship, and enterprise development.

Skills Development and Vocational Training

Given the notable skills gap in the region, as observed in the often-reported skills mismatch, job-relevant skills training—whether focused on vocational training or more broad-based soft skills training—is a priority area for social investment and one where recent evidence from other countries supports the efficacy of these programs (Attanasio, Kugler, and Meghir 2011). Boudarbat and Egel (chapter 11) show that traineeship programs in Morocco are successful in leading to better employment outcomes. Skills training has also proven to be a fairly straightforward entry point for organizations seeking to create programs for regional youth. Whether done in cooperation with formal school systems or in parallel, such programs have the potential to fill in important gaps left by traditional curricula and methods of instruction. These gaps vary from country to country, but notable needs include the following: basic business skills, computer training, up-to-date vocational training and, perhaps most important, soft skills training, including communication, teamwork, negotiation, and self-expression.

Formal school systems in most countries of the region have been willing to introduce skills training as add-ons to traditional curricula. For example, the International Labour Organization's "Know About Business" curriculum has been introduced in the school systems of six countries in the region, and plans for it are under way in another five. Ease of entry has led to the creation of scores of technical and soft skills development initiatives by NGOs and corporate citizenship arms of the private sector, such as Royal Dutch Shell's program Intilaaqah. Whether vocation-specific or not, such training programs should be informed by local market needs and integrate the perspective of the business sector in order to be effective in improving the job readiness of youth. In addition, given the rigidity of labor markets, firms must be able to ensure that graduates of such programs have developed the required skills, or they will not respond with significant hires.

A promising example of such an effective collaboration between the public sector and the private sector, which helped align the incentives of the education system with those of the private sector in order to develop the skills that matter, is the Association Tunisienne Pour la Communication et la Technologie (TACT) in Tunisia. In 2011–2012, TACT developed a program to retrain 200 unemployed university graduates in the field of information communication technology (ICT), with the guarantee of an ICT job at the end of a 10-month training program that developed specific ICT skills as well as general business skills, including English and French language skills. The government paid the tuition of these students, but only after TACT selected them, made sure that they were properly trained, and ultimately placed them in ICT jobs. In fact, if a candidate was not placed, then TACT would not request the reimbursement from the government of the tuition (Nucifora and Rijkers 2014).

Service-Based Learning and Experience Building

Young people entering the labor market in the Arab world lack not only marketable skills but also relevant experience and knowledge of the working world. While in school, young people are encouraged to focus on getting high grades and preparing for national exams in order to secure coveted university slots that can help them gain access to sought-after formal sector jobs. While the goal of the test-based system (as described in chapter 2) was to decrease favoritism and increase equality of opportunity, it has clearly failed to continue to do so. Thus, a system that is based less on rote memorization will be one way to move toward emphasizing behavioral competencies, such as having a strong work ethic, being willing to take criticism, being a good teammate, and having strong communication skills. These workplace soft skills are not acquired through schooling as much as they are learned through experiences starting at an early age. Little emphasis is placed on gaining experience and exploring different career options. As a result, most young people find themselves unprepared for the world of work on graduation.

Government approaches to dealing with this issue have centered around active labor market programs and public works, which may address a share of the immediate needs of youth, particularly those leaving school early, but do little to prepare them for work beyond the end of the program (Betcherman, Olivas, and Dar 2004). Short of reforming the incentive structure in each country, public sector efforts should at least focus on providing opportunities for young school-leavers to engage in service activities in a way that helps build job-relevant skills and experience while ensuring that youth are engaged in activities that support national development priorities. At a basic level, this means creating a larger window for NGOs and civil society groups to engage young people in community service, while promoting volunteerism among youth (Sherif 2014). More dynamically, governments should work toward the establishment of national service programs. Designing such programs in a way that allows youth to develop and implement their own local projects not only ensures that such programs meet local needs but also provides youth with valuable learning experience and skills that enhance future market readiness. A similar orientation toward skills-building can be applied to national military service programs.

Facilitating Job Information and Career Guidance

Intermediation in the job search process has seen only marginal improvement in recent years, due in part to the traditional orientation of educational systems and government control over labor market information. As a result, young job seekers are mostly searching blindly for matching opportunities, relying heavily on informal channels of family and friends, and appear to have little knowledge of how to go about searching for work outside the public sector. Compounding this is the fact that few schools in the region provide any effective career guidance and job placement programs. As late as 2012, some 70 percent of the Arab youth surveyed for the Silatech Index by Gallup reported not having availed themselves of any of these services. Similarly, part of the private sector's challenge in identifying skilled workers is a lack of systematized information on applicants and the ability to screen talent and match skills to available jobs.

As seen recently around the world, there is a particularly important role for online talent platforms (websites, mobile apps, etc.), which are slowly transforming labor markets for individuals and companies. A recent McKinsey report (Manyika et al. 2015) argues that these platforms have the potential of enhancing the efficiency of the job matching process by expanding the pool of job seekers and providers and by improving the available information about individuals' skills. The report estimated that online talent platforms could increase employment levels in Egypt and Saudi Arabia over the next 10 years by as much as 3.2 and 2.5 million, respectively. Over the last few years, several of these platforms have now begun to appear in the region: Bayt.com, the regional equivalent of Monster.com, continues to be the largest and most widely known commercial job matching site. In addition, an increasing number of new entrants are beginning to fill a variety of different labor market niches, be they in terms of geographic focus or the kind of job seekers and employers they seek to attract.

Ta3mal.com, a regional employability portal established by Silatech and Microsoft, focuses primarily on entry-level jobs for first-time job seekers and youth with less than three years' work experience. It also offers psychometric assessments to help youth chose the right career and hundreds of online courses in topics such as project management and entrepreneurship. Nabbesh.com helps businesses across the Arab world find freelancers online; the Moroccan stagiaires.ma offers internship opportunities; Najja7ni is an SMS-based mobile platform offering job matching services and "m-Learning" (educational services on mobile devices) to youth in Tunisia. Several countries now also feature both government-sponsored as well as private/commercial platforms. The national employment agencies of Algeria, Tunisia, and Morocco maintain their own platforms (anem.dz, anapec.org, and emploi.nat.tn); Palestine has both 3amal.pna.ps (public) and jobs.ps (private); and Jordan is in the process of launching a new government jobs portal alongside the privately owned Akhtaboot.com.

Fostering Youth Entrepreneurship and Access to Finance

In the context of general frustration with the ineffectiveness of traditional approaches to job creation, entrepreneurship is widely seen as key to addressing the employment challenge. There is considerable merit to the argument that the promotion of youth entrepreneurship will promote self-employment, and there is exceptional interest in entrepreneurship among the region's youth. According to survey data from the 2009 Global Entrepreneurship Monitor, young people from the region were more likely than in other regions to indicate an interest in starting their own businesses in the next three years, ranging from 24 percent of youth in Yemen to 68 percent in Tunisia, compared to a worldwide average of 24 percent. However, youth in the region were less likely than their counterparts elsewhere to actually take steps to start a business. Thus, while the entrepreneurial spirit is alive among Arab youth, it remains constrained by a myriad of barriers, including lack of access to sustainable forms of finance and effective business support services. For example, the most recent Global Financial Inclusion Database reveals that financial access for youth in the region is the lowest in the world, with only 13 percent of young people using formal financial services (Demirgüç-Kunt and Klapper 2012).

While evident gaps remain, the region has seen a proliferation of programs aimed at entrepreneurship training (e.g., INJAZ Al-Arab throughout the region, Help Leads to Hope in Somalia, and Khadija in Yemen, to name just a few) and of business competitions to promote an entrepreneurial culture among youth (e.g., the MIT Enterprise Forum). A growing number of microfinance institutions are actively and intentionally targeting younger clients, although most of them do not provide dedicated products to youth, in part because of perceptions, not supported by actual data, that youth are more risky borrowers (Coury and Qazi 2015). Alternative and more innovative sources of financial support for entrepreneurs are emerging, especially in the crowdfunding space. Kiva Arab Youth, for example, since its launch in 2012 has raised $6.7 million from 140,000 global lenders that has fully financed 4,800 youth-run enterprises in six Arab countries. More specialized crowdfunding platforms continue to emerge that also provide nonfinancial support to entrepreneurs, including Zoomal in Lebanon, Shekra in Egypt, and Aflamnah in the UAE.

Among these diffuse efforts, what is clearly missing—and where considerable scope for innovation lies—is the creation of mechanisms to form an enabling enterprise ecosystem (Isenberg 2014). Basic business training and access to capital are important but need to be complemented with access to business development services, mentoring, incubation, loan guarantees, and a proentrepreneurship policy response, a response that might include tax breaks for youth-run businesses, community workspaces, subsidized lines of credit to youth-serving finance institutions, and temporary exemption from labor regulations (Soriano and Castrogiovanni 2009). Egypt and Tunisia have recently adopted legal frameworks for the micro-finance sector, an important step toward regulating the industry, integrating it into the formal financial system, promoting innovation in the product space, and incentivizing the entry of domestic and foreign investors.

Enabling Small and Medium Enterprises

Beyond youth entrepreneurship, small and medium-sized enterprises (SMEs) represent a huge potential for job creation, productivity, and economic growth. The region is no exception, with this sector accounting for 20–40 percent of all private sector employment and 50 percent of regional GDP, a contribution that is much higher if enterprises in the informal sector, which employ a growing number of first-time job seekers, are taken into account (Gatti et al. 2013). Historically, SMEs have struggled to expand in the face of the privileged position enjoyed by large companies, public and private, who have tended to dominate product markets, enjoy access to banking systems, and shape the rules of competition to their advantage. In addition, risk aversion by banks, high collateral requirements, licensing and registration requirements, and high processing costs have meant that SMEs' access to financing is highly constrained and represents less than 10 percent of total bank loans in the region (McConaghy 2013).

As a result of their historical disadvantages, targeted policies and programs that stimulate the growth of startups and SMEs across much of the region have been in short supply. These interventions may not make the legal environment friendly for SMEs, but they can introduce flexibility in the regulation of startups, improve access to finance, enhance the business skills of entrepreneurs, provide strategic guidance to companies, and support the introduction of innovative business models. Although starting from a low base, there are a growing number of platforms aimed at providing business and financial support to SMEs through private equity and venture capital vehicles. Building on these efforts—and steering these efforts toward investments that have a more direct impact on job creation—requires a more coordinated effort among the diverse players in this space, which includes not only public and private sector entities but also regional NGOs and international donors. Large multinational corporations as well as public sector companies are also experimenting with SME development through procurement policies for products and services in specific sectors, and through the creation of public-private partnerships aimed at incubating new firms. Finally, a number of micro-finance platforms are transforming their lending models to support larger enterprises and combining their services with financial literacy and business skills.

Expanding the Impact of Social Innovation

New organizations that serve private interests in addition to a societal need, known as social enterprises or social entrepreneurship, can serve as models for the policymaking communities, though they are not substitutes for economic reforms. The social innovations they champion can bring about real change in the lives of the region's youth, especially if they are scaled up. In this regard, several core principles should guide ongoing efforts to generate success in the youth employment space (Huddart 2010; Isenberg 2010). First, solutions should be localized. While the lessons of experience in other regions have not been examined and provide a wealth of innovative policy and programmatic interventions to draw on for various aspects of youth inclusion, effective and sustainable solutions depend on local ownership and should be informed by the particulars of the local context. Second, a holistic approach is needed: no matter which sector is targeted, creating opportunities for youth requires a mix of inputs that are integrated so as to form an ecosystem that will enable change.

Third, partnerships are key, especially in the fragmented public space that characterizes the region today and determines the scale of the challenge. While innovative solutions may be developed—and even tested—in a bubble, ensuring that innovations are implemented successfully and scaled up properly requires cooperation among and support from the government, the private sector, and actors in civil society. Fourth, while technology has facilitated tremendous advances in economic growth and globalization, it is not being adequately exploited to address youth employment. Innovative ideas should be supported by innovative technology-based approaches to ensure that solutions are implemented efficiently and targeted widely. Finally, innovations in youth programs should avoid past mistakes and make sustainability an operating objective. This requires organizations to steer away from their traditional dependence on large donors and on funding sources that are subject to shifting priorities.

Conclusion

In the wake of the Arab Spring, governments will continue to respond to popular pressure and economic dislocation in the short term through public-sector-led employment and investment. It would be wishful thinking to expect anything else, given the fragility of the political arena and loss of confidence among policymakers. Since countries are unlikely to undertake comprehensive institutional reforms in the near term, a second-best approach to addressing the challenge of youth employment involves identifying and developing innovative, sustainable programs, demonstrating success through rigorous monitoring and evaluation, and bringing successful programs to scale. Moving to scale should be done in a holistic fashion that addresses key elements of the local ecosystem for jobs and business development, requiring the development of coalitions of local partners from the government, the private sector, civil society, academia, and the wider public to effect change. While change through such an approach will be incremental, the cumulative experience of successfully piloting and scaling up programs, through inclusive processes and implementation by a diverse community of actors, can eventually tip the balance of public support in favor of more comprehensive projects and help shape the contours of future reforms.

THIS CHAPTER DRAWS HEAVILY ON A PREVIOUS ESSAY, YOUSEF (2012).

REFERENCES

Amin, M., et al. 2012. *After the spring: Economic transitions in the Arab world*. New York: Oxford University Press.

Attanasio, O., A. Kugler, and C. Meghir. 2011. Subsidizing vocational training for youth in Colombia: Evidence from a randomized trial. *American Economic Journal: Applied Economics* 3(3): 188–220.

Bell, S. 2011. *iMENA: An Innovation Agenda for Jobs*. Washington, DC: World Bank.

Benhassine, N. 2009. *From privilege to competition: Unlocking private-led growth in the Middle East and North Africa*. Washington, DC: World Bank.

Beschel, R., and T. Yousef, eds. 2015. *Public sector reform in the Middle East and North Africa: The lessons of experience*. Washington, DC: World Bank.

Betcherman, G., K. Olivas, and A. Dar. 2004. Impacts of active labor market programs: New evidence from evaluations with particular attention to developing and transition countries . Washington, DC: World Bank.

Coury, T., and Q. Rashid. 2015. Youth microfinance services in MENA. http://www.silatech .com/docs/default-source/report/youth-microfinance-services-in-mena-ar.pdf?sfvrsn=4.

Demirgüç-Kunt, A., and L. Klapper. 2012. Measuring financial inclusion: The global financial database. World Bank policy research paper 6025. Washington, DC: World Bank.

Dhillon, Navtej, Paul Dyer, and Tarik Yousef. 2009. "Generation in waiting: An overview of school to work and family formation transitions." In *Generation in waiting: The unfulfilled promise of young people in the Arab world*, ed. Navtej Dhillon and Tarik Yousef, 11–38. Washington, DC: Brookings Institution Press.

Dhillon, N., and T. Yousef, eds. 2009. *Generation in waiting: The unfulfilled promise of young people in the Middle East*. Washington, DC: Brookings Institution Press.

Gatti, R., M. Morgandi, R. Grun, S. Brodmann, D. Angel-Urdinola, and J. M. Moreno. 2013. *Jobs for shared prosperity: Time for action in the Middle East and North Africa*. Washington, DC: World Bank.

Gause, G. 2011. Why Middle East studies missed the Arab Spring: The myth of authoritarian stability. *Foreign Affairs* 90: 81.

Huddart, S. 2010. Patterns, principles, and practices in social innovation. *Philanthropist* 23(3): 221–234.

International Monetary Fund. 2014. *Toward new horizons: Arab economic transformation amid political transitions.* Washington, DC: International Monetary Fund.

Isenberg, D. 2014, May 19. What an entrepreneurship ecosystem actually is. *Harvard Business Review.* https://hbr.org/2014/05/what-an-entrepreneurial-ecosystem-actually-is/.

Isenberg, D. 2010. The big idea: How to start an entrepreneurial revolution. *Harvard Business Review* 88(6): 40–50.

Lynch, M. 2014. *The Arab uprisings explained: New contentious politics in the Middle East.* New York: Columbia University Press.

Malik, A., and B. Awadallah. 2013. The economics of the Arab spring. *World Development* 45: 296–313.

Manyika, J., S. Lund, K. Robinson, J. Valentino, and R. Dobbs. 2015. McKinsey Global Institute report: A labor market that works: Connecting talent with opportunity in the digital age. file:///C:/Users/Ward/Downloads/MGI%20Online%20talent_A_Labor_Market_That_Works_Full_report_June%202015.pdf.

Mazarei, A., and T. Mirzoev. 2015. Four years after the spring. *Finance and Development* 52(2): 55–57.

McConaghy, P. 2013. Supporting job creation and innovation through MSME development in MENA. World Bank quick notes series no. 89. https://openknowledge.worldbank.org/handle/10986/16130.

Murray, R., J. Caulier-Grice, and G. Mulgan. 2010. The open book of social innovation. Social Innovator Series: Ways to Design, Develop, and Grow Social Innovation. http://blog.eisco2012.eu/home/european/library/literature/Social_Innovator_020310.pdf.

Nabli, M. K. 2007. Breaking the barriers to higher economic growth: Better governance and deeper reforms in the Middle East and North Africa. https://openknowledge.worldbank.org/bitstream/handle/10986/6914/439690PUB0Box31100nly109780821374153.pdf.

Nucifora, A., and Bob Rijkers. 2014. *The unfinished revolution: Bringing opportunity, good jobs and greater wealth to all Tunisians.* Washington, DC: World Bank.

Salehi-Isfahani, D., and N. Dhillon. 2008. Stalled youth transitions in the Middle East: A framework for policy reform. Middle East Youth Initiative working paper no. 8. Washington, DC: Wolfensohn Center for Development and Dubai School of Government.

Sherif, D. 2014. Responsible leadership in the Arab world: Youth, volunteerism and community service. Unpublished paper. American University in Cairo.

Soriano, D., and G. Castrogiovanni. 2009. The impact of education, experience, and inner circle advisors on SME Performance: Insights from a study of public development centers. *Small Business Economics* 38(3): 333–349.

Yousef, T. 2012. After the spring: New approaches to youth employment in the Arab World. In *Addressing the 100 million youth challenge: Perspectives on youth employment in the Arab world in 2012,* 4–7. Geneva: World Economic Forum.

Yousef, T. 2011. Youth unemployment: Staying ahead of the twin challenge. In *Compendium on economic governance in the Arab world,* 2–4. Geneva: World Economic Forum.

NOTES

1. For a framework on the broad challenge of youth inclusion in the region see Dhillon, Dyer, and Yousef (2009).

2. This, in essence, poses two possibly conflicting goals faced by Arab societies, especially those in transition. The first is to ensure that the voice of youth is integrated into a rapidly changing political context and the second is to ensure that their expectations are embedded in policy formulation.

3. Murray, Caulier-Grice, and Mulgan (2010, 10) adopt a broad definition of social innovation as "innovation that is explicitly for the social and public good. It is innovation inspired by the desire to meet social needs which can be neglected by traditional forms of private market provision and which have often been poorly served or unresolved by services organised by the state."

4. A number of organizations, including Synergos and Ashoka, are supporting social entrepreneurs in the region through programs that offer financial awards, technical assistance and capacity-building workshops, mentorships, and peer networks.

Index

Page numbers in italics indicate figures and tables.